Flexible Learning and ICT

A Reader

Lynda Hall
&
Malcolm Ryan

Published in 2000 by Greenwich University Press and prepared for publication by:

Procurement and Business Services Department
University of Greenwich
Woolwich University Campus
Wellington Street
London SE18 6PF

ISBN 1 86166 075 8

Cover designed by Pete Birkett

Text design and layout by Christine Murray

In the majority of cases the contents of the readings and extracts in this volume have been reproduced as they appear in the publications from which they have been taken.

Every effort has been made to trace all the copyright holders, but if any have inadvertently been overlooked the publishers will be pleased to make the necessary arrangements at the earliest opportunity.

University of Greenwich, a charity and a company limited by guarantee, registered in England (reg no 986729). Registered Office: 30 Park Row, Greenwich, London SE10 9LS.

Contents

Acknowledgements

Acknowledgement is made for permission to reproduce the extracts quoted:

Brown A, Galloway A & Brennan C (1999) 'Videoconferencing: active reflection on new technologies when lecturing' *Active Learning* Issue 11, December, pp36–39

Cuthell J (2000) 'The online learner' *Computer Education* No 94, Feb 2000, pp8–12

Eraut M *et al* (1991) *Flexible learning in schools* Department of Employment, pp17–21; 23–29

Further Education Funding Council (1996) *Report of the Learning Technology Committee – the Higginson Report* FEFC, paras 48–51; Annex E, pp67–75

Further Education Funding Council (1998) *The use of technology to support learning in colleges* FEFC, pp2–17; 23–24; diagram from p36

Halsall R, Harrison I & Owen R (1998) 'Flexible learning: the needs and perceptions of young people' *Journal of Education and Work* 11 (1), pp57–75

Helm P (1997) 'Teaching and learning with the new technologies: for richer, for poorer; for better, for worse' in J Field (ed) *Electronic pathways: adult learning and the new communication technologies* National Institute of Adult Continuing Education, pp41–49

Her Majesty's Stationery Office (1997) *Higher education in the learning society – the Dearing Report* HMSO, paras 8.20–8.36; 8.71; 13.24–13.25

Kay J (1996) 'FlexiStudying for a flexible society' *Open Learning Today* Issue 33 Sept/Oct 1996

Lincoln H (1996) *GNVQ: integrating IT* National Council for Educational Technology, pp4–15

Mason R & Bacsich P (1996) 'Computer conferencing university teaching' *Open Learning Today* Issue 33 Sept/Oct

Parhizgar S (1999) 'Using videoconferencing as a multi-purpose tool in further education' *Learning Resources Journal* 15 (1) February, pp19–22

Race P (1992a) *Never mind the teaching feel the learning* Staff and Educational Development Association, pp85–90; 91–107

Race P (1992b) *53 interesting ways to write open learning materials* Technical and Educational Services Ltd, pp29–33; 95–99; 111–125

Rowntree D (1992) *Exploring open and distance learning*, Kogan Page, pp13–33; 234–250

Sankey K & Dibble D (1997) 'Low-cost computer-mediated conferencing for part-time evening degree students' in J Field (ed) *Electronic pathways: adult learning and the new communication technologies* National Institute of Adult Continuing Education, pp68–70

Somekh B & Davis N (eds) (1997) *Using information technology effectively in teaching & learning* Routledge, pp14–26; 122–124

The School of Post-Compulsory Education and Training

The School of PCET, as it is known, has its origin in Garnett College in London, one of three institutions set up by the Ministry of Education in the late 1940s for the initial training of technical college lecturers. After many developments and organisational changes over the past 50 years, its future within the University of Greenwich will be from a campus on the banks of the River Thames in Christopher Wren's former Royal Naval College.

The School's services and students, though, are not only locally based, but nationwide and international. PCET is a leader in distance provision for lecturers, trainers, administrators and other support staff from all sectors of post-school provision, as well as from the public services and voluntary and commercial training organisations. It has associated centres in various parts of the United Kingdom, and there are projects in China, South Africa and Russia, and leadership of research and information networks within the European Union.

We aim, in both our teaching and our research, to relate professional practice to learning theory and current policy issues. This permeates all of the School's programmes – from initial training on Cert Ed/PGCE programmes, through professional development at BA/BSc and Masters levels and the work of our Training and Development Office, to our portfolio of short courses and bespoke in-house provision. There is a thriving group of research students, and the School has been at the forefront of innovation in computer mediated communication. We provide a comprehensive service for further, higher and adult education, helping people to help others learn through life.

Ian McNay
Head of School

Lynda Hall taught Computing and Information & Communications Technology (ICT) in a further education college for a number of years before becoming involved in teacher education at the University of Greenwich. She specialises in the teaching of computing skills and in training future teachers of ICT. A current responsibility is running the attendance mode of the part-time in-service Certificate in Education/PGCE at Greenwich.

Malcolm Ryan is Flexible Learning Co-ordinator in the School of PCET at the University of Greenwich. He is closely involved in working with students at a distance and in exploiting ICT in support of learning and teaching. He has a particular research interest in using computer mediated communication (CMC) within the context of continuing professional development in both the Health and the Education services.

Introduction

Flexible learning is not a new concept, having its roots in the early commercial correspondence courses of the 19th century and in subsequent manifestations of individual learning systems in the United States, with the Dalton Plan of the 1920s (based on individual or small group work, worksheets and libraries) and the Keller Plan of the 1960s (offering university teaching through self-instructional materials). But it was in the last quarter of the 20th century that we saw renewed interest in adopting more accommodating and imaginative approaches to learning and teaching in the post-compulsory sector in the United Kingdom, led perhaps by the extraordinary success of the correspondence-based courses of the Open University. The reasons for this are various, though some writers suggest that political, financial and technical factors have outweighed the philosophical and pedagogical ones. The growth has been characterised by a move away from physical, standard-sized classrooms supervised by the ever-present teacher, through an increasingly adaptable use of learning spaces and materials within colleges, an expanding provision of resources designed or adapted to facilitate study at home, towards the emergence at the turn of the century of the virtual campus and the possibilities offered by 'e-learning' and the electronic superhighway.

However, as a perceptive report by the former Further Education Unit in 1983 pointed out, the development of flexible programmes of learning does not necessarily depend upon high levels of investment in technology: 'there is much that can be done without large-scale interventions' (FEU, 1983: iii). Many of the initiatives which are recorded in the contributions to this Reader are characterised by the inventiveness of their originators rather than by the generosity of their sponsors. As the FEU went on to observe: 'progressing towards flexibility is dependent on personal and organisational attitudes as well as on resources' (FEU, 1983: viii).

The selection within this Reader presents a cross-section of views, opinions and commentaries on current practice. One of the first issues that has to be addressed is: what name do we give to this movement towards a recognition that we must make our systems increasingly responsive to the needs of existing and potential learners? While acknowledging the special meanings of terms such as 'open', 'resource-based' and 'student-centred' learning, we have chosen to use the wider and more inclusive phrase 'flexible learning', though you will see that this is by no means the preferred terminology of all the contributors to this volume. For a similar reason we have tended to write of 'Information and Communications Technology' (ICT) rather than IT, though once again there is no universal agreement on this.

The first three extracts in Part One give us a summary of such alternative viewpoints and argue the case for organising learning along more flexible lines. The next three are concerned more specifically and practically with the design and development of the materials and packages – both low-tech and high-tech – without which no flexible learning scheme can be operated.

Part Two looks particularly at what this means for the participants in the teaching and training process – the students or trainees, the teachers, and their managers. The perceptions of these 'stakeholders' are of prime importance, for if it is not seen that flexible learning approaches and schemes widen opportunities and give learners greater control over their learning, then we seek to adopt them in vain.

No-one involved in teaching or training during the past five years can have failed to notice the explosion of interest in Information and Communications Technologies, and the opportunities which these developments offer to the opening up of learning. The contributions to Part Three survey the use and potential of these technologies in specific curriculum contexts in both further and higher education. Government bodies associated with the management and funding of post-16 education and training have played an important part in promoting the development of learning technology, and selected extracts from research documents produced by these agencies are also presented.

Part Four examines the potential of on-line technology in the development of flexible learning – 'e-learning' as we have chosen to call it. There are now increasing opportunities for students to exploit not only the World Wide Web but also the growing number of internal college networks, as the case studies presented here will show.

We hope that this Reader will help to move all those concerned with post-16 teaching and training confidently into the first decade of the 21st century.

Lynda Hall & Malcolm Ryan
May 2000

Reference

Further Education Unit (1983) *Flexible learning opportunities* FEU

Part One – The Theory and Practice of Flexible Learning

The contributions to Part One are concerned firstly with trying to clarify the terms and concepts that we use in discussing open/flexible learning and secondly with providing very clear advice on the practical issues faced by those involved in the selection and preparation of materials to support particular flexible learning schemes.

Derek Rowntree leads us into the debate by exploring a range of definitions of open/flexible learning. He suggests that open learning incorporates not only a set of beliefs in the purposes of education and training, but also a methodology concerned with how these purposes can be best achieved through a variety of approaches to learning and teaching. Generally, practitioners who adopt such an open approach are concerned with widening participation by reducing barriers to access and by increasing learner autonomy. The selection and production of materials is a core process associated with open learning together with the associated issue of tutorial support for open learners, in particular when students study at a distance. Rowntree suggests that 'openness is an ideal for which we must keep striving rather than the state we can expect to attain', and presents the idea of an 'open learning continuum' by which we can measure how far any particular system can be said to be open. He considers, in conclusion, whether a new and changing society, ready and willing to accept the challenges of lifelong learning, can continue to be served by old approaches to teaching and learning.

The short piece by Judith Kay provides one answer to this question, through her account of a well-established and accessible application of the principles of flexibility within the further education sector – the FlexiStudy scheme. She alerts us to some of the financial implications of adopting such an approach, both for the students and for the providing institutions.

In the third section Rowntree engages with some of the arguments which can be ranged against the use of open/flexible learning methods. Whilst there are clearly benefits to be gained by learners, by employers and by providers, he warns us against a too enthusiastically uncritical acceptance of the 'increasing opportunities and access' argument. Too much of an emphasis on the learner as individual may not be in the interests of those who need motivation, direction and support (i.e. those who traditionally lose out in their experience of the formal education system). Too much of a reliance on well-produced and authoritative materials ('the perils of the package', Rowntree calls it) can actually reduce the opportunity to engage in debate, to challenge received ideas and to acquire personal knowledge.

Phil Race begins the three extracts which form the second half of this Part by relating theories of how people learn to the design and production of learning materials which

1

can go some way to resolving these problems of motivation and learner support. He provides a number of practical strategies designed to help anyone engaged in the development of open and flexible approaches to teaching or training. At the heart of his approach is a focus on learning by doing and the provision of feedback. He gives characteristically down-to-earth advice on writing study guides and presents a checklist for judging the quality of flexible learning materials – whether produced by us or by others. In his final contribution Race offers specific advice to all learning resource producers, whether the chosen medium is text, visuals, audiotape or videotape.

1.   So What is Open Learning?

Derek Rowntree

Before we go any further, perhaps we should try to agree what it is we are talking about. Our problem here was clearly stated some time ago by the observers (MacKenzie *et al.* 1975) who called open learning:

> *an imprecise phrase to which a range of meanings can be, and is, attached...*
> *It eludes definition. But as an inscription to be carried in a procession on a*
> *banner, gathering adherents and enthusiasts, it has great potential.*

All these years later it is still imprecise. It still eludes definition. And it has certainly gathered plenty of adherents and enthusiasts. They may all have their own views about what is special about open learning. And so may you.

Some definitions of open learning

> *An open learning system is one in which the restrictions placed on students*
> *are under constant review and removed wherever possible. It incorporates the*
> *widest range of teaching strategies, in particular those using independent and*
> *individualised learning.*

(Coffey, 1977)

> *Open Learning: arrangements to enable people to learn at the time, place and*
> *pace which satisfies their circumstances and requirements. The emphasis is*
> *on opening up opportunities by overcoming barriers that result from*
> *geographical isolation, personal or work commitments or conventional course*
> *structures which have often prevented people from gaining access to the*
> *training they need...*

(MSC, 1984)

> *'Open learning' is a term used to describe courses flexibly designed to meet*
> *individual requirements. It is often applied to provision which tries to remove*
> *barriers that prevent attendance at more traditional courses, but it also*
> *suggests a learner-centred philosophy.*

(Lewis & Spencer, 1986)

> *... a wide range of learning opportunities that both aim to assist learners in*
> *gaining access to knowledge and skills they would otherwise be denied and to*
> *give learners the optimum degree of control over their own learning.*

(Dixon, 1987)

> *Open learning is a state of mind rather than a method with particular*
> *characteristics.*

(Jack, 1988)

> *Open learning is not just about access alone, it is also about providing people with a fair chance of success.*
>
> (Holt & Bonnici, 1988)

Thinking about them, and many other words that people have uttered on the subject, it seems to me that open learning is two different things. It is:

- a philosophy – a set of beliefs about teaching and learning
- a method – a set of techniques for teaching and learning.

Much of the confusion arises because people don't always realise that the philosophy can be practised without using the method. And, more commonly, the method can be applied without the philosophy.

Open learning – the philosophy

In one sense, 'open learning' is a rallying cry – a slogan that implies commitment to shared educational beliefs. But people in open learning express a variety of different beliefs. They can be beliefs about the purposes or ends of education and training – the Why? They can be beliefs about the best means of achieving such purposes – the How? People may agree about the means but disagree about the ends, and vice versa.

The most widely agreed beliefs are about opening up learning opportunities to a wider range of people and enabling them to learn more congenially and productively. This involves reducing barriers to access and giving learners more control over their own learning.

But why do we want a wider range of learners? Some may say: 'Because we need more students/skilled workers.' Others may say: 'Because we must try to meet the needs of individuals who are not getting the education or training opportunities they could benefit from.' The former may be hoping to find additional learners who can cope with whatever programmes are currently being offered. The latter perhaps admit the possibility that they may need to develop radically different programmes.

And why do we want open learners to have more control over their learning? Is it simply a means of making the learning more palatable to them – and thus helping keep them in the system? Or is it something to do with the respect we have for them as people with their own preferences and purposes – and with encouraging them to take responsibility for their own lives? Does it touch on what we'd like to see our learners become (the Why?) as well as on how we believe they might best learn (the How?)...

Open learning – the method

Learner-centred aims could be pursued through a variety of different methods. For instance, they can be, and are, pursued in adult education classes, in one-to-one literacy coaching, and in community development projects. There seems no reason why such experiences should not be called open learning. But usually they are not.

The role of packages

For most people, open learning implies that the learner's work is based around self-study materials – the package. As Lewis & Spencer (1986) pointed out: 'in nearly every case specially prepared or adapted materials are necessary'.

These packages may involve any of a variety of media – e.g. print, audio-cassettes, television, computer 'courseware' and practical kits. And the learners using them will be provided with various amounts and kinds of help from other human beings – e.g. tutors or line managers.

Packages are designed to help the learner learn with less help than usual from a face-to-face teacher. They can contribute to openness by:

- enabling more people to learn – by economising on the amount of teacher time required
- using a variety of media appealing to different learners
- enabling learners to study when and where they choose
- enabling them to work at their own pace
- setting learning activities in the learner's home, community or workplace
- giving learners responsibility for their own progress...

How packages are used

How will learners use packages? Some will be using self-teaching packages on-site – in colleges or training centres, or at their workplace. Others may be using them at home, in pubs or on buses. And all of these may be using them alone or in company with fellow-learners.

And what proportion of their learning will come from the package rather than through contact with other people? Some learners will be using 'stand-alone' packages with no organised support. Some will keep in touch with a tutor by telephone or correspondence. Others may be supported with occasional face-to-face coaching sessions or classwork. Yet others will be using packages as one element in a programme that involves as much or even more learning in a class.

Your learners may be using packages on-site or at home (or both) – and they may or may not have contact with other learners and tutors. Which of the following sounds most like *your* practice or intention?

- 'They'll be using *stand-alone* packages, e.g. no organised contact with tutors or other learners.'

- 'They'll be using packages with *support,* e.g. they will be backed up by correspondence tutoring, occasional tutorials or classwork.'

- 'They'll be using packages *alongside* regular class teaching, e.g. as preparation or follow up for class meetings'...

Packages are not enough

Some companies have tried stand-alone packages (bought in or home-made) as a means of training staff. Usually, as the Open Tech programme clearly demonstrated (Tavistock Institute, 1987), unless the students are highly motivated, the drop-out rate is unacceptable. For example, Austin Rover set up an open learning centre at its Cowley works, using CBT [computer-based training] packages but with no-one for learners to turn to if they had problems. The trainers soon found it necessary to add tutorial support.

All the national providers – e.g. Open College, Open University and National Extension College – can make packages available to users on a stand-alone basis. But their reputation depends on supported packages, e.g. using FlexiStudy or correspondence tuition.

Packages used in the third way mentioned above – alongside class sessions – can be an important means of saving on expensive contact time. They can also ensure such time is reserved for activities that learners cannot do on their own...

So, learners need not only packages but also support. In addition, to some degree or other, they may need the 'real world'. Although its potential role in open learning programmes is rarely highlighted, the learner's world of work, family or community life may be both a rich resource to draw on in learning and a test-bed for trying out new ideas. (After all, most of us do get much of our most important learning out of this local world, unaided by either packages or support.) Packages and support systems that do not tie in to what the learner can draw on locally may be neglecting a vital means of helping him or her become autonomous...

How open is open learning?

No learning system or programme is ever fully open. Nor is any fully closed. Openness is an ideal for which we must keep striving rather than a state we can expect to attain.

Open v closed systems

What might a fully **open** system look like?

- Whatever you wanted to learn about, you would be able to get a programme tailored to your wishes and at an acceptable price.

- You would get it when you wanted it, where you wanted it, and at your own pace.

- You would be able to set your own objectives, choose the content and sequence of your programme, and decide when and how your learning was to be assessed.

- You would also be able to decide how you wanted to learn, e.g. with others or on your own, from books or from videos, with the emphasis on theory or on practice – and who might help you in what kind of ways.

And how would you get on in a fully **closed** system? Strictly speaking, you wouldn't get in at all – you'd be too old, too young, short of the required educational background or of the required fee, or you'd be in the wrong organisation (or in the right organisation but the wrong job). But if you did get in – and you might find you'd been put in whether you wanted to be in or not – then you'd have few of the choices mentioned in the previous paragraph:

- The programme organisers would tell you what you had to learn about, the objectives you were expected to attain and how you would be assessed.

- You'd have to learn in a specified place, at specified times and the pace would be set by the organisers.

- The learning methods and sequence would also be set by the organisers and they would decide who might help you and what sort of help they might give. Your wishes or preferences would not be taken into account when these decisions were made.

The open learning continuum

Clearly, these are two extreme scenarios. Most learning programmes and systems lie somewhere on a continuum (Lewis & Spencer, 1986) between these extremes. Some systems and programmes are more welcoming and accommodating than others. Those that are more welcoming and accommodating – that is, more open – may be so in a variety of ways.

So how do we compare the openness of one system with that of another? Lewis & Spencer (1986) suggest some 30 questions to help decide how far a system lies along the Closed–Open continuum. I find it more revealing to ask about a smaller set of factors under three main headings: Who? What? and How?

- *Who?* How easy is it for someone to become a learner without restrictions of age, qualifications, wealth, job, etc? And to what extent will success depend on the learner possessing already the same learning skills and motivation and cultural background as the learners the system is used to dealing with?

- *What?* To what extent is the learner free to decide the content and objectives of the programme and when and how he or she will be assessed?

- *How?* To what extent is the learner free to decide where, when and at what pace he or she will learn, the teaching/learning methods to use and the routes to take, and how he or she will call on other people for support?

For each separate factor we might question under these three headings, a learning system or programme will lie somewhere along the continuum from very closed to very open. For example, under the 'What?' heading, consider the factor of programme content. A programme is:

- *very closed*: if all learners must study exactly what they are told to study

- *not quite so closed* (or somewhat open): if they can make up their programme by choosing from a range of modules

- *even less closed* (more open): if the range of modules is very varied and each module is quite short

7

- *yet more open*: if they can choose topics within a module
- *very open*: if the entire content is tailored to suit the wishes of each learner.

I leave you to think up your own 5-point scale for each of the other factors mentioned – together with any additional factors that occur to you.

If you haven't considered such factors before you may like to apply them to a learning system you know – e.g. the system you are working in or a programme you are thinking of setting up. Towards which end of the continuum does it lie on each of the factors under each heading – and overall?...

I think I'd be safe in betting that your system is some way from the open end. There aren't many systems that are open enough for learners to decide exactly what and how they want to learn. For comparison, try imagining the learning programme you might devise for yourself if you wanted to learn how to grow your own vegetables or find out more about antiques. Where would that lie on the continuum?

How open is the Open University?

Many people assume that, given its name, the Open University must be pretty open. But is it? As a matter of fact, I don't remember any of my colleagues using the term open learning before the early 1980s. Prior to that we always said we were in distance education – and most of us still do.

So let's ask just how open the OU actually is. We'd get a rather different answer according to which of the university's activities we looked at. But let's consider how the questions above relate to the OU's undergraduate programme (which covers about 70% of its students):

Who can learn?

The Open University has no entry requirements, so anyone over the age of 18 can enrol for undergraduate courses – if they can afford the fees and other expenses. They may have to wait a year or more though, because applications always far exceed the number of places available.

What can they learn?

OU students have free choice among courses from a wide range of disciplines. Within a course, however, there is rarely any chance for students to choose or negotiate what to study in the light of their personal interests. Once embarked on a course (some entailing 100, some as much as 400, hours of learning), students usually cannot risk omitting any of it.

What they learn is heavily constrained by the objectives implicit or explicit in the assessment requirements. And they have little or no control over that. Courses have both continuous assessment (usually through essays but often with computer-marked objective questions as well) and an examination. Students have to perform satisfactorily on both. Except on some project-based courses, there will be little opportunity for them to negotiate an individual assessment theme to fit in with their own interests.

How can they learn?

OU students are mostly free to learn wherever they like. Occasional attendance at tutorials and day-schools is optional. However, the compulsory attendance at summer school on some courses remains a barrier that may exclude many potential students.

But undergraduates have no choice as to when they start and finish. All undergraduate courses start in February and end in November. Once in, students have some day-by-day choice of when to study, but their overall pace may be influenced by the timing of television and radio broadcasts and will be heavily controlled by the cut-off dates (ominous term!) for assignments.

Nor do they have much choice of teaching and learning method. At least 90% of their learning on most courses is driven by specially-developed workbooks and published texts. Television, audio, practical work and computers may also be used — but typically to present additional content rather than provide an alternative approach for those who don't take easily to reading. In addition, course structures are usually quite controlling — students are constrained to follow a fixed sequence, reinforced by the order in which batches of material are sent to them and by the sequence in which assignments are to be completed.

OU undergraduates are allotted a succession of tutors depending on which courses they take. They do not have a choice and tutors vary in how responsive they are to the needs of an individual student.

The overall reckoning?

So even the Open University is open only to a limited extent, and scarcely at all in some aspects. Compared with most other institutions of higher education, the OU is much more open on Who? and to a lesser extent on What? and How? But the gap is less wide than it was when the OU took in its first students in 1971. The need to attract more students, and the successful example set by the OU, have prompted many other institutions to allow easier access and enable more learner choice by offering shorter, modular courses.

How open is in-company training?

For comparison, let's consider the openness of a typical in-company open learning scheme:

Who can learn?

Most in-company programmes are open only to people in the company. In fact, they are probably not even open to everyone in the company. For example, few training departments would consider it wise (even if they could afford it) to let everyone join a management training scheme. Furthermore, even those who are eligible may need to be nominated. They may even be put on the programme whether they desire it or not. (I remember running workshops for one group of professionals who told me they had, in their local parlance, been 'warned to attend'.)

What can they learn?

Nor do in-company schemes usually offer much choice over objectives, content or assessment. The employers decide what knowledge and competence will suit their objectives, and the programme is tailored accordingly. From the employer's point of view, this is one of the advantages over sending people away for courses elsewhere.

How can they learn?

Trainees are not likely to have much choice about teaching and learning methods, or about who might help them. In fact, the openness of most in-company schemes lies solely in the aspects of 'time, place and pace' promoted by Open Tech. Though even this is limited if the programme is based on computers and other kit or involves attendance at a learning centre.

There may be little sign of the four learner-centred aims listed by Lewis & Spencer. The focus is usually on satisfying the needs of the employer and the job rather than the needs of the learner.

Are they open?

Is 'open learning' something of a misnomer for such schemes? Some organisations seem to think so, preferring to use the term 'flexible learning' or – as at British Gas, the Post Office and the police service – 'distance learning' or, where appropriate, 'computer-based training'.

Perhaps we could say that they are using open learning *methods* but without drawing much on the *philosophy*. With a few interesting exceptions – e.g. the 'personal development' approach at Ford, Rover and Lucas – open learning in industry may be more clearly described as 'packaged training' or, to varying extents, 'supported packaged training'.

This is not meant to disparage such programmes. Supported packages are usually a more cost-effective way of achieving the employer's objectives than trying to get people onto classroom-based courses. This may suit the learners' purposes better, also – providing them with a more user-friendly means of attaining new competences and greater confidence in their work.

But are they open enough to be called open learning? And is the OU undergraduate programme for that matter?...

The Rumble-Lewis debate

During 1989/90, such questions as those above gave rise to a fascinating tussle for ownership of the term 'open learning'. It took the form of a debate that ran over four issues of *Open Learning*. Writing from the Open University, Greville Rumble (1989) started it with an article that concluded thus:

> *The term 'open learning' is now being used to describe systems which are anything but open. This is a monstrous misuse of language which needs to be stopped now.*

Roger Lewis (1990), writing from the Open College and with an interest in industrial training as well as education, scolded Rumble for suggesting that the OU's access policy set the standard for openness. He quoted another OU writer, Ian McNay (1988), to the effect that the OU's admissions policy 'skews the entry towards the socially adept systems players'. In any case, he suggested, openness in terms of 'choice over the content of learning and over the means by which it is delivered is currently more important' than being open to the general public. As he said:

> *There may be little use in gaining access to a scheme when, once in it, choice is restricted at almost every point.*

Lewis also reminded Rumble that changes in the use of language cannot be 'stopped'. People will apply the term open learning to systems as they see fit. Rumble (1990) replied that certain uses would be 'misleading' as when 'dictatorships are called democratic republics'. The Rumble-Lewis debate continued through numbers 2 and 3 in volume 5 of *Open Learning* with new pundits entering the fray. If you haven't yet looked at these articles, you may think them worth your attention. Their clash of viewpoints caused quite a few of us to re-examine our prejudices.

What sort of openness do YOU want?

Of course, we could all go on for ever with the sophisticated equivalent of 'We're more open than you' – 'No you're not' – 'Yes we are'. But none of us can afford to be complacent. However differently we define openness, we all need to ask ourselves: Are we open enough?

What might we do to become more open? Is it enough just to let more people have a go at the same old standard programmes? Or must we develop new programmes to ensure the success and satisfaction of the newcomers?

Think about the system you are working in, or the particular programme you are developing for your learners:

- How might it be made more welcoming to learners who are not at present being attracted?
- Might it be possible to give learners more choice about what they are learning and how it might be assessed?
- What more might be done to enable perhaps new kinds of learners to learn in the ways that are best for them?

Or will you settle for flexibility?

Some providers have begun to hedge their bets (fudge the issue?) by saying they're offering 'open or flexible learning'. This leaves us to decide which of the two is on offer in a particular programme – or whether all their programmes offer both at once.

And it still begs the question: 'Flexible in what ways, and to what degree – compared with what?'

An approach labelled 'flexible learning' (without explicit mention of openness) is now very much up and coming in schools and colleges. It has been propelled by the Employment Department's TVEI Flexible Learning Development programme. Already it has inspired a minor flood of publications, many of them government-sponsored (e.g. Eraut *et al.* 1991; FEU, 1992; Tomlinson & Kilner, 1991). The chief aims of the TVEI Flexible Learning Development programme are:

> *... to meet the learning needs of students as individuals and in groups ... and to give the student increasing responsibility for his/her own learning within a framework of support...*

What are the limits to openness?

We cannot expect any one institution to be wide open to all potential learners in every aspect. We are all limited by what our budgets and talents enable us to offer. Besides which, we may be daunted by certain tensions and contradictions within the ideals of openness. What may make the system more user-friendly for some learners may make it less so for others.

For instance, suppose we let anyone enrol, regardless of whether they have already gained the prior competences that the programme has previously reckoned to build upon. If we are to help them catch up and keep up, we'll need to divert resources from the teaching of other students. But this may impoverish the teaching we can offer them and so make it less responsive, less open for them.

Again, we may decide not to pace our learners with timetabled meetings and regular assignment deadlines. This flexibility may appeal to learners who are already experienced and well-organised. But what about those who have not yet acquired the self-discipline needed for truly independent learning? Might they suffer by losing this encouragement to find time for study?

And how much control over what and how they learn are our learners ready to take? If we insist they make too many choices, too soon, some may be frightened off. Reporting his experience with mature learners, Lewis Elton (1988) says: '... many students find the greater freedom and responsibility given to them hard to handle.' He recommends offering learners gradually more and more openness as they progress through a programme (or through their learning careers).

As open learning providers, we are all entitled to set our own limits: 'These are the learners to whom I can open new opportunities. These are the ways in which I will make learning more productive and satisfying for them. More than that I cannot do – as yet.'

How far might we reach?

But we must remain aware of the gap between our rhetoric and reality. And I don't just mean that learner-centred, autonomous, self-directed learning is more talked about than practised. I mean also that there are still many potential learners whose needs we have not begun to consider. So far, as Winifred Hirst (1986) pointed out:

... the practice of open learning has had little impact on movement toward learning appropriate to an open society.

Even though each of our institutions limits itself, we are entitled to raise our eyebrows if the open learning movement as a whole fails to provide learning opportunities that might help transform the lives of people who are not attracted to what we currently have to offer. I'm thinking here of people who don't have much clout in the market-place – e.g. people who are homeless, housebound, imprisoned, retired – the unwaged, unwooed and often unwanted.

Many large organisations are looking to open learning to cut training costs and/or increase productivity. Perhaps some of them will be public-spirited enough to invest a little of the proceeds in promoting open learning in the community around them – starting perhaps with their redundant ex-employees or by helping local people improve their basic skills. (Marks & Spencer has already made some money available to promote local open learning.)

Do you think open learning should reach out to people who are not even aware that learning might help them improve their lives? Can you identify groups that your organisation might work with? Can you imagine what kind of provision you might be able to offer them?..

What is distance learning?

So far, I have scarcely needed to mention distance learning. Perhaps, it is now time we defined it and compared it with open learning.

Distance learning is learning while at a distance from one's teacher – usually with the help of pre-recorded, packaged learning materials. The learners are separated from their teachers in time and space but are still being guided by them.

The biggest and best-known distance learning systems are part of the distance education movement. This embraces the hundreds of world-wide schools, colleges and universities who cater for learners studying at a distance. The movement has spawned several specialist journals and numerous books. Oddly enough, with the exception of the journal *Open Learning*, which was once called *Teaching at a Distance*, the literature on distance education rarely refers to the literature on open learning, or vice versa.

Desmond Keegan (1990) prefers using the term 'distance education' because it includes both distance learning and distance teaching. Unfortunately it doesn't include all distance learning. Distance learning is used not only in education but also in much industrial and professional training.

How open is distance learning?

And what is the connection between open learning and distance learning? Simply this – if the philosophy of open learning is to do with improving access and learner-control, then the method (thanks to self-study materials) usually involves some element of distance learning.

However, while open learning usually involves distance learning, not all distance learning systems are particularly open. As I said earlier, it is possible to use the method without the philosophy.

Theoretically, distance learning needn't be open at all. A few years ago, the film *Superman* demonstrated an extreme example of distance learning. Our infant hero, on his solitary spaceship journey from Krypton to Smallsville, USA, was kept occupied with a packaged course that taught him all he would need to know about Earth and its inhabitants. The learning programme was totally closed.

In the real world, most distance education programmes are fairly open, as we've seen with the British Open University. But they may be open in different ways and to different extents. For example, the equivalents of the Open University in Germany and Spain demand exactly the same entry qualifications as other universities. Where distance learning is used in vocational and professional training it may be even less open.

What kind of distance?

As with openness, a learner's learning may be more or less distant, and in a variety of ways. We need to ask exactly what the learner is distant from and for how long.

There is often some element of distance even in a classroom-based, on-site course. For example, which of the following will *your* learners be distant from?

- the teachers/trainers who developed their programme
- someone who can respond to their individual concerns or difficulties (e.g. a tutor or mentor)
- the people who will assess their learning for accreditation
- other learners with whom they might pursue joint learning and mutual support
- equipment or facilities that might aid their learning
- the context in which, or 'clients' with whom, their learning is meant to be applied (e.g. student teachers learning in college rather than in school)?...

The feeling of distance

Not all distance learning systems involve all these kinds of distance. The demands and opportunities within a learning system will differ according to which factors the learner is at a distance from and for how long.

Notice that it is accessibility rather than geographical distance that matters here. The on-site learner having difficulty with a CBT package may know that the people who wrote it are in the next office. But if they are not available for consultation, he or she may feel as distant as if they were on the other side of the moon. Conversely, the learner in a Basic Skills Open Learning Centre may be happy to work alone with workbook and tapes knowing that a tutor is within call if needed.

Similarly, learners who can telephone a tutor any evening or get face-to-face feedback once a week may feel less distant than those who can only get written comments once a month. And learners who can easily meet other learners learn differently from those who are working alone. A hutful of villagers in China or Africa watching a satellite television broadcast in company with a trained animateur are experiencing 'distance' differently from the Open College student watching a video alone at home.

Such factors help explain why some on-site learners can feel 'distanced'. Many higher education students are very much aware, especially in these days of worsening staff-student ratios, that they are largely having to teach themselves, with sparse and infrequent feedback from tutors.

I also remember one course for third world health workers – a lengthy residential course held in Europe – whose organisers were turning it into a distance learning course so that (paradoxically) the new approaches would not have to be learned at a distance from the patients and co-workers with whom they were to be used. For them, the 'real world' would play a more potent role in the package-support-world 'triangle' than it does in many open learning programmes.

Is there a key factor among those I've listed? I suspect one's sense of distance depends chiefly on how quickly and satisfactorily one can get individual help or feedback from another human being whose viewpoints seem relevant – e.g. a teacher, an assessor, another learner or a co-worker...

Final remarks

- All open learning (even on-site) involves some degree of distance learning.

- Not all distance learning involves much openness – except perhaps of time, place and pace.

- But many so-called open learning systems don't involve much of any other kind of openness either.

- And some learning systems that don't call themselves open are actually more open than some that do.

I leave you to ponder how much more open our learning systems might have to become if they are to cater for the world of 'new work' envisaged by Michael Young (1988):

> *Quite soon over half the adult population will be over 50, and with earlier and earlier retirement, coupled with increased life expectancy, many millions of people are going to have over 25 years of active life ahead of them without much prospect of getting ordinary paid work again. There is going to be a second society and second careers, still based on 'work' but on a different kind of work in which people help themselves to new skills, new disciplines and new fulfilments. The old education fed by the acquisition of book knowledge will not be appropriate for many of them.*

... In the new era, people will not be limited by the habits and timetables they have for centuries been drilled into at school and in their ordinary workplaces. They will be less the creatures of the greater and lesser bureaucracies and more their own men and women, still working but to unfold more of their own span of capacities, their own ability to create, their own sense of beauty, their own sympathy for each other than any society has ever before tolerated...

References

Coffey J (1977) *Open learning for mature students* Council for Educational Technology

Dixon K (1987) *Implementing open learning in local authority institutions* Further Education Unit

Eraut M *et al.* (eds) (1991) *Flexible learning in schools* Employment Department

FEU (1992) *Flexible colleges: access to learning and qualifications in further education* (two volumes) Further Education Unit

Hirst W (1986) 'Melbourne to Manchester: a look at openness in some open learning situations' *International Journal of Lifelong Education* 5 (4), pp327–46

Holt D & Bonnici J (1988) 'Learning to manage through open learning: a case study in international collaboration' *Programmed Learning & Educational Technology* 25 (3), pp 245–57

Jack M (1988) 'The Strathclyde open learning experiment' *Open Learning* 3 (1)

Keegan D (1990) *Foundations of distance education* 2nd edn Routledge

Lewis R (1990) 'Open learning and the misuse of language: a response to Greville Rumble' *Open Learning* 5 (1), pp 3–8

Lewis R & Spencer D (1986) *What is open learning?* Council for Educational Technology

Mackenzie N, Postgate R & Scupham J (1975) *Open learning: systems and problems in post-secondary education* UNESCO

McNay I (1988) 'Open learning: a jarring note' in N Paine (ed) *Open learning in transition* National Extension College

MSC (1984) *A new training initiative* Manpower Services Commission

Rumble G (1989) '"Open learning", "distance learning" and the misuse of language' *Open Learning* 4 (4), pp28–44

Tavistock Institute (1987) *The Open Tech programme development review: final report* Tavistock Institute of Human Relations

Tomlinson P & Kilner S (1991) *Flexible learning, flexible teaching: the flexible learning framework and current educational theory* Employment Department

Young M (1988) 'Education for the new work' in N Paine (ed) *Open learning in transition* National Extension College

2.   FlexiStudying for a Flexible Society

Judith Kay

One of the positive things about open learning is its flexibility. It's the ideal way of studying for shift workers and people who work unsociable hours, busy professionals who find it difficult to attend classes on a regular basis, parents with small children and people who are house-bound open learners. Open learners also include many people who make it their first choice because it offers so much more flexibility.

However, one disadvantage of any form of open learning is being isolated from other learners. Distance learning in particular can be a very solitary way of studying, with little opportunity for the cross-fertilisation of ideas and debate that face-to-face learning offers. But one scheme called FlexiStudy is providing the best of both worlds by giving students the flexibility that distance learning offers plus face-to-face contact with a tutor.

FlexiStudy began in 1978 when five further education colleges started using materials from the National Extension College (NEC) together with access to other college facilities. It recently underwent a relaunch followed by an expansion of the scheme.

The system works like this. Basically, the student enrols at a college in the normal way for an open learning course. As part of the 'package' the student gets pre-course guidance from the college, face-to-face tutorials (instead of just telephone contact) and end-of-course assessment. They can also use the college library and other facilities. The main advantage for the colleges is that, providing they have included open and distance learning in their strategic plans, they can claim funding from the Further Education Funding Council for successful students. In most cases, this funding will adequately cover the likely cost of delivering programmes, including the purchase of open learning materials if these are included within the course fee. This effectively means that the course is subsidised and the student pays reduced fees.

To join the FlexiStudy scheme colleges pay £500 a year, which qualifies them for large discounts on materials and free preview packs. More than 70 colleges have contracted. Hastings College of Arts and Technology, for instance, has around 300 FlexiStudy students – most of them on A level and GCSE courses, with others enrolled for accounting, study skills, book keeping and a range of NVQs. Students pay around £80 for tutorial support on an A level course, plus between £55 and £90 for the materials. Stockport College has 900 students on FlexiStudy courses with another 3,000 on other open learning courses, almost a 100 per cent increase over the past three years. 'We did little separate publicity for open learning, but the students came flooding in. Open learning is a huge growth area, with a notable increase in employer-sponsored students,' says Jackie Robinson, Manager, Flexible Learning Service.

Barnet College in north London, one of the original five FlexiStudy colleges, currently has around 300 students on FlexiStudy courses using NEC materials. 'A lot of students are people who want a fast track route to a qualification in under nine months; others are people who can't study on a regular basis at college because of family commitments or irregular work patterns', says open learning co-ordinator Evelyn Thomas. 'Then there are those who have had a bad experience of school (called 'school refusers') and are intimidated by the idea of studying in groups. Where a student lacks confidence, a one-to-one relationship with a tutor can help. Finally we have a lot of students with physical disabilities or variable health difficulties for whom FlexiStudy enables them to study when they feel well enough.'

But does FlexiStudy and open learning in general have any particular benefits to the colleges? The answer is 'yes'.

Each student has a price-tag attached to them and the FE and sixth form colleges are under enormous pressure to attract more students onto courses in order to stay solvent. The message from the funding council is 'invest in open learning'. 'Open and distance learning is likely to be of lower cost than face-to-face learning. It saves capital and running costs,' says the Director of Finance at the English Further Education Funding Council. The new funding formula, he says, rationalises the use of open and distance learning within colleges by providing rates of funding independent of how courses are delivered and supported.

At Eastbourne College, which runs a successful FlexiStudy scheme, each student receives a minimum of seven hours of support for each GCSE subject to each learner, as well as telephone contact and tutor-marked assignments. The college also offers optional study skills classes in the evening. Most of the students on the scheme would have been unable to study by more traditional methods.

3. The Pros and Cons of Open Learning

Derek Rowntree

Package-based training, distance education, open learning – whatever it calls itself, has won a great many followers in recent years. Where is the attraction? Who gets what benefit from it? Perhaps the most obvious ones to benefit are:

- individual learners
- learners' employers
- providers.

Benefits to the learner

Here are some of the possible benefits that are often mentioned. Which of them might appeal to *your* learners?

- *Access*. Some learners simply would otherwise not have been able to learn what they wanted to learn.
- *Flexibility*. Short, modular packages and 'accreditation of prior learning' may mean that learners don't need to spend time and money on topics they are already familiar with.
- Available any *time* – so learners can learn when they wish, rather than to suit someone else's timetable.
- Available any *place* – unless fixed equipment is involved, packages may be used in a learning centre, at home, or even while travelling.
- Own *pace* – individual learners are not held up or hurried on by other members of a group.
- *Private learning* – less danger of 'loss of face' such as might be feared in certain kinds of group learning.
- More *choice* as to what they will learn in the programme and how they will assess their own progress through it.
- Better *quality* teaching – both in content and treatment than they might get from any local conventional course.
- A chance to use *media* that better suit their preferences or seem more motivating.
- *Individualised tutoring*. Support staff can respond to each individual's needs and interests, rather than aiming their discourse at what they hope is the 'average' level of a group...

Benefits to employers

Employers who sponsor open or distance learning for their staff may also get a wide range of benefits. As Hilary Temple (1991) suggests, though, each may have different priorities:

One goes for the chance to train a large number of staff in a short time; another for parity of standards at different plants or branches throughout the country; a third for offering training to those who have never previously had access to it; a fourth because it is the only way of enabling trainees to accomplish an individual action plan; a fifth because they contrast the cost-benefit and visible qualities of open learning with that of conventional training; and a sixth to meet specialised needs which generic training programmes do not satisfy.

Whatever their main reason for getting into open/distance learning, employers may also benefit from knock-on effects. For instance, line managers may get more involved in training. And staff may begin to take more of an interest in learning and self-development throughout the organisation.

A major study of the use of open learning in 50 companies – ranging in size from 17 to 36,000 employees – was carried out in 1988 by the Open University and Coopers & Lybrand Associates. According to OU/ED (1990):

Although open learning was found to be substantially cheaper, the most frequently cited reasons for choosing it were:

- *because trainees were scattered around the country*
- *because they were on shift work*
- *because they were difficult to release from their jobs*
- *because large numbers had to be trained in a short time*
- *because the firm could not provide any other form of training.*

Companies that used open learning identified:

- *higher pass rates than before*
- *line manager's satisfaction*
- *better retention of information*
- *a better record of promotion*
- *an increase in the number of employees working towards vocational qualifications, from 43% to 75% of workforce.*

Various firms in the survey also reported such business benefits as the following:

- *financial performance improved in 70% of branches*
- *error rates in manufacture down by 3%*
- *reduced customer complaints*
- *increase in the success rates of calls (sales engineering)*
- *fewer 'helpline' calls (microcomputer firm)*
- *sales increased by 50% (chemical industry).*

Many firms in the survey reported that open learning had made a measurable impact on business performance indices such as improved productivity and profitability. We may want to ask, however, whether the employees shared in these proceeds. After all, we are told that 'Virtually all of the cost savings were achieved through the use of the trainees' own time ... frequently at home'.

Such productivity and profitability benefits are also reported by Forté as a result of an open learning programme on wine service for hotel and restaurant staff. In addition, they offer evidence of increased satisfaction among customers and of greater interest in further self-development among staff.

Benefits to providers

A specialist provider like the Open University or National Extension College owes its existence to open learning and distance education. For other providers, like further education colleges and training departments within a firm, the benefits sometimes centre around saving jobs and finding enough new learners to keep its existing courses running...

Here are some of the benefits that providers have mentioned to me. If you are concerned with providing open or distance learning, which of them might be relevant to *your* organisation?

- responding more easily to local needs
- exploiting new sources of funding
- catering for new types of learner
- catering for greater numbers of learners without a proportionate increase in cost
- cutting contact hours on existing courses
- getting more use out of existing facilities
- providing new development opportunities for staff...

The price to be paid

Clearly, open learning offers many benefits. But, as always, there is no gain without some degree of pain. Open learning will not suit everyone. Some potential learners, sponsors and providers may feel they simply cannot meet its demands...

Here I am referring not so much to the financial costs (which may themselves be considerable) but to the human costs. In particular, for most organisations, open learning means change. And the degree and kind of change is not always predictable at the outset. In the words of Ian McNay (1987), the introduction of open learning can be both 'disruptive and revolutionary'.

Learners too may baulk at the price to be paid. Again, I am not talking simply about fees, though these may indeed be a matter of concern to the learners. Equally or more challenging, however, is the matter of self-discipline. Not all potential learners will have the experience and motivation to control their own learning programme to the degree called for by many open learning schemes. Such self-discipline may be especially hard for learners whose near ones or dear ones (whether at work or at home) are unsupportive...

21

Now let us look at some rather more fundamental concerns about open learning and the dangers that may lurk behind its beneficent front.

Where the dangers lie

Open and distance learning has already changed the lives of thousands of people around the world. Every week, more and more are joining the procession behind MacKenzie's banner [see quote on page 3 above]. If we are to join them, we need to keep our critical wits about us and watch where we put our feet.

We cannot afford to regard open and distance learning simply as a technical fix. It is not a tool we are free to use in our own well-meaning way exactly as we please. As in any other area of human affairs, there may be hidden agendas, undeclared interests and unintended side-effects. Perhaps we shan't always be able to do anything about these factors. But we'd do well to keep aware of them for they can easily put us at cross-purposes with people whose aims turn out not to be the same as ours...

Now that the first flush of enthusiasm has had time to dissipate, people are starting to ask if open learning is always quite the 'good thing' it is usually portrayed as. (For example, see Boot & Hodgson, 1988; Edwards, 1991; Fox, 1989; Harris, 1987; Hirst, 1986.)

These concerns are to do with who pays for open learning, who can learn, who decides what is to be learned, and what effect open learning is having on the teachers and the taught.

Who pays for open learning?

To begin with, we have to recognise that open learning is largely a government enterprise. The Wilson government begat the Open University and the Heath government begat the Manpower Services Commission and the Thatcher government begat the Open Tech Unit and Open College.

The current government still funds the promotion of vocational open learning through the Employment Department and subsidises the Open University through the same Funding Council as other universities. The open or distance learning activity in many other countries around the world is also underwritten by their governments.

Investment in open learning has many benefits for a government. Chiefly, it offers the prospect of updating or re-skilling the workforce at a speed that would be impossible by traditional methods. At the same time, the economies of scale and the shift to pre-recorded media promise vast cost savings. The combination of large numbers of learners and high visibility of projects – especially perhaps where new technology is upfront – can have high public relations value. In fighting for economic survival, a government can be seen to be big, bold and innovative.

To the extent that government is paying the piper, we can expect to find it calling the tunes. What sort of tunes does government want to hear? Usually the ones defined for it by industrial interests – that is, skills and competences capable of giving the economy 'competitive edge'. Here, the chief goal is not an educated population but a healthy economy.

Who can learn?

In the UK, open learning has been promoted by a government devoted to privatisation and the market economy. Students who choose open learning rather than conventional courses are likely to get very much less financial support (if any). For instance, three quarters of Open University students get no help with fees. (And the state subsidises the OU at only about 60% of the rate per student allowed to other universities.) This is in spite of the fact that most OU students are living at home (so no maintenance costs), working full-time (thus contributing to the economy) and paying taxes (part of which go to subsidise full-time students in conventional universities).

Thus, access gets biased towards the well-heeled middle-class and learners whose employers will pay the fees. The Open University has a 'hardship fund' but this will never be big enough to invite an influx from the huge army of people who have more time than most on their hands and who may be more in need than most of a new stimulus in life, e.g. the unemployed, the house-bound, and the retired.

Instead, the OU, like other providers, is under pressure to seek out new (paying) 'markets' and now runs one of the biggest business schools in Europe. Similarly, Open College ... had to backpedal on providing vocational courses for unwaged or self-financing students and ... operate chiefly through companies who [would] sponsor their employees.

So, who is meant to benefit from open learning? There has clearly been a shift of focus – from the needs of learners to the needs of their employers or sponsors. Open Tech Unit seemed to change its mind quite early about who the customer was. At the start (MSC, 1982), they said:

> The main thing is that learner needs and circumstances are paramount and determine the system to be used in each instance.

But a year later we see the real customer emerging from the parentheses (Tolley, 1983):

> Open learning provides the opportunity for the student to learn at a pace, time and place which satisfy the student's circumstances and requirements (or alternatively, the employer's circumstances and requirements).

Perhaps you see no harm in such a shift of focus. Even in higher education, many people now seem to be committed to 'the new vocationalism'. On the other hand, you may agree with Alan Tuckett (1988) that:

> The ability to attract students from the least powerful, least privileged classes and groups is a useful measure of the openness of a course, institution or system...

What can they learn?

Who decides the content of open learning? Who decides what is worthwhile knowledge in our supposedly democratic society? Increasingly, providers are having to bow to market forces. As Ros Morpeth (1988) points out:

> *It does not take much imagination to see that this will lead to an expansion in vocational courses which the government or employers are prepared to pay for and a reduction in courses which encourage students to think, question and learn for its own sake. Certain categories of students who do not have much economic power – for example, older people, women, ethnic minority groups and the unemployed – are bound to find that their needs are not given proper consideration.*

Learning for life or for work?

More and more, the content of open learning programmes (like many others in education post-16) is being influenced by industrial interests. So what is the prospect for courses that encourage the pursuit of knowledge for its own sake? And what about courses that encourage critical reflection on moral, social and political issues or challenge the status quo?

Those who wield economic power in society are unlikely to encourage critical, non-conformist thinking. The public nature of open learning material even facilitates censorship. In 1984, for instance, the government's Education Secretary protested about alleged Marxist bias in some of the Open University's teaching materials (Richards, 1984) – and those materials were revised rather sooner than is usual.

Perhaps there will always be some employers with more liberal views about what knowledge is worthwhile – like the many police forces who pay the fees of officers to take whatever Open University courses they choose, or the Ford 'EDAP' programme which pays for employees doing general continuing education courses. But, especially in times of recession, training departments may have a hard time getting funds for schemes that have no obvious business payoff.

Such economic priorities may also be voiced by learners. So what? some may say. If we encourage open learners to choose what they want to learn about and they choose on the basis of what might improve their work prospects, who should worry? Those of us, perhaps, who believe that lifelong education – of a kind that we all need to live self-respecting lives in an open, democratic society – cannot be attained merely through education for work.

Neglected opportunities?

We may be especially concerned if the hype about open learning is blinding people to the underfunding of certain other educational opportunities that (for some learners at least) may be more appropriate. For example: the setting up of the Open University allowed other universities to offer fewer part-time degree courses.

Non-vocational and basic adult education is also short of resources. The 75 Open Learning Centres devoted to improving adult literacy and basic skills (ALBSU, 1991) are doing good work but are themselves too underfunded to make up for funding deficiencies elsewhere. Even the public libraries (once called 'the universities of the people') are having to buy fewer books, reduce their opening hours and, in too many cases, close down altogether.

Richard Edwards (1991) implies that the economic promise of open learning may be something of a con, anyway. Open learning cannot make everyone a skilled worker because our post-industrial economy will never be able to provide skilled, secure jobs for more than about 25% of the potential workforce. Open learning will serve to promote the regular re-skilling of this core. But:

> For the rest of the workforce, it will be there to support the movement of people in and out of employment, or to keep them busy with the revolving door. How real these opportunities are or whether they are taken up is not the point. Open learning is there to maintain the appearance of opportunity...

Can it be true that the majority of the population cannot look to open learning to improve their long-term employability? If not, what can they look to it for? Is there a danger that market forces – directed at the work-worthy minority – may lead to only a restricted and unbalanced curriculum being available to potential open learners?

If open learning does get itself a lop-sided curriculum it will be so much less open. As Ian McNay (1988) points out, 'unless it is used to educate and not indoctrinate, to encourage people to be critical, not conformist, it will be closed before it has had the chance to become more than barely ajar.'

How will they learn?

We may be reasonably happy about who can get access to open learning. We may even feel they have adequate freedom to choose its content. And yet we may still have reservations about the actual processes of open learning. We may wonder about the possibility of unwanted side-effects.

Let's consider four typical aspects of open learning:

- Open learners work mostly on their own
- ... and rarely in groups
- ... using pre-recorded materials produced by teachers who do not know their life or work context and whom they may never meet
- ... with support from people who did not produce the materials.

The individualism of the do-it-yourself learner

Open learning is usually a private affair. Course materials address themselves to the individual learner. The learner is given responsibility for his or her own learning. The individual needs to be self-motivating, self-directing and relatively self-sufficient.

It is interesting that this do-it-yourself approach came to maturity during the years of Thatcherism. That ideology deemed the individual responsible for his or her own fate. It denied the existence of social forces beyond the individual's control that might excuse any lack of success. Hence, for instance, it is the fault of individuals rather than that of society if they fail to become part of the skilled core workforce – especially since they've now been offered (user-friendly) open learning. As Richard Edwards (1991) puts it:

> *Being part of the core is the goal, as it is 'normal' to be a high skilled worker. Persons can strive for this goal, but if they do not achieve it, it is because they lack the skills. Education and training opportunities are available to them through open learning, as and when they need them, so the responsibility for not participating in the core of the economy lies with them.*

Thatcherism also championed individual self-interest beyond the interests of any collective 'society'. Is there an underlying danger that open learning could promote a similar spirit of 'I've got on all right, Jack – so the jobless can't have been trying'? If so, we may want to look for ways of making open learning more of a collaborative experience.

The perils of the package

Packaged learning can easily become passive learning – especially if the learners are to be assessed on what they have learned. The learner can become dependent, distanced from his or her own experience of the subject, concerned only to soak up the message or – slightly more actively but no more creatively – suss out which bits of it are likely to be assessed. Whatever the intentions of the authors, a package's well-structured exposition of carefully-sifted ideas can encourage the learner in servile (if sometimes cynical) compliance.

The package – especially if it is glossily expensive – clearly embodies the wisdom of the expert (perhaps even a team of experts) whose view of things seems to be authoritative. Learners may feel too overwhelmed to challenge it or offer alternative views based on their own experience.

Packages lend themselves to what Richard Boot & Vivien Hodgson (1987) have called the 'dissemination' model of learning. Here, they say, 'knowledge can be seen as a (valuable) commodity which exists independently of people and as such can be stored and transmitted (sold)'. This contrasts with what they call the 'development' model whose purpose, they suggest, is 'the development of the whole person, especially the continuing capacity to make sense of oneself and the world in which one lives'.

It is easier to write packages that encourage people to learn what they are told than packages that help them make their own personal knowledge. Lewis Elton (1988) gives useful guidance on how to overcome this problem.

The absent group

People often find they are better able to challenge received ideas, and struggle towards new ideas of their own, when they can do so in company with other learners...

Sadly, group interaction – allowing an opportunity to relate the package's ideas to a known context, to hear and perhaps grapple with other people's contradictory viewpoints or experiences, to articulate and get feedback on one's own, to engage in collaborative enquiry – is what the open learner gets relatively little of. In the absence of such live 'process', many home-based learners may feel, as Winifred Hirst (1986) suggests, that packages are like fast food take-aways – seeming to lack that 'real honest-to-goodness flavour'.

Some sponsors of packaged learning may be quite pleased to ensure that learners are studying alone and learning what they are told to learn. Alan Tait (1989) reminds us why distance teaching was brought into higher education in Iran and Turkey. Reportedly, the rulers wanted to avoid the kind of political dissent that had been common where students spent time together on campus.

Most providers and sponsors of open learning have no such fear of the collective. But how much of it can we afford? The more often we expect learners to come together in groups, the more constrained (less open) some may feel. Contrarily, others may see it as the most attractive feature of the course. (And if we also expect those groups to have a paid leader, we risk eroding the cost advantages of open learning.) Yet if group meetings are infrequent, learners may not know or trust one another enough to disclose their thoughts and feelings or listen with empathy to others.

The human touch?

What about the human media – tutors, mentors, counsellors, and so on? Can they help overcome any tendency to dissemination in the package materials and undue deference in the learner? Can they provoke the learner to challenge the materials, relate them to their own experience and develop their own stance on the subject?

Quite possibly. Many Open University students have told me how their subjects came to life in arguing the toss with their tutors – either face-to-face, by correspondence or on the phone. Such tutoring in turn demands considerable attention to recruitment and staff development. Not all teachers take easily to the nurturing, developmental role. An unreconstructed pedagogue might simply add his or her weight to the dissemination model – increasing the learner's dependence on authorities.

The danger to teachers

Nurturing the teachers in an open learning system may be almost as important as nurturing the learners. Just as packaged learning can dehumanise the learners (in the sense that they may be reduced to dutiful data processors), so too it can de-skill and alienate, or even supplant, the teachers. Some people – perhaps those who suspect that the only open learning with a chance of catching on will be cheap learning – seem to hold out the ideal of a teacher-proof package, e.g. Temple (1988):

> ... *without adequate support even quite satisfactory open learning material is badly received. The present solution is seen to be the proper training of teachers, trainers and tutors, whose services are, however, expensive for*

anything other than their technical expertise. A more economical far-reaching alternative is to develop better learning materials whose interactivity will provide the necessary support and to ensure that learners have access to – and are not embarrassed about using – peer groups and other 'non-experts' for most of their general needs.

The plight of the teachers in open learning can be seen as an aspect of what Otto Peters (1989) calls 'industrialisation'. He points out that large-scale distance education has been made possible only by introducing principles and practices developed in manufacturing industry – e.g. project planning, mass production of teaching materials, quality control, division of labour and mechanisation.

Those last two items may pose a special threat to teachers and, through them, to learners. Division of labour means specialisation within the workforce. The course-writers have to share the task of making a package with a number of other specialists – editors, graphic designers, educational technologists. And none of the course producers may have any teaching contact with learners. Indeed, the task of supporting learners may be passed to another set of specialists (e.g. tutors) who have had no say in deciding what is to be taught. Assessment may be controlled by yet another group of specialists (who neither plan nor teach the programme).

Otto Peters warns us that teachers may thus be alienated. Each one's involvement is limited and he or she is no longer responsible for the whole process. Thus teachers may be left feeling isolated and frustrated, coping with uncertainty and loss of control while, at the same time, learning new skills and keeping up the high level of motivation expected of them in what may be an innovative and risky undertaking.

As for mechanisation, open learning teachers and trainers may be only too aware that the ultimate form of mechanisation is automation. How long, they may wonder, before packaged learning puts us out of work altogether? Staff in colleges and universities, which the government is now demanding should process many more students without employing extra teachers, may increasingly find they are having to make the acquaintance of new packages rather than new colleagues...

Final remarks

I do not want to end this unit on a down beat. In the last few pages we have warned ourselves about some dangers that may imperil open learning. It may lend itself to use as a tool of social control. Packages may promote dissemination rather than development. Isolated learning may limit exposure to conflicting ideas. Both learners and teachers may feel they've lost some vital spark of humanity and creativity.

But traditional education and training are not perfect either. That is at least partly why open learning has taken off. It still has enormous potential to transform people's lives. Can we overcome the dangers and harness that potential? Can we make learning more productive and satisfying – both for existing learners and for people who have never previously thought of themselves as learners and may even think of themselves as non-learners? Can we develop an open learning fit for the kind of society we'd like to live in? That is the challenge.

References

ALBSU (1991) *Open learning centres in England and Wales* Adult Literacy & Basic Skills Unit

Boot R & Hodgson V (1987) 'Open learning: meaning and experience' Chapter 1 in V Hodgson, S Mann & R Snell (eds) *Beyond distance teaching – towards open learning* SRHE & Open University Press

Boot R & Hodgson V (1988) 'Open learning: philosophy or expediency?' *Programmed Learning and Educational Technology* 25 (3), pp197–204

Edwards R (1991) 'The inevitable future? Post-Fordism and open learning' *Open Learning* 6 (2), pp36–42

Elton L (1988) 'Conditions for learner autonomy at a distance' *Programmed Learning and Educational Technology* 25 (3), pp216–24

Fox S (1989) 'The production and distribution of knowledge through open and distance learning' *Educational and Training Technology International* 26 (3), pp269–80

Harris D (1987) *Openness and closure in distance education* Falmer Press

Hirst W (1986) 'Melbourne to Manchester: a look at openness in some open learning situations' *International Journal of Lifelong Education* 5 (4), pp327–46

McNay I (1987) 'Organisation and staff development' in M Thorpe & D Grugeon (eds) *Open learning for adults* Longman

McNay I (1988) 'Open learning: a jarring note' in N Paine (ed) *Open learning in transition* National Extension College

Morpeth R (1988) 'The National Extension College: present and future' *Open Learning* 3 (2), pp34–6

MSC (1982) *Open Tech task group report* Manpower Services Commission

OU/ED (1990) *How to profit from open learning – company evidence* Open University/Employment Department

Peters O (1989) 'The iceberg has not melted: further reflections on the concept of industrialisation and distance teaching' *Open Learning* 4 (3), pp3–8

Richards M (1984) 'OU's head on the block' *Times Higher Educational Supplement,* 13 July

Tait A (1989) 'The politics of open learning' *Adult Education* 64 (4), pp308–13

Temple H (1988) 'Open learning: helped or hindered by Open Tech?' *Programmed Learning and Educational Technology* 25 (3), pp241–4

Temple H (1991) *Open learning in industry* Longman

Tolley G (1983) *The Open Tech: why, what and how?* Manpower Services Commission

Tuckett A (1988) 'Open learning and the education of adults' in N Paine (ed) *Open learning in transition* National Extension College

4. Designing for Open Learning

Phil Race

... The present chapter is intended to help teachers and trainers who are thinking about developing flexible learning materials of their own. My discussion of the design of open learning materials relates to [my own] model of learning.

How do people really learn?

In the last two thousand years or so, quite a lot has been written about how people learn. Indeed, people have been learning for some millions of years, and my guess is that while we have changed the nature of *what* we learn, we have not changed much regarding *how* we learn. In recent times, most of the theories of learning have been detailed and complex, written by psychologists, and it has become fashionable to use long words to describe learning. However, ... I've recently been advancing my own 'universal theory of learning' (in short words), based on the response of *real* people to questions about how they learn.

People are already 'open learners'

My first conclusion is that most of the learning people do is by what, nowadays, we call 'open learning' processes – in other words, at their own pace, in their own way and at times and places of their own choosing. So, designing open learning materials is simply a matter of designing materials from which people can learn in their own natural ways. However, there's a lot more to it than simply writing all the knowledge down – textbooks have been around for most of recorded history and we've all experienced how easy it is to spend hours with textbooks *without* any substantial learning payoff being derived from them. Learning resources need to contain much more than just information, and looking at how people learn is the best way to determine what needs to be added.

Linking open learning to how people learn

[Here is my] model of learning, which can be expressed in a few lines – there are four main stages, as follows:

1. wanting to learn, and knowing what to learn, and why
2. learning by doing
3. learning from feedback
4. digesting what has been learned.

In short, it's a sequence of wanting, doing, getting feedback and digesting. Each of these four natural stages in the learning process has implications in designing open learning materials. In this article, I'd like you to think about each of the four steps in turn and relate them to the components of open learning materials.

1. Creating the 'want' (and responding to 'what?' and 'why?')

Motivation is a key foundation for successful learning, and in plain words motivation is about 'wanting'. It's no use just 'wanting' vaguely, however. People need to be able to see exactly what they can learn from an open learning package and why it will be useful to them. Several ingredients of an open learning package can be polished up, so that people are attracted towards it and stimulated to begin it.

The title

Titles can be attractive – or off-putting. Which would you choose from a selection of packages with the following titles?

'Elements of Chemical Thermodynamics IV'
'Getting to Grips with Thermodynamics'
'Introductory Accountancy for Turf Accountants'
'Balancing your Betting-shop Books'

It helps, too, if the package *looks* interesting, with a stimulating and attractive cover design. After all, the title and cover also play a big part in helping people to *choose* a package in the first place.

Aims, objectives, competence statements

People (not surprisingly) want to know exactly what they will become able to do when they have worked through an open learning package. They need to be helped to *want* to achieve the objectives – and not to be frightened off by them. They need to see the relevance of the competences that the package will enable them to demonstrate. *'When you've worked through this package, you'll be able to write a good short story'* is a much more attractive objective than *'The expected learning outcome of this package is that the student will be able to compose a short work of creative fiction'* (at least, I think it is!).

The introduction

I'm always telling authors of open learning materials: 'You never get a second chance to make a good first impression'. It's obvious really. That first paragraph or two sets the mood in which learners proceed. The first page or so should be written with a great deal of care (preferably *after* the whole of the rest of the package has been written, so that it can point firmly towards things to come).

But I know this already

No-one comes to a new subject completely ignorant. Everyone knows *something* about a topic – even if it's just a series of questions they want to find out the answers to. In addition, people don't like to *feel* ignorant! Therefore, to help sustain the 'want', people need to be given credit for what they know already – it needs to be valued. One of the best ways of valuing what people already know is to give them the chance to tell you, then reply to them along the lines 'well done, you're absolutely right'. It's perfectly possible to do this in open learning materials, by setting early exercises which most people should be able to do correctly, and responding positively to what they do with the exercises. But, we're overlapping already into the second and third phases of my model of learning: doing and getting feedback. (People aren't simple; all four stages overlap!)

2. Learning by doing

The heart of open learning

Surprising as it is to many people in the world of education (and not surprising at all to trainers), people don't learn much by sitting at the feet of the master or mistress. In addition, people don't learn much just by *reading* the fine words of experts. People learn by having a go themselves. They learn by *doing*. They learn by getting things right. They learn even more by getting things wrong – and getting feedback on what was wrong. It's particularly helpful to learn by getting things wrong *in the comfort of privacy* – one of the most powerful strengths of open learning.

'Doing' is more than just 'recalling'

Designing an open learning package is essentially a case of designing things for learners to do, from which they can learn. Admittedly, sometimes we have to tell them a little information before they can do something useful – though usually this information can be quite minimal. Sadly, writers too often feel that they have to write down everything that they know – not much help to people who learn by doing, not reading.

What can learners do?

It's not just a matter of giving learners some information, then giving them the chance to tell it back to you. Here are a few ideas, all of which can be built into tasks for learners to do: deciding, choosing, prioritising, summarising, arguing, defending, attacking, backing, proposing, creating, suggesting, illustrating, explaining, expressing, discussing, planning, exploring, fault-finding, criticising, evaluating.

How soon should the 'doing' begin?

As soon as possible! It's often possible to begin an open learning package with something interesting for learners to do – for example to map out what they can already do (and can't yet do) using a checklist. When learning-by-doing is built into a package right from the start, learners quickly get the idea that the package is not just another text book.

Self-assessment questions, activities, assignments

As soon as learners have a go at some 'learning by doing' they need to be able to find out 'was I right?' or 'was my choice a sensible one?' So, any good learning activity will be one where it is possible to learn by doing *and* it will also be possible to learn by getting feedback on what has been done. In short, the most important parts of any open learning package are those that learners *do*, not just read.

Getting the tasks right

When you're there in person to tell people what to do, they've got more than your words to help them work out *exactly* what they should be trying to do. They've got your tone of voice. There's your facial expression. There's your body language.

When you're writing tasks for open learners to do, the words need to be particularly well-chosen, to compensate for all those other clues that aren't available to learners. The best way to get the wording of tasks right is to try the written tasks out on 'live' people in a face-to-face situation, watching how they respond to the words and asking them whether the purposes of the tasks are clear.

3. Learning from feedback

Throughout this book I've mentioned this. Learners need feedback to help them feel good about what they have just learned successfully – and to help them find out what they have not yet learned successfully. When learners have a go at self-assessment questions or activities, they need a lot more than mere answers. Look at it this way: all they can tell from an answer is whether they were right or not. True, that's feedback of sorts. But it's possible to give much more useful feedback if we try to *respond to what learners do*. In other words, if we ask them to make a choice, we need to be able to comment on whether they made a good choice and explain the justification supporting the best choice and explain to anyone making a different choice exactly what is wrong with doing that.

Praise and sympathy

When people do something well, it helps enormously to say 'well done'. There are thousands of ways of wording 'well done' messages – there's no need to be repetitious and boring about giving praise.

When people get something wrong, especially working alone as open learners, they need a few well-chosen words of 'sympathy' along with the explanations to help them on their way. The danger is that someone who gets something wrong may be thinking *'am I the only idiot in the world who would have got this wrong?'* Words such as *'this was a tricky question'* or *'most people have trouble with this at first'* can make *all* the difference.

Write 'responsable' questions

Sorry about the shock of a 'new' word that looks very much like a spelling mistake, but I've found it a useful term to use in open-learning writing workshops – people remember it! By 'responsable', I simply mean 'able to be responded to'. The need for feedback places limits on the sorts of questions which can be useful to learners. It's little use asking them to *'list four causes of inflation'*. They may list four completely different ones from the ones we want them to list – and they may be right. Far better to ask them *'which of the following are the four most important causes of inflation?'* (giving eight possibilities, say), then responding exactly why four are more important than the others, and including explanations of any of the possibilities they may have chosen which are not causes of inflation at all.

Various sorts of feedback

Learners can benefit from printed feedback comments which *respond* to what they do with self-assessment questions or activities. They can also benefit from 'human' feedback, for example that given by a tutor responding to a tutor-marked assignment.

However, there are even more possibilities for ensuring that learners get sufficient feedback to make them feel good about their learning.

Other people can be a vital resource. Learners can give feedback to each other. Friends, supervisors, bosses, managers, employees, and all sorts of other people can be a resource to learners regarding getting feedback. Learners may indeed need help in working out who to ask what, for feedback.

Help learners to receive feedback well

'There is no such thing as criticism, there is just feedback' – if only it were as easy as this. However, it can make all the difference if some time can be spent with learners convincing them of the value of feedback even when it's 'negative'. Simply helping them to receive critical comment as 'criticism of something I did' rather than 'criticism of me' is a major step.

4. Digesting – making the learning one's own

Some revered theorists of learning have referred to this as 'reflection'. For years, I happily went along with them. To learn something, we do indeed need to make sense of it, take stock of it, and allow it to fit in among all the other things we know. However, the more I thought about it, the less happy I became with the word 'reflection' for these processes. 'Reflection' implies something rather passive. And in any case, a mirror only gives one back what is placed before it (the wrong way round horizontally, yet alright vertically – no wonder 'reflection' can cause confusion!).

Then I thought of *digesting*. This useful word describes what we really want to help people do to consolidate their learning. It implies 'making it one's own'. It implies taking stock and making sense of what has been learned. It implies giving it time. It implies sorting it out into what one needs to keep – and discarding in due course the parts that are not useful or relevant. Sadly, our education system does not seem to have been good at helping digestion. In particular, we tend to have tried to 'fill people up' with all sorts of things they don't really need and not faced up to the need for them to sort out what they needed, then dispose of the rest. Perhaps (to take the analogy one step too far?) there are a lot of people who steer clear of opportunities to learn simply because they have become constipated?

Summaries and reviews

These can be a big help in the 'digesting' stage. Summaries and reviews help learners to decide what they need to retain. It can even be useful to read the summary or review *before* starting a topic as a way of finding out what it's *really* going to be about (especially if the objectives aren't clearly spelled out). Sadly, many open learning materials are skimpy on summaries or reviews. However, it's relatively easy – and very useful – to 'add-on' summaries and reviews by writing study-guide material to help learners to navigate an existing open learning resource.

'Hiccups'

If we overload our digestive systems, hiccups give us a useful message. The same can be true of learning. It is possible to build into open learning materials, from time to time, an activity that will 'catch' anyone who is going at it too fast and help them to consolidate things they really need.

Indigestion remedies

Every now and then, a good open learning package will give learners the chance to find out how their 'digesting' is going. This can take the form of an exercise which helps them to detect any parts that are not being properly digested, offering helpful suggestions about how to go about putting the situation right.

Supporting open learners

In this short chapter, I've been concentrating on those components of learning packages which can help open learners to learn productively, using their natural ways of learning. However, even the best open learning package can work even better if it is well supported from 'outside' – for example by tutors or mentors. Human helpers can be even more responsive than print when it comes to providing learners with feedback on what they have done. Moreover, human helpers can help maintain open learners' motivation – in other words, 'keep them *wanting* to learn'.

Summary

When designing open learning materials – whether print-based, computer-based, or multimedia packages – what matters is 'how it works'. This is much more important than the 'content' of the materials. The keys to quality are the elements of the materials which mesh with the ways that people actually learn. The best materials will create the *want* to learn, provide abundant opportunities to *learn by doing,* provide a great deal of *useful feedback* to learners and take account of the fact that learning does not happen instantly, but needs time for *digestion.*

5. Moving from Traditional Teaching to Flexible Learning

Phil Race

This chapter aims to help teachers develop flexible learning materials from the resources they already use with their students. The chapter suggests how to make an 'additionality' approach at least as effective as employing off-the-shelf flexible learning resource materials. This chapter contains various ideas relating to moving teaching/learning processes towards open, flexible or distance learning.

When you've applied these ideas to your own situation, I hope you'll be better able to:

- decide whether to adopt, adapt, or start from scratch, as you track down and examine existing flexible learning materials in your subject areas;

- work out *which* of the materials you are already using in your teaching lend themselves to being adapted into something that will work as a flexible learning resource;

- build on existing resources at your disposal, adding to them components which will allow them to work in independent-study mode;

- choose or develop high quality flexible learning resources.

Flexible, open and distance learning

Each of these terms has been defined in different ways by different writers. Perhaps the simplest way to explain the similarities, differences, and overlaps between them is to describe how the respective types of learning usually happen.

Distance learning

Learners are separated by distance from providers for some, most, or even all of the time. Examples include the Open University (UK), various correspondence learning agencies, and some in-company training schemes where trainees are studying at their own base rather than in a training centre. Usually (but not always) distance learning is done by people working on their own.

Open learning

This term is broader, and includes all the examples of distance learning given above. Open learning usually means that learners have some control over three primary factors: time, place and pace, or in other words:

- where they learn
- when they learn
- how they learn.

'Open learning' can sometimes also be taken to mean 'open to all comers'. For example, the Open University takes people without the formal entry qualifications required by many traditional institutions of higher education. However, in practice, most open learning programmes need learners to have already reached particular levels of competence or experience, as laid down in the 'prerequisite knowledge and skills' listed in the materials.

Flexible learning

This term is even broader, and includes all forms of open and distance learning, but also includes other learning situations which at first sight appear more traditional. For example, 200 people in a lecture theatre can be 'learning flexibly', if (for example) they are spending five minutes where everyone is working through a handout and trying to answer some questions. In other words, flexible learning involves people taking some control regarding how they learn. Flexible learning should be considered as part of a toolkit of ways of developing successful learning outcomes and demonstrable competences in our students. Essentially, developing flexible learning processes from traditional teaching processes is largely a matter of putting into print not only the content of the syllabus, but particularly the *support* which would be offered to the students by teachers. Since it is recognised that most learning occurs by doing, the key aspect of the development of flexible learning resource materials is the *interaction* between learners and materials – in particular how well the materials respond to learners' attempts to answer self-assessment questions.

'Doing' and 'feedback' in flexible learning

Important aspects of the support and interaction which can be built in to flexible learning resources are:

- the *tasks* and *exercises* whereby learners gain competence
- the *feedback* learners receive on their progress
- the *guidance* learners are given regarding use of textbooks and resources
- details of the *assessment criteria* which will be indicative of successful outcomes.

The end of traditional teaching?

It is not suggested that flexible learning should replace all traditional teaching. For many purposes, face-to-face learning situations have advantages over learning alone, and peer group interaction is a vital part of many kinds of learning. In particular, it is possible to arrange that learners receive feedback from their peers – far more feedback than could be received from tutors or lecturers (even if not the 'expert' feedback which they need in addition). It would be sensible to examine which parts of our curriculum are best handled through each of several alternatives including:

- large-group teaching and learning
- small-group tutorial work
- small-group unsupervised work
- individual self-study on campus
- individual self-study at a distance
- small-group self-study.

Each of these learning situations should be used for those purposes particularly suited to it. For those curriculum elements where self-study pathways or components are feasible and desirable, we can develop or acquire flexible learning resources of a suitable quality and standard.

By far the best situation in which to develop flexible learning resource materials is by being involved face-to-face with 'traditional students'. The ultimate aim may be to produce resources which can promote learning without the presence of a tutor, but the hand over of control is best done one step at a time, with thorough monitoring of each move towards learner autonomy. A longer-term aim should be to establish distance learning pathways, built initially from those flexible learning resources which prove their worth with conventional students.

Ten reasons for moving towards flexible learning:

1. Increasing competition between institutions of higher education and training means that we have to be able to *cater more flexibly* for a wide variety of student needs and expectations.

2. With increased need for *collaboration* between providers of education and training, resource-based learning provides an easier basis for such collaboration.

3. The availability of a substantial proportion of curricula in *packaged* form significantly helps progress towards a modular structure and allows increased choice to students.

4. Increased pressure on funding will mean we need to be able to cater both for *larger class numbers* and for *new target groups* of part-time and distant students.

5. As the proportion of *mature and non-traditional entry students* increases, we need to complement traditional teaching and learning approaches by creating additional flexible learning pathways and to replace entirely some traditional approaches disliked by mature students.

6. With increasing use of supported self-study in secondary education, *student expectations* are likely to move away from that of being taught mostly in lectures.

7. With the increased franchising of our programmes in further education colleges and in-company training departments, the availability of flexible learning resource materials provides an excellent means of ensuring that the *quality of learning* is maintained and controlled.

8. In *commerce and industry*, open and flexible learning is becoming much more attractive than traditional training (many central training departments have been restructured or even closed down).

9. It is increasingly realised that, in many disciplines, higher education students are *seriously 'over-taught'*, and that this produces surface rather than deep learning and limits students' development of highly valued transferable skills.

10. Perhaps the most important outcome of higher education should be *the development of the ability to manage one's own learning*; flexible learning pathways develop this ability – being taught inhibits such development.

Adopt, adapt, or start from scratch?

- *Does something suitable exist already?*

  If the 'perfect' open learning materials (perfect for your learners' needs) exist already, the most logical thing would seem to be to adopt them. This may mean negotiating with whoever owns the materials to get quantity-discounts. If (as is often the case) there are materials which nearly meet your learners' needs, you may well be able to 'make up' any deficiencies with tutorial support, or with things you add-on to the materials. There are various catalogues and databases which can be valuable in helping to identify and locate materials which already exist. However, there is no substitute for getting your hands on existing materials, before deciding whether they can be used as they are, or whether they lend themselves to adaptation for your students. You may need to use all the tricks you can think of to get a good look at such materials. Better still, it's worth trying a small-scale pilot before committing yourself to the purchase of large quantities of materials.

  Another way of tracking down potentially relevant learning materials is through informal contacts with colleagues from other institutions. Coffee-breaks at conferences can be very profitable if used to help find people with whom you can exchange resources and information! A good checklist should be useful in helping you decide which materials may be good enough to adopt. You could use the checklist at the end of this chapter as a starting point and refine it to tune-in better to the needs of your learners.

- *Have you time to start from scratch?*

  Writing open learning materials from scratch takes time – a lot of time! Open learning writing has often been paid for on the basis of ten hours to write up the equivalent of one hour's learning. In practice, it may take more like a hundred hours to write up one hour of learning, when preparation, piloting, editing, adjusting and so on are taken into account. If something fairly close to what is needed already exists, it can be more economical to adapt rather than start from scratch. However, you'll learn many valuable things from having a go at writing your own materials. If you really want to create new materials, the time issue seems to take care of itself.

- *Could the 'not invented here syndrome' affect you?*

  Most teachers and trainers feel a little uncomfortable working with materials written by others. We tend to prefer to work with materials where we have a sense of 'ownership'. Even if alternative materials are better than our own, our instinct is to prefer our own, and it's only too easy for us to see all sorts of weaknesses in other people's materials. This can be a reason for starting from scratch and writing new flexible learning resource materials. However, the *real* reason should be based on the needs of our learners. If these needs are best served by writing new materials specially for them, starting from scratch is indeed justified.

- *What are the advantages of adapting?*

  Adapting existing resource materials can have many advantages, including the following:

  - it can save time and expense;
  - you probably already own materials which can be adapted;
  - you can adapt materials a bit at a time;
  - you may be able to try out the adapted bits face-to-face with conventional classes to gain feedback and enable improvements to be made quickly;
  - you *may* be able to use small pieces of published material without copyright problems or payments – but seek expert help and advice; librarians often know a lot about copyright rules and regulations;
  - you'll still feel a considerable amount of 'ownership' of the materials if you've done all the fine-tuning yourself (i.e. avoiding the 'not invented here' feeling);
  - it can be much less expensive than having to purchase complete packages for each of your learners;
  - adapting can be excellent practice towards writing some materials from scratch in due course.

'Learning by doing' – the heart of flexible learning

Most learning happens when we actually try to do something. Learning doesn't happen efficiently when we merely read about something or listen to someone talk about it. The measure of a good open learning package is *what the students do* as they work through it. Therefore, preparing to put together an open learning package (or adapting something which exists already) is not so much a matter of collecting together all the things students need to read – it's about collecting together a set of things for students to *do*.

When you already teach a subject face-to-face, you are likely to have a considerable collection of tasks and activities you give your students – in other words you are already well on your way to having one of the most important ingredients of your open learning packages. Don't forget the words you say when you introduce a task to students. Though you may already use printed sheets for the task briefings, any additional oral briefing is likely to play a very important part in helping students see exactly what they are intended to do as they approach a task. With oral briefing you have the additional advantages of tone of voice, emphasis, facial expression and body language. When translating tasks for flexible learning usage, it helps considerably if you can capture as many of these 'extra dimensions' as possible and wrap them up somehow in printed words.

What have I already, that can be used or adapted?

When you're already teaching a subject using traditional or face-to-face methods, it is not a mammoth task to translate your experience into the design of flexible learning resource materials, particularly if you are able to make the transition a little at a time. For example, it is possible to translate small elements of your normal teaching into flexible learning mode and try them out in traditional lectures or tutorials, gaining feedback from your observations of how your learners get on with the materials, questions, and feedback. Also, you can design mini-modules to give to learners, covering things you decide not to do in face-to-face mode.

The list below is an attempt to show how well you are 'armed' for making the transition towards flexible delivery of subjects you already teach. You will have many of the following – and probably more:

- your experience of teaching – probably the most valuable resource in this list
- your knowledge of students' problems
- your ability to help students to find solutions to their problems
- syllabus objectives or competences you work with already
- your own handout materials:
  - usually no copyright problems
  - often already contain central material
- existing resource materials
- class exercises
  - often adaptable to make self-assessment questions
- case study details
  - usually already the basis for learner activity – the essential part of flexible learning
- your own lecture notes
  - these may cover most of the content your learners need, already in concise form
- textbook extracts
  - it may be possible to obtain clearance to include small extracts without charge
  - OR it may be possible to get learners to refer to books (bought or borrowed from libraries)
- manuals
  - usually are already some way towards being interactive material
  - it may be possible to use extracts without copyright difficulties
  - it may be easy to re-compose extracts to avoid copyright difficulties
  - it may be possible to refer learners to 'available' manuals directly
- worksheets and assignments you give your students already
- problems and projects you design for your students.

What may need adding for flexible learning usage?

Some or all of the principal features of the best open learning materials can be added to transform your existing materials into flexible learning resources.

User-friendly objectives

- warming up things like 'the expected learning outcome is that the student will...' to 'by the end of... you'll be able to...'

- making objectives more directly relevant to learners' needs
- making them appropriate to the assessment criteria involved.

Responses to questions/tasks/activities

- not just model answers, but *responses* to what learners *do* when they have a go at the questions/tasks/activities
- discussion of anticipated errors/difficulties
- positive, encouraging comments for learners who have succeeded
- reassuring and encouraging comments for learners who did not succeed.

Additional questions/tasks/activities

- in self-assessment format, with responses as above.

Written study-skills help

- the *sorts* of help and support you'd give face-to-face learners informally.

Assessment criteria

- to link with objectives, learning outcomes and performance standards
- to alert learners to what counts and what could lose them credit
- to build learners' confidence, allowing them insight into 'the rules of the game'.

Summaries/reviews/checklists

- provide 'repeats' of crucial points, allowing learners to see what is most important
- provide useful revision aids.

Feedback questionnaires

- these should be short, structured, and in easy-to-complete format, but with additional space for comments from learners who *want* to expand on the basic questions.

Audiotape commentaries and discussions

- relatively cheap and simple to produce
- can make it less lonely for learners working on their own
- can be useful for talking learners through things like textbook extracts, derivations, complex diagrams and so on
- can also be used to help learners self-assess more complex tasks they may have done as part of their work – i.e. talking them through good answers and common mistakes (can be more friendly than a long printed response).

Briefings

- showing learners how best to use external resources such as textbooks, manuals, audiotapes, video, or practical kits.

How can a package be put together efficiently?

Turning your existing resources into an open learning package can be done more easily than you might have imagined. It's best to get the various separate components of your package into good working order, trying them out with groups of your students whenever you can, then gradually build the components together into a draft package and see how your students cope with it.

At first, the task of putting together an open learning package may seem formidable – especially if you want to equal the best published packages. However, Rome wasn't built in a day, and the best open learning materials were created gradually, step by step – with a great deal of piloting at each stage.

Most of these steps are simple extensions of things you do in your day-to-day work with your students. The following sequence can save much time and trouble:

1. Design *self-assessment questions* and *activities* for your open learners, based on the class-work exercises you presently use and the assignments and projects you set your existing students, linking these to the syllabus *objectives* or *competences* in the same way as you already do. Adjust the wording of all these components as you go, so they become as straightforward and clear as possible, so that learners don't need you to explain what the words mean.

2. Write *responses* to each self-assessment question and activity. Base these responses on the way you deal with your live students. Write in the explanations you give them when they make mistakes. Keep striving to make the questions and responses as self-explanatory as you can so that you don't need to be present in person. Try out each draft with your live students and observe any difficulties, adjusting questions and responses as necessary.

3. Start turning your notes and handouts into short sections of text. Make these sections bridge the gaps between the *response* to one question and the next question. Each chunk of text therefore has a distinct function – to lead up to the next student activity.

4. When there are questions or activities which really do need a human response rather than a prepared one, turn the questions into *tutor marked assignments* and build these in to your package.

5. Go through the bits and pieces of your package, adding *summaries* or *reviews* at key points. Make such additions every time your students may need reinforcement of principal ideas and concepts.

6. Now that your package is nearing a 'working' form, go through it again, adding *short introductions* or *'lead-in'* paragraphs, preparing your students for what is to come in each part. It's far easier to write well-tuned introductions when you've already written the parts you're leading up to.

As you can see from the above sequence, writing an open learning package is not done in the same way as writing a textbook. It's not a matter of starting by writing page 1 and working through in a linear sequence. Open learning packages are designed around the *learning* that students will gain from them. This takes the emphasis away from the text itself and means you don't need to try to write everything you know about the subject, only the things your students *need* to gain.

It's often advisable to start working on the middle of your package, then work outwards in both directions. Writing the very beginning is one of the most crucial tasks – this is much easier to do if you've already written later parts of the package – you know then exactly what you're introducing.

Responses – not just answers

The responses you write for self-assessment questions and activities are by far the most important ingredient of your open learning package and therefore you should give them careful attention. (It's sadly all too easy to tell that questions and responses have been added to many open learning packages at the last minute – almost as an afterthought).

If you think about the best quality face-to-face teaching, some of the most important skills include:

- explaining to students what to do when they can't yet answer a question
- helping students to feel a glow when they do something correctly
- helping students find out exactly what went wrong when they make mistakes.

Writing open learning materials gives you the chance to package up these valuable skills, so that your help is extended to students even when you're not there in person. The response to a good self-assessment question should enable each student to find out two things:

> *'Was I right?'*
>
> *'If not, why not?'*

When open learning materials are scrutinised by professional open learning writers, the first thing that they turn to are the responses to self-assessment questions and activities. If these responses are working well, the package is a good one.

Structured questions are easier to respond to!

Responding to open-ended questions is possible – but usually difficult. A good response needs to cover every answer that learners may reasonably have given – and more. Structured questions involve learners making a decision such as:

- which is the correct option?
- which is the most sensible course of action?
- which is the best order in a sequence?

With such questions, you can respond directly to learners who choose a 'wrong' or 'less-good' option, explaining exactly why their choice is not the best one.

Some guidelines for briefings

'Briefings' represent one area of support and advice that is normally handled quite informally in face-to-face sessions. Students at such sessions have the extra advantages of tone-of-voice and facial expression, helping them find out more about exactly what they're intended to do with the textbooks and literature references they're given. The same level of support needs to be put into print if students studying by flexible learning pathways are to derive the same amount of benefit from briefings to resource materials. The following suggestions give some ways of ensuring that printed briefings serve learners effectively.

- *Keep them short and specific*
  It is better to have briefings to *short extracts* than to whole books or chapters: e.g. 'Now work through Sections 2.3 and 2.5' is better than 'Now read Chapter 2'.

- *Make briefings active*
  i.e. don't just ask learners to 'read' things, but give them things to do *while* they read them – or even *before* reading things (not just *after* they've read them).

- *Include 'commentary' elements in briefings*
  e.g. 'Chapter 3 gives a good overview of ... ... watch out particularly for the way ... is discussed. Don't worry about ... at this stage, you don't need to know the sort of detail that you'll see in Section 3.5!'

- *Include 'signposting' in briefings*
  e.g. 'In Section 4.8 we've already seen why ... happens. In Section 4.9 you'll find out what happens when ... which is useful when you need to work out how to ...

- *Plant questions in learners' minds*
  When learners have already got some questions in mind before reading something, they have a subconscious 'thirst' for the answers to the questions. This means that when they come across the 'answers' as they read, those parts are more memorable to them. This makes reading far more efficient.

  e.g. 'As you study Section 6, try to find answers to the following three questions:
    Why does...?
    How could...?
    When might you find...?

- *Include 'steering' in briefings*
  e.g. 'You don't need to spend much time on Section 7 unless you want to.' 'The heart of the matter is explained very well near the end of Section 5.7.' 'Aim to spend about half an hour simply getting the feel of Chapter 4 before having a go at the next set of self-assessment questions.'

- *Help learners to find out for themselves which parts they need to concentrate on*
  This can be done by using self-assessment questions to measure how much different learners already know about a topic and by using the responses to route each learner accordingly. For example:

Before you move on to Chapter 3 of the textbook, have a go at SAQ 23 below.

SAQ 23

Before studying 'waldefaction' in Jones & Smith, try to answer the following six questions to see if you already know something about it (don't worry if not – it's all in Jones & Smith!):

1.

2.

3.

4.

5.

6.

Response to SAQ 23 [out of sight of the question]

1.   [correct answers]

2.

3.

4.

5.

6.

If you got all of these right – well done – and you only need to look at Sections 3.7 and 3.9 in Chapter 3; you already know all you need to from the other sections.

If your only mistake was to ... you'll find out what to do about it at the beginning of Section 3.2. The only other parts of Chapter 3 you should give particular attention to are Sections 3.7 and 3.9.

If you didn't get much of this SAQ right – don't worry – it's all covered in Chapter 3. As you work through this Chapter, take particular note of Sections 3.2 and 3.4 – these contain what you need to do questions like SAQ 23...

Writing study guides

Some flexible learning programmes hardly 'contain' any subject matter in the normal sense of the term, but are written to guide learners through an existing resource such as a 'reader', or through a selection of resource materials. The Open University, for example, often adopts key reference books as the major source of information in a course. The open learning packages then become interactive guides to the books. All that I said earlier about briefings continues to apply to this sort of guidance. It remains particularly important that when learners have completed a task or activity based on the reference material, the study guide provides them with true responses to what they have been doing.

The 'books plus study guide' format solves several problems. Copyright is taken care of, as learners purchase (or are loaned) the original source material. Economies of scale are possible, as mass-produced books tend to be less expensive than open learning modules produced in runs of only hundreds. Any study guide is much slimmer than the corresponding material would have been if it had been put together in fully-interactive open learning style.

The study guide format depends, of course, on the availability of the resources to be used. If a textbook goes out of print, or becomes dated and superseded by new work, the study-guide will at once be redundant. However, it remains less expensive to revise or renew a 'slim' study guide than to redesign a full open learning module.

Some general tips for writers

- Avoid sitting thinking about writing – write! Set yourself stage deadlines – better still, let other people know about your deadlines. Work on small manageable jobs – don't try to work on the whole package at once.

- Show your writing to other people (students, colleagues, friends) long before it's 'ready'. Critical feedback on an early draft is easier to swallow than criticism of your completed masterpiece.

- Keep the tone relatively informal. Use *'you'* for your students. Use *'I'* as the author. As far as you can, try to make the printed page 'talk' to your students in the same way as you would have talked yourself – particularly when explaining things.

- Remind yourself now and then that you're not writing a major treatise, or a paper for an esteemed journal in your field. You're writing for your students. Don't stand on your professional dignity in your writing.

- Use plenty of *white space*. Leave room for your students to write into the material their answers to your questions and their own notes and comments. Your students will develop an important sense of ownership of the materials as they write all over them.

- Use short words rather than long words where possible. Get your meaning across as directly as you can (there's no 'tone-of-voice' or 'facial expression' to help your open learners).

- Use short simple sentences rather than long complex ones. Aim to get your meaning across on the first reading of each sentence. Be particularly careful when setting questions and tasks. Make sure that students will know exactly what they are intended to do with each task.

- Include headings and sub-headings so that students can see at a glance what each page is doing. If your students can see where they're going – and where they've been – their journey through your open learning package will be more likely to be successful.

- Include illustrations wherever they help students to understand things. Illustrations also help to keep students going – a page with something visual on it looks more enticing than a solid page of text.

Piloting – the best guarantee of quality

You may have seen many open learning materials which *look* marvellous – but which don't work! These are packages which were 'glossed-up' and published long before they were ready.

The more feedback you can get about how your package works, the better you can make your final version. The best open learning packages owe as much to the experiences of students who tested them out as to the skills of the authors.

You don't have to wait until you've got a finished product before starting to gather feedback. You can try out each small part as you compose it. For example, with the help of your students, you can test your self-assessment questions and responses. You can try out your tutor-marked assignments. You can change things every time you find a problem.

When eventually you have a first draft of your package assembled, it's useful to try this out on some students (and on some colleagues), deliberately seeking detailed feedback by providing questionnaires (and by talking to your piloteers).

Among other things, make sure you ask questions such as:

- *What is the best thing about the package?*
- *What do you like least about the package?*
- *What do you think is the hardest part of the package?*
- *What do you think of the tone and style of the package?*
- *How clear are the objectives of the package?*
- *How useful are the self-assessment questions and activities?*
- *How helpful are the responses to the self-assessment questions and activities?*
- *Do you think there are sufficient illustrations?*
- *How useful are the summaries and reviews?*
- *How long do you think the package takes to work through?*
- *Suggest some changes which can improve the package.*

A checklist for flexible learning resources

The checklist which follows is quite powerful! If all the answers are 'yes' or 'very well indeed', you're looking at an exemplary piece of open learning material. However, even when some of the criteria below are not met, all is not lost. In fact, it's very useful to identify exactly which criteria aren't met by a particular piece of flexible learning material; you are then in a position to compensate for whatever's lacking. It often only takes a few extra words or lines to 'plug a gap' in some material, or to help learners to make better use of it.

If you are writing your own material, you should find this checklist a useful self-editing resource. I've clustered the 30 checklist questions under sub-headings representing the main elements of flexible learning materials identified earlier in this chapter.

Objectives or statements of intended learning outcomes

1. Is there a clear indication of any prerequisite knowledge or skills?
2. Are the objectives stated clearly and unambiguously?
3. Are the objectives presented in a friendly way? (i.e. *not* 'the expected learning outcomes of this module are that the student will...'!)
4. Do the objectives avoid 'jargon' which may not be known to learners before starting the material?

Structure and layout

5. Is the material visually attractive?
6. Is there sufficient white space? (for learners to write notes, answer questions, do calculations, and so on.)
7. Is it easy for learners to find their way backwards and forwards? This is sometimes called 'signposting' and includes good use of headings.

Self-assessment questions and activities

8. Are there plenty of them? (Remember that flexible learning – like any other learning in fact – is largely dependent on 'learning by doing'.)
9. Are the tasks set by the questions clear and unconfusing?
10. Are the questions and tasks inviting? (Is it clear to learners that it's valuable for them to have a go rather than skip?)
11. Is there enough space for learners to write their answers?
12. Collectively, do the self-assessment questions and activities test learners' achievement of the objectives?

Responses to self-assessment questions and activities

13. Are they really *responses to what the learner has done?* (i.e. not just answers to the questions.)
14. Do the responses meet the learners' need to find out:
15. 'Was I right?'
16. 'If not, why not?'
17. Do the responses include encouragement or praise (without patronising) for learners who got them right?
18. Do the responses include something that will help learners who got it wrong not to feel like complete idiots?

Introductions, summaries and reviews

19. Is each part introduced in an interesting, stimulating way?
20. Do the introductions alert learners to the way the materials are designed to work?
21. Is there a clear and useful summary/review?
22. Does it provide a useful way to revise the material quickly?

The text itself

23. Is it readable and unambiguous?
24. Is it relevant? (for example, does it keep to the Objectives as stated?)
25. Is it 'involving' where possible? (i.e. plenty of use of 'you' for the learner, 'I' for the author, 'we' for the learner and author together.)

Diagrams, charts, tables, graphs, and so on

26. Is each as self-explanatory as possible?
27. Does the learner know what to do with each? (i.e. to learn it, to note it in passing, to pick out the trend, or even nothing at all.)
28. A sketch can be more useful than 1000 words: is the material sufficiently illustrated?

Some general points

29. Is the material broken into manageable chunks?
30. Does the material avoid any sudden jumps in level?
31. Does the material ensure that the average learner will achieve the objectives?
32. Will the average learner enjoy using the material?

Helping learners use flexible learning materials

The following suggestions can help learners adjust their approach to using flexible or open learning materials. I suggest that you fine-tune and develop your own advice to your learners, starting from the list below, by adding-in comments relating to the particular style and format of the materials they will be using.

1. Check whether there are things you should already be able to do before you start working through the open learning materials. Information such as 'prerequisites' is often given at the start.

2. If the material gives objectives one way or another, pay particular attention to these and keep returning to see how well you are getting on towards mastering them. Objectives are usually phrased along the lines 'when you've completed this package, you should be able to...'

3. Most open learning materials (good ones) are 'active' and contain things for you to do as you work through them. These active parts are sometimes called self-assessment questions or activities. However tempted you are to skip these and read on, don't skip them! Even if you think you know the answer, jot it down, then compare what you did with the answer or response given in the material.

4. When you get a question right, be pleased with yourself. When you get one wrong, be even more pleased – you've found out something useful. Find out exactly why you didn't get the right answer – and remember this for next time.

5. When you come to a bit that has you stumped, don't struggle with it for ages. Skim ahead and see what's coming next. The next bit may be straightforward. Make a note of exactly what you don't understand about the bit that stumped you, and plan to find out from someone how to deal with that bit. It's probably quite simple when you've got someone who can explain it to you, even though you may never have worked it out on your own.

6. Open learning materials often contain a great deal of information – don't try to learn it all as you proceed. Make decisions about what is required to be learned, as opposed to the things you are merely required to understand as you read them. It's very useful to work with fellow students for this – you'll all have slightly different views about exactly what is important and what isn't – the truth will be closer to the average than to one person's view.

7. If you've been given your own copy of the open learning material, make it belong to you, by writing your own comments and notes all over it (as well as by writing in the answers to questions and activities). You'll often remember the things you added to the material – a useful way of boosting what you remember about the topics involved.

8. Keep looking back – remind yourself of the things you've already done. The more often these things have been through your mind the more firmly you'll understand them.

9. Keep glancing ahead to see what's coming next. You'll often understand why you're doing something only when you see where it's leading towards.

10. Have another go at all the self-assessment questions and activities – again and again where they are difficult. Your ability to do something difficult depends more on how often you've tried doing it than on how thoroughly you did it once.

Conclusions

If you're already working face-to-face with students, you have several advantages when it comes to gradually turning parts of what you know into flexible learning resources:

*   You know your students – i.e. one of your target audiences.
*   You can try things out and get quick feedback on whether they work or not.
*   You can turn existing class-exercises and homework questions into self-assessment questions and activities.
*   You can turn the feedback you would give orally or in comments on marked work into printed responses to self-assessment questions and activities.
*   You can transform your own notes into the textual parts of flexible learning materials.
*   You can continue to use face-to-face sessions for the things that are difficult to wrap up in print.

Increased use of flexible learning within conventional programmes of study allows learners more opportunity to learn in 'high-quality' ways:

*   learning by doing, rather than by being taught;
*   learning at their own pace, rather than at yours;
*   learning in their own style, rather than in the way you happen to teach;
*   learning again and again from their materials where necessary, rather than once as you teach.

6.   Print and Other Media

Phil Race

Open learning packages can be made up of print materials alone, or can be computer-based programmes, or can be any combination of a wide range of media possibilities. Choice of medium or media depends on many factors, including the nature of the subject matter, the sort of people who make up the audience, and the way in which they will be able to learn most effectively.

It's wise to think about media before writing anything at all. If you decide to include non-print media in your package, you don't want them to appear to be last minute add-ons. You need to design the ways you put media to their best use from the outset.

Here we look [at the production of text and visual materials], and two other media: audiotapes and videotapes...

Text

Shorter sentences

... One of the ways to make material more readable is to use shorter sentences. Sadly, most of us have been trained to use long sentences. Think about it. At school, we were rewarded as our command of language grew. We were praised for writing longer sentences, with more clauses of various kinds in them. It was increasingly expected that we would not only have a subject, an object and a verb in each sentence, but that we would use conditional clauses, adverbial clauses, adjectival clauses and appropriate punctuation marks to string all these together in a way that would be impressive to whoever might read our work: in fact we were trained to write in an elitist kind of way, gradually narrowing the range of people who could understand our writing.

Phew! I deliberately made that a long sentence. It used to be one of my faults to write long sentences. I still tend to use a lot of commas, as you have probably noticed. Sorry!

One of the ways of getting sentence length down is to try to get rid of most of the commas. They can be replaced in a number of ways, including:

- Miss them out when the meaning will be just as clear without them.
- Replace some of them with full stops. Then start a new sentence.
- In sentences which have a series of commas, replace them with a list set out as here.
- Replace some of them with dashes – like this – creating separate bits of the sentence; dashed bits may count as separate sentences as far as the eye ... is concerned; we tend mentally to process such bits separately.

A good rule for sentence length is that a sentence should communicate a single idea.

But won't short sentences be patronising?

If sentences are too short, they could make for jerky reading. But that doesn't necessarily mean they would be found patronising as short sentences are often used to convey complex ideas.

It's best to think back to your target groups of learners. They may not be as skilled with advanced language as most authors. Maybe some learners will be studying in English as their second language. All the more reason to give them straightforward, direct English.

Now let's try getting rid of some commas in the long sentence in the first paragraph of this item.

> *It was expected that in each sentence we would have:*
> * *a subject*
> * *an object*
> * *a verb*
>
> *and increasingly we would be expected to have:*
> * *conditional clauses*
> * *adverbial clauses*
> * *adjectival clauses*
> * *appropriate punctuation marks.*
>
> *We were expected to string all these together in a way that would be impressive to whoever might read our work.*
>
> *In fact we were trained to write in an elitist kind of way, gradually narrowing the range of people who could understand our writing.*

You'll recognise the above as a new version of the long sentence from the previous page. All but one of the commas have gone. A better layout has been used to make the ideas stand out more. And it's easier to read...

I, you and we versus them and us

Textbooks are usually written in third person passive voice.

'It is found that when iron corrodes, a red-brown surface coating gradually grows on its surface. If the coating is abraded, it flakes off pitting the original metal surface.'

That is the sort of language we were trained to write. It was claimed that it was an objective way of presenting information. Reports were expected to be written in this sort of way. On no account should the author's humanity get in the way of being objective and dispassionate!

When writing learning materials we need to think again about such precedents. [One] way of helping learners to feel involved in the materials is to use first person (I or we) for the author(s) and second person (you) for learners whenever possible or appropriate.

Even when the materials have been written by several authors it may be better to use 'I' rather than 'we'. The latter can come across rather condescendingly, like the royal we. The time to use 'we' is when it means 'the learner together with the author'.

I used the phrase 'them and us' in the title of this item. I was referring to the feeling engendered by many formal textbooks, where the learner feels very much on one side of the teaching-learning process, with the author of the book on the other side.

It takes a little effort to drop inhibitions about writing 'I' as an author. It's somewhat easier to develop the habit of referring to the learner as 'you'. Using 'you' also has the advantage that it doesn't matter whether the learner is male or female, or whether one or more learners may be working together.

Delatinising your English

Long words where shorter words may do

One of the fascinating things about the English language is the variety of origins of words in everyday use. This means that we have several different words for most meanings as well as several different meanings for most words. In our own education we were gradually trained to use longer and longer words even when shorter ones would have done. Our language skills were measured to some extent in terms of the size of our vocabulary, and our ability to use 'difficult' words correctly. The problem is that it's easy to stick with this and continue to use longer words than necessary. This can get in the way of communicating effectively when writing learning materials.

Quite often, people writing open learning materials are authorities in their fields. This means they may often submit papers to learned journals, where referees may expect a 'high' level of language. Perhaps they feel it beneath their dignity to descend to a straightforward level of language. Perhaps they feel that they may lose their prized ability to communicate with their peers. Writing open learning material appears to do no irreversible damage to such abilities – unfortunately!

To some extent, words deriving from Latin origins tend to be longer than those of Anglo-Saxon origin. Of course, this is only part of the problem. Even with short words sentences can be far too long. I'm sure you'll have noticed that in the small print in all sorts of contracts the purpose would seem to be *not* to communicate efficiently!

Of course, I'm not suggesting avoiding long words altogether. Learning materials would be very boring that way. What I'm suggesting is to keep a general watch on your use of long words, and when a shorter one would do just as well, use it. Of course, if it is clearly on the agenda as part of your learners' objectives to extend their vocabulary and use of English, don't go out of your way to avoid the long words.

In my lists which follow I've randomly chosen a few long words, paired with some shorter words which in some instances would do just as well. You may like to compose a short sentence including a few of the shorter words, then 'translate backwards', replacing them with longer words. Whenever I've used this as a writers' workshop exercise, there have been hilarious results.

longer word	shorter word
unprecedented	new
advantageous	useful
commencement	start
disadvantage	snag
consequently	so
facilitate	help
subsequently	later
utilisation	use
expenditure	cost
furthermore	and
considerable	much
illustrate	show
comprehend	know
ascertain	find out
deliberate	discuss

The examples above are only the tip of the iceberg! Have a look at some of your own writing. We've all got favourite words that could be replaced by something simpler now and then.

Getting rid of rambling phrases

It's not just single words which cause problems. There are many phrases in everyday use which could be replaced by shorter ones, or could even be missed out altogether sometimes, without changing the meaning of sentences. You may like to experiment with my list below – and add to it.

establish a connection between	link
paying appropriate attention to	noting
in the immediate vicinity of	near
achieve a consensus	agree
at every available opportunity	whenever
maintained in a perpendicular alignment	held upright
with a fair degree of probability	probably
it may well turn out to be that	probably
unable to proceed further	stuck
aligned in a horizontal position	lying flat
socially withdrawn and inhibited	shy
at the present moment in time	now
on a subsequent occasion	later
render assistance to	help
ascertain the exact location of	find
reach a stationary state	stop
and in addition	and
due to the fact that	because

The lists I gave are only a start. We've all got our pet words and phrases. Sometimes we're alerted to them only when working with people learning English as a second language. It's very useful to have a friend or colleague willing to look at a piece of something you've written with a single task of highlighting those of your longer words or phrases which may not be needed.

What I really mean is...

Have you noticed how often, when you're explaining things to people, someone will ask you what you mean? Or someone will give you a puzzled look? Or it will be obvious to you that your meaning hasn't yet got across? When you find out you're not getting your meaning across, you probably often continue with a phrase like: 'what I really mean is...'

It's well worth doing this all the time as you write learning materials. Imagine someone questioning what you're about to say. Say to yourself 'What I really mean is...' then write what you would have said.

There are further ways of making sure learners know exactly what you mean. When, for example, there's a necessarily complex piece of writing (for example a definition, a regulation, a statute and so on) it's helpful to add:

> 'What this really means is...'

It's so easy for meanings to get lost! That's why it's well worth double checking that what you write really does get your meaning across. Even with face-to-face communication meanings can get lost. For example, in lectures (at least those where the communication is mainly one way) the problem of students seeming to write the wrong notes can be attributed to:

> *What you wrote*
> *about what you thought you heard*
> *is not really*
> *what I meant to say!*

Even this problem is alleviated by the use of 'What I really mean is...'

Play it again

One of the problems with text in open learning packages is that your learners may not get your message first time. This is a problem with almost any printed material, no matter how much skill and care you have used to make sure that the messages are coherent and well presented.

Classical composers like Mozart, Beethoven and Brahms used the sign conventions of music to show exactly where they wanted the orchestra to repeat a section. Your readers have the choice of re-reading any piece of the text which they feel they have not understood. However, in spite of your efforts as a teacher and author, a particular piece of text may not get through to every learner. Mere repetition may not be enough.

In face-to-face teaching learners often ask: 'Would you mind saying that again?' Teachers in turn expect to say things again. The old adage about lecturing deals with this:

> Tell them what you're going to tell them.
> Tell them.
> Tell them what you've just told them.

Perhaps a military instructor might just say exactly the same thing three times over. A teacher would expect to say it again in different ways. It is this re-working of material in different ways and in different situations which contributes to effective learning.

What does this mean in terms of an open learning text?

Tell them what you're going to tell:	Objectives, Introductions
Tell:	Main content
Tell what you've told:	Reviews and Summaries

This strategy is further adapted for open learning materials:

Tell them what you're going to ask:	Objectives, Introductions
Ask:	SAQs, Activities
Tell what you've asked:	Responses, Summaries

Learning is achieved more effectively when ideas pass several times through one's mind, particularly if there are different slants each time. So writing it just once, however brilliantly, may not be enough for your learners.

Signposting

Signposting is about helping your learners to find their way around your materials. It's a term used for ways of doing three things for your learners:

- helping them to find out exactly where they are now
- reminding them of where they're coming from
- pointing them towards where they're heading.

It is possible to add on much of the signposting your learners need in the final production stage. However, it is better to think about it as you write and, indeed, to build in right from the start some of the signposts which will help learners.

Words

Just a few written asides in your writing can make a lot of difference to your learners. Write the sort of things you'd have said to a group of learners. For example:

- 'Now that we've seen how ... , let's go on to explore how we can...'
- 'For this next part you'll need to remember what you learned about ... , and it would be useful if you had your ... handy.'
- 'We'll soon be exploring ... , but first we need to think about ...'

Flags

These are small visual symbols (icons) used in many open learning materials to help various features to stand out. Flags can be used for all sorts of things including:

- objectives
- self-assessment questions
- activities
- responses to self-assessment questions or activities
- reviews or summaries
- key points
- tutor-marked assignments.

But don't go overboard on flags. If there are more than about half a dozen different symbols on a page learners may find it confusing, not helpful. Flags may well be designed at a later stage, and by someone other than the author, but there's no-one better than the author for ensuring that flags appear in the right places.

Headings

Headings are a very useful way of helping learners find their way around learning materials. Headings help to break the material into manageable chunks and give learners a sort of menu. There are several ways of using headings to help learners keep track of exactly where they are in your materials.

- *Running headings* (at the top of each page) can remind learners of the main topic and can make it easier for them to find their way around your materials.

- *Question headings* can be particularly useful. They plant questions in learners' minds, so that as they work on they are more receptive to the answers to such questions. Question headings can play a useful role in helping to alert learners exactly to what they should be getting out of their learning materials.

- *Sub-headings* can make it easier for learners to scan backwards and forwards through the materials, adding to their understanding of where they've been, where they now are, and where they're going.

Numbers

All sorts of things may need to be numbered, including:

- self-assessment questions
- activities
- responses
- diagrams
- tables
- sections
- assignments.

But be careful not to have too many systems going at once. For example, it would be confusing if page 6 of section 1 contained SAQ 4, figure 2 and Activity 3. It would be more logical to have SAQ 1.4, figure 1.2 and Activity 1.3.

Some materials put numbers on all paragraphs. I think headings or sub-headings are a more effective way of helping learners to find particular paragraphs.

Visual material

Most good open learning units are visually interesting. Part of the interest is in the way graphs, charts, diagrams, pictures, cartoons, tables, and other illustrations are used. This applies as much to screen-based learning materials as it does to printed booklets. This [section] explores some reasons for including visual elements in your open learning materials.

The impact of visual material can be lost, however, if it is in the wrong place. It is surprisingly easy for this to happen. You're certain to have met illustrations that were not where they should have been. Typical causes of annoyance are:

- illustrations where you have to turn over a page to read text that relates to them
- tables of data continued from one page to another
- illustrations that have got onto the wrong page altogether, often with the wrong caption as well.

Sometimes this is the fault of the author; at other times it has happened somewhere along the journey to production.

No one is in a better position to decide exactly where an illustration should appear than the author. Editors and publishers may think they know better, but they don't. Editors and publishers may be more concerned that the pages look balanced than whether illustrations are in the right place from the learning viewpoint. If you're writing materials and passing drafts to someone else for laying-out and publishing, be very dogmatic about where you want your illustrations. Write something along the lines 'Figure 2 here please' and possibly show as a highlighted line down a margin exactly what text needs to be in sight at the same time as each illustration. When the proofs come back to you, it's crucial to check the following points:

- is each illustration in the right place?
- have the captions got mixed up or missed off?

I've been using the phrase right 'place', but this can vary of course. It's sometimes worth having an illustration before the point at which the text takes up the points it raises, for example when you want to plant some ideas in your learners' minds before going on to develop the ideas in text. The illustration needs to be seen during the textual discussion when learners need to refer to details of the illustration several times as they work through the text. An illustration may be saved until after the text when you want the illustration to bring together various concepts or ideas in a form which serves as a memorable summary.

Ten reasons for making it visual

... We've been dealing so far with things your learners use rather than the main content of the open learning materials. Now we come to illustrations. The danger is that they can so easily become things your learners don't use. What's worse, they can actually cause problems for learners.

In this discussion, we're thinking of all the non-text parts of open learning materials, which can include diagrams, charts, tables, pictures, sketches, cartoons, and so on. With every illustration, there should be one or more purposes. Here is a list of ten possibilities. You may well be able to add others.

1. *To give your learners a break*
    For an open learner, there is nothing worse than being confronted with a double page spread of unbroken text. This looks like hard work. There isn't a stopping place in sight, there isn't a rest. Almost any kind of illustration helps to give your learners a break from reading.

2. *To give your learners something to hang on to*
    If there's a difficult idea coming up, an illustration can set the scene for your learners, so that as the idea unfolds they can glance back at the illustration and remind themselves where the idea fits into the broader scene.

3. *To help your learners make sense of what they've learned*
    A picture can be worth a thousand words. When learners can see what you're getting at, as well as read about it, they've got much more chance of understanding it.

4. *To show things that can't be shown with words alone*
    All sorts of illustrations do this: graphs, diagrams, charts, tables, pictures. But don't forget, your learners need to know what they're expected to get out of each illustration. More about this later.

5. *To show how one thing depends on another*
    Graphs and tables show how things are related to each other. Learners can see things far quicker than they could read about them.

6. *To help learners collect things together*
    When there are lots of things learners should have grasped, an illustration is often the best way of helping them to turn the information into something that stays in their minds.

7. *To show your learners where they are*
    Illustrations can be used to show learners where the present topic fits into the whole picture. Flowcharts are useful for this, with the box representing the present position shaded in, so that learners can see what's coming next, and so that they can be reminded of the links with things they've already studied.

8. *To act as the basis for a task*
    Illustrations can be turned into self-assessment questions or activities. For example, learners can be asked to:

    fill in missing labels on a drawing, or numbers on a table

add to a diagram

find out what's wrong with a circuit diagram

draw graphs using information from a table

work out what the trends are from graphs

choose which one of four illustrations is correct.

There are many more possibilities. Giving learners something to do with illustrations ensures that they're used actively, rather than merely being glanced at and forgotten.

9. *To encourage your learners to use illustrations themselves*
When learners need to be able to illustrate their own answers, for example in exams, the more active practice they've had the better. It's no use expecting learners to be able to sketch graphs or draw cross-sections unless they've had practice.

10. *To make your learners smile*
Most learners like a few cartoons, though some academics feel insulted by them. Learners who don't like cartoons tend not to notice them anyway. Some learning materials make excellent use of cartoons to reinforce main ideas in a way that is memorable and amusing. A word of warning, however. Many cartoons involve a victim, someone at whose expense the smile is produced, and it's easy to upset readers by being racist or sexist

Audiotape

Some advantages of audiotape

Audiotapes, if used actively, can add a lot to your learning package at relatively little cost. For subjects such as music or languages the benefits of audiotape are obvious.

Here are some of the more general advantages of audiotape:

- You can assume that learners have access to a tape player.
- It can be used on the move, in cars, on trains, while jogging etc.
- It can stimulate the imagination in ways not possible with print.
- Tone of voice can give vital 'extra' information.
- It can show how unfamiliar words should be pronounced.
- It can be used where dramatic information is to be conveyed.

Some disadvantages of audiotape

- It is relatively difficult to get to particular sections quickly.
- It is non-visual. It's hard to get an overview of what's on a tape as you cannot skim read.

Some suggestions for using audiotape for Open Learning

- Make it clear when the tape should be used. Have clear instructions in the printed materials, maybe using a 'flag' so that learners know when to play the recording.

- Make it active. Don't just have 'sit back and listen to this' episodes; they will soon be forgotten.

- Tell learners when to stop the tape and do something. If you don't stop them, they're likely to carry on listening and become passive.

- Explain why audiotape is being used. Alert them to the special learning that the tape will enable them to achieve.

- Plant questions in learners' minds before they listen to the tape. If they're listening with an agenda, they'll pick up much more than if they're simply listening.

- Use it (when helpful) in conjunction with visual information. For example, use it to talk learners through complex flowcharts, to explain key steps in mathematical derivations they have before them, to describe aspects of illustrations or models, and so on.

- Give them some way of checking that they've achieved the purposes involved. For example, include self-assessment questions on things they should have got out of listening to extracts, give responses so that they can find out whether they've got the message, or whether to listen to the tape again.

- Keep the audiotape episodes short and sharp. A long audiotape discourse can have all the disadvantages of a lecture.

- Make it easy for learners to revise the learning they should have derived from the tape. Include a printed summary, perhaps in an appendix. It could be worth providing transcripts of the tape; some learners will otherwise make their own, which is not a very effective use of time.

- Take care to label it informatively. If there are several tapes, learners may otherwise find it difficult to locate the part they want to listen to for a second or third time.

Standards of production

If the tape sounds amateurish, learners may not take the content of the tape seriously. There are ways to make tape sound more 'professional':

- Have someone used to radio broadcasting record the tape for you.
- Script the tape and rehearse it well before recording it.

That said, for some audiotape purposes production standards are less important, for example:

- lively debates and discussions
- examples of what a machine sounds like.

Videotape

Some advantages of videotape

There are numerous advantages to things that can be seen and heard at the same time, particularly when it comes to showing people and things moving. Videotape can:

- show personalities, attitudes, body-language, as well as give tone of voice
- demonstrate 'real' situations which it would be impossible to convey in print, such as surgery, nuclear power generation, and so on
- provide a wealth of case-study information.

Some disadvantages of videotape

- It can be all too easy to sit back and watch.
- Not all learners can be assumed to have easy access to playback facilities.
- It can't necessarily be used in learners' normal study places.
- It can be expensive to produce.
- Broadcast television trains us to forget much of what we see on our screens.

Some suggestions for using videotape for Open Learning

- Where possible, don't produce it from scratch. It's usually possible to arrange copyright so that you can edit together extracts from materials that are already available. This can save a lot of time and money.

- Make it clear when the video should be used. Have clear instructions in the printed materials, maybe using a 'flag' so that learners know when to watch the video.

- Make it active. Don't just have 'sit back and watch this' episodes: they will soon be forgotten.

- Tell learners when to stop the video and do something. If you don't stop them, they're likely to carry on watching and become passive.

- Explain why video is being used. Alert them to the special learning that the video will enable them to achieve.

- Plant questions in learners' minds before they watch the video. If they're watching with an agenda, they'll pick up much more than if they're simply viewing.

- Use it (when helpful) in conjunction with printed information. For example, have a workbook to be used while playing the video, listing questions to consider while watching, things to decide after seeing an episode, and so on.

- Give them some way of checking that they've achieved the purposes involved. For example, include self-assessment questions on things they should have got out of watching, give responses so that they can find out whether they've got the message, or whether to have another look at the video.

- Keep the episodes short and sharp. People tend to be well trained in forgetting what they see on broadcast television.

- Make is easy for learners to revise the learning they should have derived from the video. Include a printed summary, perhaps in an appendix. It could be worth providing transcripts of key discussions included in a video recording: some learners will otherwise spend time making their own.

Standards of production

It is important to ensure that video is produced to a professional standard. We're all conditioned by the high standards we see on our television screens. Anything less than this tends to cause us to devalue the content as well as the quality of what we see...

Part Two – Learners, Teachers and their Institutions

This Part is concerned with the general implications of flexible approaches to learning for the teachers, the learners and the institutions of education and training. While it remains true that small-scale innovations can often be initiated through the actions of one or two enthusiastic and inventive teachers, there comes a point when the support of managers is necessary if the impetus is to be maintained.

Michael Eraut's first contribution emphasises the variety of issues which have to be encountered by both teachers and students in facing what he describes as 'the challenge of learning'. The prime responsibility of teachers, he says, is to give learners 'ownership of their own learning', and it is through flexible learning that such a state of independence can be achieved. He identifies ways in which both the classroom and the external world can be the focus of flexible learning activities, and maintains that the changes which this implies in the role of teachers leads to an extension of their professionalism. Though the immediate context of this extract is the school, there is nothing in it which does not apply to the post-16 sector.

Arguments supporting moves along the open learning continuum towards greater student-centredness arise from the research project carried out by Rob Halsall and his colleagues, as reported in the next extract. Their survey of the perceptions and articulated needs of a sample of nearly nine hundred young people aged 14 to 25 revealed problems associated with low participation rates and poor standards of attainment. Flexible learning was seen as a way of addressing these concerns by helping the young people to overcome some of the obstacles which lay in their path. The findings confirmed the researchers' view that we must aim for greater inclusiveness and we might be able to achieve this by paying a little more attention to the content and wider purposes of education, and not simply concentrating on the delivery and management of learning.

For the final reading in Part Two we return to Michael Eraut, who considers the issue of how to go about managing innovation within institutions of education and training. He evaluates the relative merits of *incremental* ('here a bit, there a bit') and *holistic* ('organisation-wide') approaches to change and outlines some of the conditions for success and some of the barriers to implementation. Flexible learning, he maintains, is 'part of a serious reappraisal of how learning occurs', and it can be regarded as successful only when it has become 'embedded' into the institution.

7. Teachers and Students as Learners

Michael Eraut

Public perceptions of the respective roles of teacher and student (or pupil) are strongly determined by people's own experience of the educational process. It is not therefore surprising that caricatures of the teacher as an instructor of knowledge, the ideal student as a well-behaved, passive recipient and the school as a means of instilling discipline into the unruly remain pictures that are still, at least partially, accepted by many who should know better.

Despite significant educational Commissions, Reports and Acts throughout the last half-century and despite many bold attempts by teachers in all sectors to move the emphasis away from an instrumental, mechanistic and purely knowledge-based view of the school curriculum, the notion persists that it is all quite simple: the teacher's job is to *'teach'* and the student's job is to *'learn'*. This truism only begins to have any meaning when the terms *'teach'* and *'learn'* are more clearly defined.

It is such a re-definition of these terms that is the concern of Flexible Learning developments. It is not the establishment of a new theory or 'school' so much as a bringing together of many concepts, experiences and practical developments in education...

Flexible Learning is driven by an overwhelming recognition that *'learning'* for young people today should not be restricted to an *'academic'* interpretation on the one hand ... nor to an instrumental notion of *'vocational training'* on the other... Rather, it is about the kind of learning which enables students to become independent learners ultimately able to manage the process and determine their own goals.

It is an approach focusing on a future which requires people who are flexible and adaptable, who can transfer from one situation to another, who can apply their knowledge and skills in a variety of contexts, who are equipped to work in a high technology society, who will be able to communicate effectively in Europe ... and in a shrinking world that increasingly has common problems to share.

Pressure for change has come both from inside education and from without. The main motivator within schools observed by this project has been the desire to help young people equip themselves as competent learners in a rapidly changing world through independence of mind as well as the ability to work co-operatively.

A ... particularly influential external view of what is required from today's young learners is provided by the CBI's Task Force, who recommended that the outcomes from all training and education should include the following Common Learning Outcomes as core elements:

- positive attitude to change
- effective communication
- application of numeracy
- personal and interpersonal skills
- problem solving
- values and integrity
- applications of technology
- understanding of work and the world.

Such a vision of education inevitably requires considerable flexibility from its teachers. It does not mean that 'tried and tested' methods have to be thrown overboard, but rather that the teacher's role has to be extended and elaborated. The practical implications of helping today's teacher to become an even more highly-skilled professional are explored later. But first let us consider further the prime purpose which such growing expertise must serve: the facilitation of learning.

Learning

All too often the word 'learning' is used as if it were synonymous with 'knowledge'. Understanding of the term is further confused by the equation of 'knowledge' with one particular aspect of knowing, that is, the capacity to commit information to memory. Such narrow definitions of knowledge and learning will not suffice for any serious discussion of education, especially one that seeks to put the learner centre stage. Education is concerned most of all with the development of understanding and the ability to access new knowledge through finding out for oneself; and with the acquisition of skills in communications and putting to practical use the knowledge one has. This encompasses both the Common Learning Outcomes listed above and the kind of knowledge which has been traditionally developed by the best subject teaching. Whether the curriculum area concerned bears an academic or a vocational label, there is a need both to learn how to do things – critical reading, writing, problem-solving, making, planning – and to develop conceptual frameworks for interpreting and understanding what one reads, hears and sees.

Another widely-held misapprehension is that learning is basically easy. Such a view is reinforced by a belief that failure to learn is due either to the stupidity of the learner or to the incompetence of the teacher. When learning turns out to be difficult, most people, including teachers, blame themselves. As a result, a large proportion of the population feel inadequate as learners. We all compare ourselves to other people whom we think find learning easy, and belittle our own efforts and achievements in contrast. The reality is that most learning is difficult and that sometimes it is extremely difficult. This is not however to support a traditional paradigm of the educational process which expects that the pupil will inevitably 'suffer' through mental effort and the teacher will only achieve his/her aims by the imposition of strict discipline. Rather, we wish to highlight the need to pay more attention to the learning process itself, openly acknowledging the difficulties, allowing time to overcome them and celebrating learning when it finally occurs.

Besides setting the right psychological tone for facing the challenge of learning, we need to provide practical support. Moreover this support has to be so managed that once a skill has been acquired or a concept understood, it has become part of the practical and intellectual equipment of that learner. However, skills and concepts do not become part of a learner's 'action knowledge' or repertoire, until they have been used in a range of contexts. Indeed, most of the learning of concepts and skills occurs not at preliminary acquaintance but during subsequent *use*. This is where we so often get our priorities wrong. We put most of our teaching efforts into communicating new ideas to students, and very little towards helping them put those ideas into use.

At this stage in our discussion, it is useful to introduce the notion of *'ownership'* as a desired end-point for learning. Learners can be said to have taken ownership of an idea when they are able to use it for their own purposes rather than for other people's purposes, i.e. only in contexts prescribed by the teacher, textbook or examination syllabus. The idea does not become part of their repertoire until they can use it as a resource for thinking, whenever it might be relevant. Indeed, it is only after a period of using an idea and working out one's own interpretation of it in a range of situations that it gets built into one's cognitive framework and affects the general way one thinks.

To put it more broadly, learners develop a sense of ownership of an area of subject matter when they begin to have some mastery of the issues rather than only a superficial acquaintance and a capacity to regurgitate on request. Such ownership brings about significant gains in confidence which in turn become an important motivator for the continuing process of learning...

There is a particular challenge here to teachers to structure the learning experiences and opportunities so that students develop a real sense of ownership of their own learning – not just the information but the processes as well...

Every parent knows the dilemma of deciding when is the right time to allow your child to take a risk in the process of learning: letting them cross the road alone or using a sharp knife unsupervised. Risk-taking is an important and inevitable part of learning. Leaving aside the issue of physical danger, where the teacher's responsibility for children's safety cannot be reduced, there should be opportunities for students to learn in ways that involve the risk of making mistakes: investigation, experimentation, trial and error, discussion, working with others, drafting written work. Only by taking the risk of giving students responsibility for their own learning, can ownership be developed. This applies not only within the safe confines of the classroom but also in resource centres and/or libraries. These are at best *'hives of activity'* to which students will come and go to take the risk of making (for them) a new discovery. It may involve teachers accepting the risk that the students may misuse the time and not look after equipment properly. The evidence is that fears in this respect are usually ungrounded – provided that the learner has a sense of ownership both for the task to be undertaken and for the resources at his/her disposal...

Imaginative teachers and managers in schools are, by the very nature of their task, looking for the best ways to help their students forward in the process of learning. The key questions here for educational practitioners relate to the delivery of the curriculum. What are the most effective ways in which students can be enabled to learn? What are the most effective ways for teachers to operate?

We look first at changes in the classroom.

Flexible features of classroom learning

[There are] certain common elements in flexible modes of learning which are described here...

Student responsibility for own learning

This does not mean the abdication of the teacher! But it does mean the student is involved in a partnership for learning and can no longer just sit and hope that the teacher will make it all happen. It will mean just as much work for the teacher. However, teachers working in this way find that there is a much higher level of satisfaction and achievement, both for their students and for themselves, which compensates for the greater preparation required. Lessons also become more interesting and stimulating for the teacher as well as the learner.

Goal/target setting

Although teachers have usually had the aim of their lesson worked out, they have not always communicated their intentions to the students. Knowing from the outset what is the goal of a particular task, module or unit gives the student an immediate sense of purpose as well as a reference point.

Variety of resources available

Teachers have usually tried to have a variety of materials for use in the classroom. What is less common is letting the student choose which particular resource is to be used and accepting responsibility for its care and return. This is the opposite of spoon-feeding and some teachers may find it hard not to organise this detail of classroom management. But the more responsibility the student has for all aspects of the learning process the greater will be the sense of ownership referred to earlier.

Student choice

This follows logically from the previous point – not only choice in resources but between alternative activities and appropriate levels. While providing choice may initially be more demanding for the teacher, the variety will give greater flexibility in management of space and resources as well as feeding back a richer range of work to the whole teaching group. It has always been seen as the teacher's task to determine what is the appropriate level at which a student should be working. But the expedience of teachers working within situations of greater student choice suggests that students are more able to make realistic assessments of their most appropriate level of working than is generally assumed. There may also be important external factors not necessarily known to the teacher, e.g. previous difficulty with work in a particular learning area and therefore a need to build confidence gradually and not take too many steps at once.

Intended outcomes to be negotiated

The involvement of the student in this level of decision-making means that s/he has to accept responsibility and be involved fully in the task. The teacher needs skills of listening and guidance to avoid imposing decisions on the student.

Student and teacher assessment of performance

This has to be a mutual process in which the student and teacher negotiate an agreed assessment. If agreement cannot be reached then that fact should be recorded along with the separate assessments.

Student evaluation of task/module

This is now a common experience in many schools but care should be taken by teachers not to let this become just a routine procedure. It is important for students to know that their observations have been taken seriously and that they receive feed-back. For teachers, although initially it may be threatening to have students' comments on lessons, the benefits of constructive observations can be considerable in further planning and modification of courses. Often there are positive confirmations that customers are satisfied!

Record of tasks attempted

The more complex the organisation within the classroom the more important it becomes for records to be kept. When students are working on different tasks or using different resources they need to be trained to keep careful records of what they have done. It is a valuable discipline for the student and also relieves the teacher from what could be a time consuming task.

Active role for student wherever possible

This is not a recipe for a chaotic situation in which all the class appear to be all over the place! This is an emphasis on work being organised so that the student is interacting with other learners, with materials or a specific environment as an essential part of the learning process – in other words, learning through use.

Learning activities and contexts

Learning activities can be broadly grouped under the following headings:

- doing
- seeing and listening
- reading
- writing
- talking and listening.

Historically the greatest emphasis in schools has been placed on the categories of reading and writing. Doing was deemed appropriate for *'practical'* subjects such as

Science, Home Economics and Crafts. Even in those areas there was a tradition of demonstration in which students watched the teacher carry out the experiment or execute the particular skill rather than being given the opportunity to find out for themselves.

It is not long since a model lesson might have included considerable periods of time in which children worked in absolute silence and the idea of talking was strongly discouraged. Now, fortunately, *'talk'* is recognised as a vital aspect of learning as is listening and observing. These are no longer the exclusive prerogative of *'English'* lessons but essential activities within all aspects of the curriculum. All five categories of activity are essential to a balanced learning programme. Flexible approaches need to ensure that a balance is maintained so that students are practising and developing all these skills across the curriculum.

Learning contexts

A flexibility of approach in planning the appropriate kinds of learning experiences should allow students to work in a variety of different contexts. The value of working in groups is usually stressed not least because it is the mode in which so much human interaction occurs. Within the school situation it is important that the purpose and function of the working group is defined.

Support groups: Working completely alone is difficult for most learners and the support of peers helps to provide a friendly and encouraging context in which to work. The size and mix of such groups will have an important bearing on the way in which work is carried out. Smaller groups are more likely to be efficient and the group members need to be personally compatible. It is not essential that they all have the same level of ability or do the same task. The teacher should be sensitive to the needs of each student within the group to ensure that those who require support receive it but not to the detriment of other learners.

Task-oriented groups: It is in the context of specific tasks that groups are most likely to be used. For example: investigating a specified problem; carrying out a survey, project or case-study; working on a role-play or simulation.

External locations

Another valuable change of context can be the use of locations away from the regular base of the school or college. This could include exploration through museum and field-work visits; working with people in the community – nursery groups, the elderly or disabled; work experience or work-oriented projects with local industry and commerce. Also, residential opportunities are widely recognised as a valuable context for learning in terms of scope and quantity of work that can be achieved as well as developing important social skills of interaction and co-operation.

Other resources

Finally, the use of a whole range of non-paper-based resources opens up the range of options and experiences available to students: audio-tape and video-tape, film, interactive video, satellite TV, word-processor, computer, reprographic equipment. Technology has a seductive charm and at worst can be used by teachers to attempt to absorb difficult students or cope with large numbers. Any additional resources, whether in simple book form or using complex technology, need to be used in ways appropriate to the particular task or course and not in any way as ends in themselves.

Changed roles for teachers and learners

In the last section of this chapter we look at the ways in which the roles of both teachers and learners have changed and developed. The diagram 'Flexible Roles' [below] summarises the main characteristics of the complementary roles. The notion of complementarity is in itself a major step forward. No longer is the relationship between teacher and student characterised by conflict and fear but by co-operation, inter-action and support.

Flexible roles	
Learner or learning group	*Teacher*
Choosing/Accepting task	Advising/Negotiating
Clarifying task and expectations	Briefing
Getting organised for task: 　planning 　searching for resources	Advice/Direction on grouping resources, sources of support Design of tasks/learning resources
Working at task: 　assessing progress 　getting support when needed	[Presenting] Monitoring Management of support
Completing task: 　evaluating achievement 　reviewing the process 　noting what has been learned 　sharing some of the outcomes	Discussion of completed task Providing feedback Reviewing process Facilitating, review and sharing of learning

This mode of working represents a major change for many teachers and it cannot be expected that all are going to alter their practice overnight. It should be emphasised that the adoption of more flexible roles means an enhancement and extension of the teacher's professionalism; it in no way diminishes the skills already possessed. Instruction and presenting will still feature but it is expected that these skills will not be as dominant as they have in the past. Advice, briefing, review, providing feedback, managing support: all these should already be part of the experienced teacher's repertoire. The subtle difference is that they need to be used as part of a two-way process in which the emphasis is on support, guidance and negotiation rather than direction and imposition. Teachers need to be prepared to be learners as well as their students.

The changes implicit in Flexible Learning methods can be just as daunting for some students as for teachers. It will very much depend on the kinds of learning experience they have had in primary school and the extent to which the early years of secondary education have continued that experience. There is a *'safeness'* in teacher-focused learning in which the student is the passive recipient. But there is no risk, limited motivation and in the long term, we would argue, limited learning.

Involving the learner through choice, planning, evaluation, assessment and review is not a series of devices devised by educationists to mollify the rebellious young! The principles behind these processes are applicable to all learners whether they are 9, 19 or 90. The real test of all these processes will be whether learning has occurred: not has the student memorised some facts or answered some questions accurately (although they may well do these things during the course of the learning) but has s/he changed as a result of the experience? Is there understanding of a new concept? Has a new skill or competency been acquired? Is the learner now, as a result of the learning experience, able to take that knowledge, skill or understanding and apply it?

8. Flexible Learning: the Needs and Perceptions of Young People

Rob Halsall, Ian Harrison & Ray Owen

Abstract

This article is based on a survey of school, college and unemployed young people in a Single Regeneration Budget area in the north of England. Its concern is with the low participation rates and standards of attainment in post-16 education and training, especially in such areas. Its main purpose is to explore the needs and perceptions of the young people regarding certain forms of flexible learning, thence to discuss the possible role that greater provision of these might play in addressing participation and attainment. The key question posed is whether current styles, patterns and places for learning adequately serve young people's needs. The article first outlines the problem of low participation and attainment. It then discusses what is variously meant by flexible learning, suggests that it is part of a commitment to promoting greater student-centredness, reviews different sets of arguments associated with this commitment, and addresses why flexible learning might be a useful response to low participation and attainment. Key findings from the study are that qualifications are highly valued by young people; that the majority wish to pursue further education and training but that many face obstacles, especially those related to financial and domestic circumstances; and that many would welcome more in the way of flexible learning opportunities, the existing provision of which is somewhat limited. Finally, the findings are discussed in relation to a number of themes: the rhetoric of developing a learning society; the limitations surrounding the greater provision of flexible learning, not least those to do with sociocultural constraints on student choices and progression; the need for an inclusive approach to flexible learning, one which is for all learners rather than for lower achievers alone; and the danger of focusing only on the delivery and management of learning, at the neglect of the content and purposes of education.

Introduction

This article arises out of a feasibility study, conducted during 1996, in relation to establishing a flexible learning centre of excellence in a Single Regeneration Budget (SRB) Project area. The broader context was a concern for the participation in, and retention of, young people in the 14–25 age group in education and training, many of whom are currently disaffected and frequently isolated from existing provision. The study included a survey of the views of a sample of local young people on what they regarded as the most helpful conditions for them to learn. This article draws on that survey.

The problem

As Smithers & Robinson (1989) suggest, from the mid-1980s a consensus emerged that the main failings of the education and training system in England and Wales were the low participation rates and low standards of attainment in education and training post-16 by comparison with our international competitors. For example, in 1987 only 35% of 16–18-year-olds were in full-time education and training as compared with 51% in Australia, 77% in Japan and The Netherlands and 82% in Belgium (DES, 1991). Charges have also been levelled that the pre-16 sector has failed to meet the nation's needs and expectations. In both sectors, this has led to prescriptions from policy makers on what should be taught, schemes for institutional self-evaluation and the inspection of institutions, teacher appraisal, institutional development planning, the introduction of National Training and Education Targets and league tables of performance.

More recently, participation rates have risen dramatically and there have been improvements in attainment at age 16 and 18. Sutton (1994) suggests that the main reasons for this include the success of the GCSE examination, the expansion of vocational training opportunities, high rates of youth unemployment and the closing down of the benefit option for young people not involved in education and training. However, it would be foolish to think that all is well. There are still significant numbers of 16-year-olds leaving school with very low, and sometimes no, qualifications. For example, about 8% of 16-year-olds in England leave school without a single GCSE at any grade, approaching 20% in some local authority areas. And whilst more young people are staying on post-16, there is a sharp drop-out rate at 17 and a high failure rate for those who 'stay the course'. Thus, the Audit Commission's analysis of full-time post-16 courses 'has shown up courses of all types with disappointingly low success rates – measured in terms of the proportion of enrolled students who achieve the qualifications they set out to gain. Typically, between 30% and 40% of students starting on a course do not succeed, and for many courses the proportion is much higher' (Audit Commission, 1993: 1). More recently, running through the Dearing Report (Dearing, 1996) on post-16 qualifications is the theme of underachievement and waste. It is, unfortunately, still the case that the UK performs 'poorly in international comparisons in both training and educational attainment ... [and that] it is what the CBI calls the "long tail of under-performance" that presents the biggest challenge to the achievement of a learning society in the UK' (Tuckett, 1997: 3).

Why do so many young people drop out of or fail their post-16 courses? The causes are many and varied, and for any individual there will be a particular constellation of factors. However, it is possible to offer some generalisations. Both Her Majesty's Inspectors (1991) and the Audit Commission (1993) have identified the problem that many young people are on courses for which they are unsuited, sometimes because of low prior attainment (see also Tymms, 1992). For example, of 638 students studied by the Audit Commission, non-completion rates for those with fewer than 32 GCSE points was 55%, between 32–36 points 12%, 37–41 points 8%, and over 42 points 4%. Although the courses included in these studies preceded the advent of NVQs and GNVQs, these too have not yet proved to be able to retain as many students as was first hoped.

Other factors at play in both the post-16 and pre-school sectors help to explain why some young people do not enter further education and training at all, in addition to dropping out of it. Thus, there is variously boredom with the subject material and dislike of teaching methods (Robinson, 1975; NFER, 1993), dislike of teachers (Bealing, 1990) and demotivation occasioned by lack of success – 'students leave because they do not have much success in school' (Wehlage & Rutter, 1986). Finally, of course, there is a range of more personal factors related to drop-out rates post-16 and to why 16-year-olds and unemployed young people do not enter or re-enter education and training. Chief amongst these seem to be the pressure of domestic responsibilities and financial pressures. On the latter, for example, the NFER (1996) concludes that money worries often have a major impact on a student's educational life beyond 16. Of the 256 English and Welsh school sixth forms surveyed, 38% reported that financial problems had at some time prevented young people from staying on for sixth form study, frequently because they needed to work to support their families. Furthermore, many students were trying to combine study and part-time jobs, and their school performance was suffering as a result.

Within all this, achievement, staying on, and retention rates all tend to be lower in inner city areas than elsewhere, and in relation to our own study there are indicators of an enormous waste of human talent in the SRB Project area. Thus, local education authority statistics for the area point to:

- relatively high levels of truancy, and more generally absence, from some of the schools – the four high schools in the area in 1994–95 had on average 22.2% half days missed through absence (range 15.5–36.1%) compared with an average of 9% for England;

- very low proportions of youngsters gaining five GCSEs at grades A–C, and high proportions leaving without even one grade A–G, in some of the schools. The average across the schools gaining five grades A–C was 19.5% (range 8–28%) compared with the England average of 43.5%, while the respective figures leaving without a single grade of any sort were 19% as against 8%;

- relatively low levels of participation in education and training post-16, and unemployment rates higher than the city average.

Flexible learning

In the current educational debate a number of concepts are used as though their meanings were self-evident. Flexible learning is one of these. It can mean, for example:

- flexible choice of routes or pathways, such as A level or Advanced GNVQ, including the possibility of combining elements from different routes;

- the opportunity for the learner to determine at least part of the programme of study within the chosen route;

- the opportunity for the learner to determine, at least in part, the learning goals, the pace of work and/or the timeframe for the completion of the programme of study;

- the opportunity for the learner to select from alternative approaches to learning and modes of study, e.g. more or less 'active' learning styles, classroom-based or distance learning; and

- related to the above, the opportunity for the learner to decide when and where study will be undertaken.

In one way or another, all of these possibilities can be seen as part of a commitment to help students take greater control of their learning or, to put it another way, to help promote greater student-centredness. Hustler & Hodkinson (1996) suggest that this commitment can be seen to be associated with different, and sometimes competing, sets of arguments. The first is to do with promoting student-centredness as a necessary, but probably not sufficient (Avis, 1991), element of democratic education. This 'is to do with challenging false hierarchies and preparing young people to participate more fully in an active democracy' (Hustler & Hodkinson, 1996: 11).

The second set of arguments is to do with student-centredness as a way of developing more effective, 'deeper' learning. Here, the focus is pedagogical, based on the work of those learning theorists who suggest that a requirement for such learning for most people is that they be given greater responsibility for their own learning (e.g. Rogers, 1969; Bruner, 1974; Kolb, 1983). Thus, Tomlinson & Kilner (1990: 9) discuss teachers' needs 'for flexible adaptation of their activities to suit the learning needs of students: teachers need to "flex" in the face of variation in learners, topics, resources, contexts, and any other interacting factor that may influence effective learning'. Learning, they say, needs meaningful active involvement; there is individual variation in motivation, and therefore the emphasis needs to be on consultation and negotiation in order to maintain the level of learner motivation. The themes of individual variation, motivation and interaction that Tomlinson & Kilner describe as being facilitated within a flexible learning approach are also reflected in Stenhouse's views on effective teaching strategies. He argues that 'If respect for the client is of central importance, we need to develop teaching strategies which embody such respect... If knowledge is to be approached as a resource and an open system rather than as an imposition by those who possess it, new styles of teaching need to be evolved...' (Stenhouse, 1975: 32). Additionally, Ball makes a number of assertions about the conditions for effective learning: 'there is a need to find ways of transferring control of the learning process to the learners themselves. It is a central theme of this report that the best individual learning ... is as far as possible self-directed' (Ball, 1991: 10).

The third set of arguments is to do with viewing student-centredness as one response to the nation's economic needs. Here emerges an intriguing consensus between the sort of 'progressive' educationalists referred to above and the 'New Right', a paradox first identified by Jamieson (1985) and partly explained by reference to an alleged emergence of a post-Fordist society in which people 'are required to master an ever widening range of complex information. What is needed, it is claimed, is the ability independently to acquire new knowledge and skill, so that learning how to learn becomes increasingly important' (Jamieson, 1993: 200). In similar vein, Avis notes that we are offered, as a response to post-Fordist economic organisation (the existence of which he queries), 'the vision of a learning society in which everyone can be fulfilled' (Avis, 1996: 71) through being able to exercise autonomy, and in which people can be adaptable and flexible through being learners who know how to learn and who are able to take greater control of, and responsibility for, learning. For him and others, though, the promotion of such a learning society is clearly to do with appropriating the curriculum to serve economic, rather than student, interests.

Finally, an associated set of arguments to do with student-centredness concerns viewing the student as consumer in the marketplace, in the broader context of what some see as the marketisation and commodification of education (e.g. Menter *et al.* 1995; Esland, 1996). Here we can note developments such as training credits and vouchers, the establishment of a post-16 three-track qualifications system, modular and credit-based learning, and flexible styles of delivery according to student need or demand. Also, on a related issue and consonant with views that recent developments in post-compulsory education and training are not genuinely student-centred, is the view that 'the chief concern ... is not primarily with improving the quality of education and training but with regulating labour markets and driving down costs' (Gleeson, 1996b: 92).

Flexible learning as a possible response to low participation and attainment

Clearly, different sorts of responses are relevant to different causes of low participation and low attainment. For example, in relation to the problem of course selection post-16, attention needs to be focused on matters of guidance and information given to students both pre- and post-entry, and to induction programmes. In relation to financial problems there is much to be said for the provision of maintenance grants to post-16 students, and for a clear definition of central and local government's duty to secure 'adequate facilities' for further education. The focus of our study, though, is the provision of more flexible learning opportunities which, in one or more of its forms, could be seen as a response to low participation and attainment. Thus, the provision of alternative routes such as GNVQs might serve to attract or retain those for whom an A level programme is unappealing. The opportunity to have a greater say in the selection of learning goals might help to 'turn on' those who react against education and training as something 'done to' them. Choice of when and where to study might appeal to those experiencing particular sorts of constraints, for example arising out of domestic responsibilities. However, this study does not attempt to address all such possibilities or all forms of flexible learning. The key question underpinning our survey was whether the current styles, patterns, and places for learning adequately served the needs of young people. We prioritised this as our focus for three main reasons.

First, whilst a new, national framework for qualifications is to be introduced as a result of the Dearing Report on post-16 qualifications and whilst this itself might have some impact on the problems we have identified, we agree with Gleeson in his demand for recognition that 'the driving force of reform is the quality of *teaching and learning* in school and post-compulsory education ... it involves embracing broader views of the student as learner rather than customer, or skills carrier ... a key feature will be in the transition from a received to a learner-oriented pedagogy' (Gleeson, 1996a: 15–16). And as Sutton argues in relation to achieving the full potential of GNVQs, 'teachers need to be comfortable and familiar with the student-centred flexible learning philosophy and methodology... If the targets [NTETs] are to be achieved, it will not be enough for institutions to become more client-centred by improving access to study and qualifications. It will be necessary to help students become more responsible for their own learning' (Sutton, 1994: 351). Here, it is pertinent to point out that the National Commission on Education (1993), in the wake of other commentators such as Ball (1991), forecast that the key task for teachers in the future will be managing the transference of responsibility for learning to students.

Second, important to any pedagogic notion of flexible learning is a belief in the need for continuity of learning experiences as people progress from school and college and on to the workplace, and continuity implies that learning will be more effective where students are familiar with the learning methods. Ball (1991) makes a particular contribution to the debate in making a general distinction between formal and informal learning and their application, respectively to education and the workplace. He points out that much of what we learn is achieved without teachers. However, within the education system, most learning is structured and formal. Ball contrasts this with learning in the workplace which is largely unstructured, informal and controlled by the learner, and suggests that a 'learning society' should use both modes and recognise the utilisation of the appropriate mode in any given learning situation. Thus, in making the link between appropriate learning experiences in education and the workplace, Ball has underlined methodology as an important transitional factor and one which can contribute to effective performance. At the same time, local education authorities throughout the UK have pursued the same theme in relation to the 16–19 sectors. For example, Manchester LEA in acknowledging appropriate methodology as being an ingredient for enhancing continuity and progression states that:

> It is likely that the participation rate post 16 and throughout adult life – and the quality of the participation – will be much enhanced if the quality of involvement pre 16, and of the curricular and attitudinal continuity can be improved. This continuity should centre on the curriculum and methodology established in the '5–16 Curriculum for Manchester Schools'. Essential features will include ... an increasingly student-centred curriculum and approach, allowing for some negotiation of content, context, style, and pace of learning, even within a national foundation curriculum.

> (Manchester LEA, 1994: 6)

Third, successful schools and colleges tend to maximise the time available for learning (e.g. Denham & Lieberman, 1980) and make best use of that time (e.g. Carroll, 1989). The provision of flexible learning opportunities is one means by which institutions can increase the time that students spend on purposeful learning. Here, a particularly relevant point in relation to our study is that one feature of recent school improvement initiatives, especially in disadvantaged areas, has been the introduction of additional learning time either during lunch breaks or after school (Stringfield, 1995).

Research design

We have said that the key question underpinning our work was whether the current styles, patterns and places for learning adequately served the needs of young people. Associated with this was a set of further questions:

- What is the extent of young people's desire in the SRB area to continue in, or resume, education and training?
- What are the key obstacles to such continuation or resumption?
- What opportunities do these young people have for flexible learning?
- Do they wish for greater opportunities to study more flexibly?

Our findings are presented below in relation to each of these questions. The research involved the use of questionnaires, administered to three different groups of young people aged between 14–25, and follow-up interviews with a small sub-sample of each group. The strategy adopted was to ascertain the views of as many of these as possible, who were resident in (the unemployed), or studying in, the SRB area. The sample divided into three categories: all 14–16-year-olds in the four high schools *(n = 745)*, a broadly representative sample of 16–25-year-olds in education and/or training in the FE college *(n = 72)*, and 16–25-year-olds accessed through the youth service who were unemployed and not in study or training *(n = 64*, hereafter referred to as unemployed).

Because of the different contexts, it was decided to construct three questionnaires, each containing a mix of closed and open-ended items, with some questions being common to all. They were piloted with 15 students from one of the 11–16 schools, ten FE students and ten unemployed persons in attendance at a local Youth Centre. Some amendments were made to the questionnaires in light of the pilot exercise and the final versions were designed to be optically mark read to expedite the task of processing the data. Additionally, interview schedules were designed for each group of young people after the data from the questionnaires had been processed and interpreted, in order to gather more illuminative data. The total number of interviewees was 55, drawn from across the three groups. Here, though, we draw largely on the questionnaire data. The chi-square test has been used to determine the statistical significance of differences between frequencies.

The findings

Attitudes towards further education and training

Because the SRB Project was largely based on a concern for supporting the progression of young people into further education, training and employment, the questionnaires included items designed to elicit the attitudes of young people to further study and qualifications, and to gain their perceptions regarding barriers to further study. All three groups responded very positively to the question on the importance of qualifications, ranging from 73% of the unemployed replying with an unequivocal 'yes' (they are important), to 95% of the school students. The figures remain relatively high for different sub-groups, though there are some notable differences. Thus, whilst 84% of the 16–17-year-old unemployed responded positively, the figure for those aged 20 + was only 58% (p <0.05). Here, some of the interview data is particularly poignant: 'there's no point training because there's no jobs at the end of it anyway'. There were also gender differences, especially amongst the unemployed where 84% of females answered in the affirmative as against 63% of males, though this difference is not statistically significant. Finally, there were differences between schools where the numbers viewing qualifications as important ranged from 89–99%, although even the lowest figure might be regarded as a very positive response given the nature of the student intakes and the socio-economic characteristics of the area.

The questionnaires also included an item relating to whether or not respondents wanted to carry on, or resume, studying/training, worded appropriately for the specific circumstances; e.g. for the school sample, 'Do you want to carry on studying for qualifications when you finish year 11?' 63% and 67% of the school and college respondents respectively expressed the view that they definitely wanted to carry on studying. Again, a pattern of gender and school differences can be observed: in schools, 51% of males as against 75% of females (p <0.01), and in the college, 59% of males as against 71% of females (not statistically significant), with figures ranging from 52–76% between the schools. However, fewer than a third of unemployed respondents expressed a definite interest in resuming study/training, though as many as 47% were as yet unsure about this. It is possible that this is related to both the issue of barriers to undertaking study/training and that concerning their knowledge of the availability of opportunities, both of which are discussed below.

Obstacles to entering, resuming or staying on

Given what might be seen as a high level of interest in pursuing or resuming further qualifications, or at least in the possibility of this (and, here, note that the figures reflecting a clear lack of interest were only 11%, 14% and 22%), why is it that more young people in this area do not actually do so? Both the college and the unemployed young people were asked to list the barriers that make it difficult for them to study or train. Forty-seven responses were obtained from the 41 college students who replied to this question. Only five stated that there were no barriers or difficulties. Only three students cited their lack of motivation and/or self-discipline as a reason, though this figure might well have been proportionately higher if everyone had responded to the item. Twelve cited barriers arising from the facilities on offer to them which ranged from dissatisfaction with the support from lecturers, distractions from others in the classroom and poor computing facilities (from one interview, for example, 'the computer room closes early and it's not available at all at weekends and the equipment's crap, there's only one printer that works in D15'). However, the majority (*n* = 27), almost two-thirds, cited personal circumstances as being the major barriers (see, on this, Banks *et al.* 1992). The major factors here were:

1. constraints arising from pressure of work upon part-time study
2. financial considerations especially travel costs, and
3. difficulties arising from family commitments and responsibilities.

The majority of the 40 unemployed respondents to this item also cited these personal circumstances as being the major barriers to resuming study or training. Thus, 'I've got three children under four and few places run courses of interest in the evening'; 'child care facilities are appalling and I can't afford it anyway'; 'I'm on my own with five children. Even so I could study and would like to but I need to work as much as possible to make enough money'. Additionally, there was an issue concerning the knowledge many of these people had of the availability of places and opportunities for study/training (the unemployed questionnaire included a separate item on this). Some 55% of the respondents claimed to know little about such availability, which might indicate that the dissemination of appropriate information is an additional barrier.

Because the school students are in statutory education, they were not asked the same question as the other young people. However, some insight into their satisfaction with approaches to teaching and learning can be gleaned from the survey, as can further insight into the FE students' responses mentioned above concerning dissatisfaction with existing provision. Thus, the students were also asked whether they would like to be more dependent on themselves to learn, and 81% of school students and 69% of college students answered in the affirmative, though the latter figure masks considerable age-related differences: 91% of 16–19-year-olds as against 57% of older students ($p < 0.01$). There was a clear view, then, especially amongst 14–19-year-olds, that they wish to possess the skills that would enable them to operate more independently of their teachers. When those involved in follow up interviews were asked to elaborate on the reasons, they offered the following sorts of comments:

- You're more willing to work.
- Your teacher is not going to be there all the time.
- The teacher doesn't always get to you in a class of thirty.
- If there are things you wanted to know that they don't teach you at school, you can find out for yourself.

Actual opportunities for flexible learning

There seems to be a realisation here that learning can go on independently of the teacher and that motivation also improves when students take more responsibilities for their learning. However, the responses to questions regarding the actual availability of flexible learning opportunities suggested that they seemed to be somewhat limited. These questions listed typical places and times for independent learning that were likely to be currently available to school and college students (hereafter referred to as, simply, locations). They were:

- the classroom at lunchtime or after school/'normal' college hours
- the school library/resource centre or college library during lessons
- the school library/resource centre or college library at lunchtime or after school/'normal' college hours
- the public library after school/college or at weekend
- the college resources centre during lessons
- the college resources centre at lunchtime and after 'normal' college hours
- the college drop-in centre/s during weekdays

- the college library, resources centre or drop-in centre/s at weekend.

It seems that, on the whole, students were restricted to working in the classroom during actual lesson time. This was particularly so for the 14–16-year-olds, only 9% of whom claimed there was quite a lot of opportunity for working elsewhere during lessons, rather than for the college students, for whom the figure was 28%. Where there was greatest flexibility for both groups was in working in classrooms or the library/resources centre at lunch time or after the timetabled day ends. Where there was least flexibility of all was in the use of college facilities by college students at weekends or by 14–16-year-olds at any time (9% and 8% respectively).

Desired opportunities for flexible learning

Did the students, though, want greater opportunities for flexible learning than they had? They were asked which of the activities they would like more opportunity to do and to explain why this was so. Out of 745 14–16-year-olds (68%), 507 responded to this question, naming at least one, and sometimes more than one, activity. The figure for college students was 25 out of 72 (35%). A high proportion of school students claimed that they did want greater opportunity to engage with at least one of the more flexible learning locations. This was particularly true of females: of the 376 school respondents we could identify as female, 82% responded positively as against 55% of the 360 people we could identify as males (p<0.01). However, the same cannot be said of the college students where the figure overall was only a little more than one-third. Perhaps this reflects, in part, the differences in the opportunities actually available, though again there is a gender difference, albeit not statistically significant: 39.5% of females as against 23.5% of males. All but the public library opportunity figured strongly for 14–16-year-olds, while the items most frequently cited by the college students related to greater use of the college library/resources centres, both during lessons and outside of lesson times during the week, and to use of the college at weekends. There was, then, particularly for school students, a real sense that many of them wished to utilise existing locations for independent work more than they say they can do at present, and exploration of the reasons they advanced for this make it clear that behind the wish was a genuine desire to work harder and improve their learning; in short, to 'do better'. This is captured no better than in one interview with a 15-year-old boy who remarked that, 'if only I was able to work more in the classroom or the library when lessons weren't on ... I'd get so much more done and get so much more out of it than I do what with the kind of behaviour there is in lessons and the noise there is at home'.

What seems clear from our data is that many of the school students claimed to want greater opportunity to undertake more work – homework, coursework, revision and catching up, generally, on missed or unfinished work – and to do so by way of having more readily available to them an environment which is either more conducive to concentration than is their classroom during lesson times or their home, and/or one which offers them fuller use, or use at all, of learning resources. In respect of the latter, the most frequently cited things were greater access to the broader range of reading materials located in libraries and resources centres, and greater, individual access to up-to-date computers (which is the main factor accounting for the high response concerning the use of the local FE college). Interestingly, it is not the case that these students have little access generally to computers. Responses to another item in the 14–16 questionnaire show that of the 200 students who reported that they worked in places in school other than classrooms and the library/resources centre, the vast majority mentioned the IT or computer room/s. Clearly, they want to, and do, use computers extensively. However, they want to use them much more, to have more individual use of them, and they want access to more 'state-of-the-art' equipment. Typical responses were:

- I find it easier to concentrate because it's quiet. There will be no one there to distract you and you get on with your work.

- I don't have a computer at home and there is work that I sometimes need to do or want to do on a computer.

- The library and computers [in an FE college] would be of more information [sic] with higher level books. They would also do more subject books that we do not do, e.g. there aren't many maths text books in our library.

- I think number 1 [work in a classroom at lunchtime or after school] is useful and if there was more opportunity to use it, you could do your homework there ... it would be very useful for people who haven't got a quiet place at home to do homework!

- I'd like to use the school library more because I have a lot of spare time at lunch so this time could be put to use. We have a school library at lunch but year 10's day is only Thursday and it's often closed on this day.

Unfortunately, the much smaller sample of college students, combined with a lower response rate to the question, means that it is not particularly meaningful to offer an analysis of their responses, other than to note that of 26 instances of reasons given for wanting greater opportunity to use the various locations, there were 11 to do with being able to do more work or catch up on work (though the issue of a quieter environment rarely figured), and 14 to do with greater use of learning resources, with specific reference in most of these cases to the wish that the college facilities be open at weekends.

So far, we have focused on, and explored students' wishes for, greater opportunity to engage in the sorts of flexible learning activities which are already available to them to one extent or another. We also explored, with the college students and the unemployed, the extent to which they would prefer different modes of 'delivery' and learning. Thus, we asked which of three methods of learning they would prefer: courses running at set times of the week, flexi-study or distance learning, 'definitions' of each method being provided. The unemployed respondents appeared to be much more interested than did the college students in the more flexible modes of delivery and learning (64% as against 30%, $p<0.01$) with flexi-study being far more popular than distance learning. This is possibly related to a stronger reluctance on their part to be associated with (traditional) learning institutions and what normally goes along with these. Indeed, some pointers are provided here by way of their responses to an item in their questionnaire which asked for things they did not like about studies in which they were previously involved. In particular, eight of the 34 respondents mentioned not liking their teachers or lecturers and seven mentioned having to take subjects they either did not like or saw no benefit in doing. More generally there was the sort of feeling expressed in one interview: 'After what school was like there's no way you'll get me back in education'. However, the 30% figure for college students who would prefer (largely) flexi-study or distance learning to 'fixed time' course provision is not an inconsiderable figure, particularly in the case of males, for whom the figure was 42%. This gender difference also pertained to the unemployed group where the figures were 74% and 51% for males and females respectively, though in neither case is the difference statistically significant.

Additionally, and of direct relevance to the purpose of our broader SRB Project feasibility study, we sought reactions, from all three groups, to the existence of a (hypothetical) new learning centre by way of the following question: 'Imagine that there was to be set up a new learning centre which wasn't part of a school/public library/FE college. The place would be equipped with learning materials and resources including computers, and someone would be there to help you learn or train. How interested would you be in using it as a way of studying or training?'

The possible responses to this question were: very interested; quite interested; so-so interested; not interested. The 'very' or 'quite a lot' of interest was substantial for all three groups, ranging from 58% amongst the unemployed (the least committed presently to any form of study or training), to 69% of the 14–16-year-olds (where two of the four schools involved rank very low nationally in terms of grade A–C GCSE results), to a very high 76% of the college students (the difference being statistically significant, $p < 0.05$, only between the first and last groups). The figures for females are even more striking: 73%, 75% and 78% respectively. Conversely, the figures for 'not interested' are very low, ranging from only 9–16%, though 18–31% for males. A key question relating to this hypothetical learning centre was whether its availability would make students more likely to study (after the timetabled day or at weekends) than was presently the case. This was only applicable to existing student groups and, unfortunately, was not asked of the 14–16-year-olds. However, the response from the college students was highly positive: 72% said 'yes' with, again, a gender difference (78% females as against 56% males, but not statistically significant).

A summary of the findings

The survey provides evidence that qualifications are highly valued by the majority of all respondents irrespective of whether they are within the school, college or unemployed samples. Furthermore the majority of respondents wish to continue with their study or training in some form although there is evidence, particularly among the unemployed, that their previous educational experience and views concerning the job market may have affected their perceptions of its value. Personal circumstances are perceived by the majority of respondents in the college and unemployed samples as being major barriers to further study. Particularly powerful here are financial considerations relating to, for example, loss of income and travel costs; inadequate and costly child care provision; and family commitments. Furthermore, dissemination of information relating to opportunities for further study or training, particularly for the unemployed, is an issue which requires to be addressed. In relation to school students there is evidence of some dissatisfaction with teaching and learning opportunities. Greater opportunities for the forms of flexible learning considered in this study might, at least in part, provide an answer to some of these problems. On this possibility, the evidence presents a fairly consistent pattern amongst 14–25-year-olds who are in education or training. Given the opportunity, about two-thirds of young people would make use of locations in schools and college, outside of normal lessons, to spend time on more independent activities. The most popular of these locations is the classroom during lunchtimes and after the end of the school/college day. Despite an overwhelming view that students do rely on teachers for their learning, there is an equally impressive majority (approximately 75%) who would wish to be able to learn more independently.

However, students, especially those in school, claim that there is relatively little opportunity to engage in more flexible patterns of learning in their current contexts. Particularly lacking are opportunities for college students to use college facilities at weekends and for school students to use college facilities at all. For the latter in particular there is also claimed to be limited scope for using existing school facilities. A considerable number of students claim they would like greater opportunity to engage in more flexible learning in their current contexts. This is particularly the case for 14–16-year-olds and even more so for females in that group. The reasons for the above reflect a widespread desire to undertake more work than is presently the case, principally through being able to study in a quieter environment than is normally possible and through being able to access, on a more regular basis, a wider range of learning resources, including more individual use of more up-to-date computers. As regards possible forms of flexible learning outside of their present contexts, significant numbers of college students and unemployed persons would prefer flexi-study to courses running at set times. This applies particularly to the unemployed and even more so to males in that group. As regards the hypothetical flexible learning centre, a substantial number of respondents in all three groups expressed 'very' or 'quite a lot' of interest, females in particular, and from the limited college sample it seems that such an opportunity would lead to an increase in the amount of time spent studying outside of normal timetable contact hours.

Concluding comments

First, our findings point to a general poverty of provision and physical accommodation for flexible learning. This stands in marked contrast to the rhetoric of developing a learning society. Moreover, whilst there is a clear desire across the whole age range for more facilities and opportunities within and beyond schools and colleges for independent study, making these available only provides part of the solution. It cannot be assumed that users are equipped with the necessary independent learning and study skills to make best use of the resources and opportunities made available to them. Nor can it be assumed that staff are able to manage flexible learning provision as effectively as is needed. Institutions need to address these matters within the context of their policies for teaching and learning and for the professional development of staff. These need to recognise that accommodating independent study is an integral part of the process of progressively developing in young people the skills which enable them to function as autonomous learners, whether those skills are applied in a traditional classroom or in a flexible learning centre or by way of flexi-study arrangements. There is also a need to recognise that as young people progress from one learning environment to the next they will function more effectively if they are in possession of those skills.

Second, as we have said earlier, different sorts of responses will be appropriate to different causes of low participation and attainment. Amongst the causes for the young people we studied are financial problems, including those to do with travel costs and with the likelihood of forgoing earned income; difficulties arising from domestic responsibilities which help prevent people from leaving the home; lack of individual attention from teachers, and distractions occasioned by others in the classroom. To varying degrees the provision of more flexible learning opportunities might help to combat these problems and our evidence is that many young people would welcome taking these up, whether in the context of their current, largely classroom-based learning situations, or by way of greater flexi-study arrangements. There seems to be, therefore, a case for further consideration of making available, on a more comprehensive basis than hitherto, more in the way of flexible learning opportunities in both post-16 and pre-16 sectors.

However, we need to be mindful that provision of opportunities does not necessarily lead to their take-up. Our findings suggest that a considerable number of people have not been able to take advantage of the opportunities that do presently exist. This has come across most powerfully in discussing the barriers to education and training take-up, especially with our unemployed sample. Many of these emanate from people's socio-economic circumstances. Moreover, of course, there are those who do not wish to take up opportunities for further learning in any form, and in this study gender is seen to be an important issue. Thus, not only do Key Stage 4 girls desire, much more than do boys, greater opportunities to engage with flexible learning, but also wish much more to continue with post-16 education and training at all. As Bloomer indicates, post-16 choices are strongly influenced by the social and cultural conditions in which they are made: rather than providing opportunities to break from class restraints, for example, the 'choice-making process itself ... serves for many students simply to reproduce class differences' (Bloomer, 1996: 148). More generally, Avis et al. (1996) argue that the whole debate about post-compulsory education and training has ignored issues of class, race and gender: recent reforms such as the establishment of a three-track qualification system reinforce the problem of past educational failures. Here, their argument is that we need to adopt a unified approach to post-14 education and training. This brings us to our next discussion point.

Our SRB Project brief makes explicit reference to a category of young people – those who are disaffected and often isolated from education and training – and suggests that the provision of a flexible learning centre will better serve their needs. Our survey, in fact, did not set out to test that hypothesis, but to find out from young people what they regarded as the most helpful conditions for them to learn. Because we drew on a sample of young people between the ages of 14–25 who were in full and part-time study and unemployed, including all 14–16-year-olds in the area, it is likely that our sample included those who are disaffected but also those who are highly motivated. Both groups, it would seem, see increased flexibility in learning provision as being desirable and motivational. This suggests that the provision of greater flexible learning opportunities should not be considered simply as a response to the problems of low participation and disaffection. Whatever is provided to serve the needs of those who are disaffected and isolated from education and training should be perceived in the community as an inclusive, integrated provision: it should not be seen as a way forward for the disaffected alone.

The fact is that flexible learning approaches, especially in schools, have been associated in particular with programmes for lower achievers. Thus, we can point to the Lower Attaining Pupil Project (LAPP), funded by the Department of Education and Science in 1982. This was an initiative which aimed at raising the achievement of the bottom 40% of 14–16-year-olds whose needs were not being met by the traditional curriculum. One important strategy in a number of the various local education authority projects was to design much more flexible teaching spaces, often called 'multi-skills bases' which became a model for many flexible learning centres in schools during the 1980s. A more flexible learning approach and the use of multi-skills bases was also evident in the City and Guilds 365 course which later evolved as the Certificate of Pre-Vocational Education (CPVE) and BTEC Foundation. The underpinning philosophy for these courses and, to an extent, the LAPP Project, was prescribed in *A Basis For Choice* (FEU, 1979). This became a seminal document because it provided a framework for a pre-vocational curriculum which embodied those characteristics which had been found successful in motivating students. Most recently, the introduction of National and General National Vocational Qualifications gives further impetus to flexible learning in that students and trainees have greater flexibility for organising their learning programmes and for using a range of learning environments within the context of a modular framework.

The strong association of flexible learning with both vocationalism and lower achievers may well have formed an impression in the minds of some people that flexible learning is only appropriate for those students who are on vocational courses and/or lower achievers. There are three reasons why we feel that it is important to counter such a view. First, the evidence from our survey suggests that young people across the board desire greater opportunities for flexible learning. Second, as Cockett (1996) argues, the history of initiatives aimed specifically at the needs of lower attainers is that they eventually wither. A period of development and commitment is followed by one of establishment during which participation in the initiative marks the students as low attainers, and in the end parents and students refuse to opt for experiences that mark them as less able. Here, then, is the problem of stigmatisation. As Raffe describes it, 'A vicious circle is thus created, and the net result ... might be merely to reinforce existing biases within education, by conveying the message that the new approaches are only relevant to those who lack ability or the motivation to try something better' (Raffe, 1985: 20–21). Third, we return to the point made earlier that current theories of learning suggest that flexible learning approaches are, in fact, appropriate for a wide range of people. We would stress that this includes the most able students. George, in describing the underpinning principles for the curriculum provision for gifted and talented children discusses the need for 'Objectives which are open-ended [which] allow for student determination in the learning process [and for] making sure that these children have some power over their own curriculum which is their entitlement' (George, 1992: 79). On teaching strategies, he suggests that the process-centred approach is more appropriate rather than overly structured work which is lacking in open-ended problem solving elements. Mentorship, using adults from the community other than teachers, counselling, flexible progression, extra-mural activities and making more efficient use of libraries and other sources of information, are all referred to by George as strategies to be used to extend the able child. Certainly, there is evidence to suggest that all students can benefit from flexible learning approaches. For example, Hughes gives an account of a four-year study where the Head of Geography at one school used flexible teaching and learning methods while colleagues taught the same curriculum more formally to students of similar ability. He writes:

The GCSE results, to my mind, offer conclusive evidence that flexible learning strategies influence outcomes and raise pupil attainment... One of the most noticeable and pleasing outcomes of flexible learning is the way in which the most able pupils are really stretched. They are not held back by whole-class teaching but are free to progress at a pace and to a depth that really challenges them.

(Hughes, 1993: 33, 73)

Finally, although providing greater opportunities for flexible learning, especially for all, might help to raise participation and attainment, what of the *content* of education? As Gleeson remarks:

Increasingly, the rhetoric is one of delivering and managing learning without real definition of what constitutes the nature of that learning ... preoccupation with improved participation, qualification and skills ... has little to do with enabling young people to think critically about themselves, their community and society.

(Gleeson, 1996b: 97)

Here, we are reminded of the argument for student-centredness as a necessary element of democratic education, the absence of which, some would argue, renders meaningless or irrelevant any attempts to address Finegold & Soskice's (1988) judgement that the nation's economy is founded on a 'low skills equilibrium'. In this context, Hodkinson (1994) suggests that what is needed is the development of:

... personal effectiveness: the ability to do things for oneself and with others; critical autonomy: thinking for oneself, including the ability to analyse and critique common assumptions;

... a sense of community: including recognising and respecting the rights and opinions of others, and contributing to community and society through individual and group efforts.

To conclude, then, there do seem to be grounds for suggesting that the greater provision of flexible learning opportunities should be considered in relation to the problems of low participation and attainment. However, it cannot be assumed that either young people or staff have the skills to make the most of such provision. Nor can it be assumed that greater provision of flexible learning opportunities will lead to their take-up. Moreover, any such provision should not be aimed at, or be perceived as being aimed at, a discrete set of lower achievers or disaffected groups. Flexible learning needs to be approached on an inclusive rather than exclusive basis, first in order to avoid the problems that arise from stigmatisation and second because it does appear to be an appropriate strategy for managing learning, irrespective of course status or academic ability of students. Finally, discussions concerning the possible role of flexible learning, for example in raising participation and attainment, should not ignore the issue of the content and purposes of education. Too narrow a focus on the delivery and management of learning can easily detract from more fundamental considerations.

References

Audit Commission (1993) *Unfinished business: full-time educational courses for 16–19 year olds* HMSO

Avis J (1991) 'The strange fate of progressive education' in Education Group II *Education limited: schooling and training and the New Right since 1979* Unwin Hyman, pp114–139

Avis J (1996) 'The myth of the post-Fordist society' in J Avis, M Bloomer, G Esland, D Gleeson & P Hodkinson (eds) *Knowledge and nationhood* Cassell, pp71–82

Avis J, Bloomer M, Esland G, Gleeson D & Hodkinson P (1996) *Knowledge and nationhood* Cassell

Ball C (1991) *Learning pays: the role of post-compulsory education and training – interim report* Royal Society of Arts

Banks M, Bates I, Breakwell G, Bynner J, Jamieson L & Roberts, K (1992) *Careers and identities: adolescent attitudes to employment, training and education, their home life, leisure and politics* Open University Press

Bealing V (1990) 'Inside information' *Maladjustment and Therapeutic Education* 8 (1), pp19–34

Bloomer M (1996) 'Education for studentship' in J Avis, M Bloomer, G Esland, D Gleeson & P Hodkinson (eds) *Knowledge and nationhood* Cassell, pp140–163

Bruner J (1974) *Beyond the information given: studies in the psychology of knowing* Allen & Unwin

Carroll J (1989) 'The Carroll model: a 25 year retrospective and prospective view' *Educational Researcher* 18, pp26–31

Cockett M (1996) 'Vocationalism and vocational courses 14–16' in R Halsall & M Cockett (eds) *Education and training 14–19: chaos or coherence?* David Fulton, pp33–49

Dearing R (1996) *Post-16 qualifications* The Schools Curriculum and Assessment Authority

Denham C & Lieberman A (eds) (1980) *Time to learn* National Institute of Education

Department of Education & Science (1991) *Educational statistics for the United Kingdom* Her Majesty's Stationery Office

Esland G (1996) 'Education, training and nation-state capitalism: Britain's failing strategy' in: J Avis, M Bloomer, G Esland, D Gleeson & P Hodkinson (eds) *Knowledge and nationhood* Cassell, pp40–70

Finegold D & Soskice D (1988) 'The failure of training in Britain: analysis and prescription' *Oxford Review of Economic Policy* 4 (3), pp21–53

Further Education Unit (1979) *A basis for choice* FEU

George D (1992) *The challenge of the able child* David Fulton

Gleeson D (1996a) 'Continuity and change in post-compulsory education and training reform' in R Halsall & M Cockett (eds) *Education and training 14–16: chaos or coherence?* David Fulton, pp11–16

Gleeson D (1996b) 'Post-compulsory education in a post-industrial and post-modern age' in: J Avis, M Bloomer, G Esland, D Gleeson & P Hodkinson (eds) *Knowledge and nationhood* Cassell, pp83–104

Her Majesty's Inspectorate (1991) *Student completion rates in further education courses* DES

Hodkinson P (1994) 'Empowerment as an entitlement in the post-16 curriculum' *Journal of Curriculum Studies* 26 (5), pp491–508

Hughes M (1993) *Flexible learning: evidence examined* Network Educational Press

Hustler D & Hodkinson P (1996) 'Rationales for student-centred learning' in R Halsall & M Cockett (eds) *Education and training 14–16: chaos or coherence?* David Fulton, pp108–109

Jamieson I (1985) 'Corporate hegemony or pedagogic liberation: the schools-industry movement in England and Wales' in R Dale (ed) *Education, training and employment: towards a new vocationalism?* Pergamon, pp23–40

Jamieson I (1993) 'The rise and fall of the work-related curriculum' in J Wellington (ed) *The work-related curriculum* Kogan Page, pp200–217

Kolb D (1983) *Experiential learning: experience as the source of learning and development* Prentice-Hall

Manchester LEA (1994) *14–19 Progression in Manchester Schools and Colleges: a policy statement* Manchester LEA

Menter I, Muschamp Y & Ozga J (1995) 'Public collusion, private trouble: the discursive practices of managerialism and their impact on primary teachers' paper presented at the annual *BERA/ECER* Conference, September, University of Bath

National Commission on Education (1993) *Learning to succeed* Heinemann

National Foundation for Educational Research (1993) *What do students think about schools?* NFER

National Foundation for Educational Research (1996) *Sixth form options: post-compulsory education in maintained schools* NFER

Raffe D (1985) 'Education and training initiatives for 14–18s: content and context' in A Watts (ed) *Education and training 14–18: policies and practice* CRAC, pp19–24

Robinson W (1975) 'Boredom at school' *British Journal of Educational Psychology* 45 (Part 2), pp141–152

Rogers C (1969) *Freedom to learn* Merrill

Smithers A & Robinson P (1989) *Increasing participation in higher education* BP Educational Services

Stenhouse L (1975) *An introduction to curriculum research and development* Heinemann

Stringfield S (1995) 'Attempting to enhance students' learning through innovative programs: the case for schools evolving into high reliability organisations' *School Effectiveness and School Improvement* 6 (1), pp67–96

Sutton A (1994) 'NTETs, GNVQs and flexible learning' *The Curriculum Journal* 5 (3), pp337–353

Tomlinson P & Kilner S (1990) *Flexible learning, flexible teaching: the flexible learning framework and current educational theory* Employment Department

Tuckett A (1997) *Lifelong learning in England and Wales* NIACE

Tymms P (1992) 'The relative effectiveness of post-16 institutions in England' *British Educational Research Journal* 18 (2), pp175–192

Wehlage G & Rutter R (1986) 'Dropping out: how much do schools contribute to the problem?' *Teachers College Record* 87 (3), pp374–392

9.   Managing Change

Michael Eraut

Over the last thirty years people in education have become used to innovations which were short-lived in their success. They did not reach the stage of adoption in the sense of permanent acceptance nor become established as an integral part of the system. Much has been learned from that experience about how best to manage change...

Flexible Learning is part of a broader agenda for change. Because it is fundamentally about the processes of learning it has ramifications for both the content and the delivery of the curriculum and the management of learning within the contexts of the classroom and the whole institution. The requirements of TVEI, GCSE, Standard Grade and the National Curriculum suggest that Flexible Learning is not just a peripheral issue of supporting 'new approaches', it is part of a serious reappraisal of how learning occurs and how it can be more effectively evaluated. The emphases on relevance, breadth, balance, differentiation, skills and competence are inseparable from the movement to make learning more effective.

We are talking here of change of some magnitude. Whether the initial change is small in scale or part of a grand design, its implications for the whole institution must be addressed if the innovation is to survive. In most schools this change will be radical, in the proper sense of that word, because it will challenge assumptions and practices that lie at the heart of the way in which that particular institution functions. Such a task does not have to be seen as daunting or impossible. But it must be recognised from the outset that change of this order does not happen overnight. Unfortunately today's technological rhetoric of getting things *up and running'* and seeing that the new system is *'in place'* does not take sufficient account of the scope, pace or process involved in changing educational organisations. Sophisticated systems and strategies will be ineffective unless they take proper account of the complex interactions of the human beings who constitute the institution.

Scope

Two patterns of change observed in Flexible Learning innovations can be broadly defined as *incremental* and *holistic*. Incremental change may be effected through one or more small-scale developments, e.g. the introduction of a supported self-study programme in Modern Languages or an integrated Science and Technology course involving co-operative group work and tutorials. Eventually such developments within discrete areas of the curriculum may become part of a wider strategy as their effectiveness is evaluated; and, if judged successful, they will act as a catalyst for changes elsewhere.

Holistic change is where the total organisation is involved from the outset in strategic planning and commitment to the innovation. Ultimately a whole-institution approach will be necessary if Flexible Learning is to become the accepted mode for delivering the curriculum; but an incremental approach may be the best way of starting. Such an incremental approach, however, should not be confused with a piece-meal approach where a variety of Flexible Learning innovations are set up within one institution without reference to each other or to any common policy, leading to major problems of continuity and cohesion.

An incremental approach is adopted when innovations are carefully planned within selected areas of the institution as important building blocks for longer-term development. The value and long-term future of these innovations is likely to be enhanced when they are integrated into a corporate strategy.

Needs

The strategy adopted by each institution will depend on how it assesses its needs. A college that has a well-established reputation within the local community which is statistically reflected in excellent GCSE and Advanced Level examination results will be cautious about losing this. At the same time, concern for students of 'average' ability may motivate the selective exploration of alternative methodologies. On the other hand, a school that is the result of a merger of two other schools with declining populations located in an inner city area may judge that it has nothing to lose and be eagerly seeking a radically new approach to better meet the needs of disaffected students.

The assessment of need depends both on awareness of other possibilities and on the review of current practice and its effect on those involved... For this, external as well as internal resources are useful. INSET can be helpful in raising awareness of approaches to Flexible Learning, especially when followed up by visits. It may also provide some assistance with developing the capacity for self-review. Where 'outsiders' are knowledgeable enough to be able to understand the organisation and can reflect that understanding back to the 'insiders' in an appropriate way, that too is extremely valuable.

Internally, the best starting point will usually be the main concerns of staff and students. Talking these through will suggest possible items for change agenda. But the talk needs to be both relevant to the purpose of the institution, i.e. the needs of its members, and constructive, i.e. discussing how the needs can be addressed through the processes of learning and the proper management of that process. When such matters become part of what people talk about (what Parlett calls the *'ideas in currency'*) then a successful change process is likely to be under way.

Pace

Innovators are likely to be impatient in their attempts to effect change and often have an evangelical zeal for their particular programme. But too fast a pace can be counter-productive. People take time to adjust and learn to do new things, and it takes longer than is usually recognised for any kind of change to take root. Hence, consideration of pace is a vital part of the planning and implementation of change.

Frequent monitoring of progress will check that the pace is appropriate and that agreed plans are being carried out. Then a formative evaluation involving all participants will provide feedback on whether their intentions are being realised in practice. Have planned goals been achieved? Are the methods used proving efficient and effective? Have attitudes changed or been modified? What evidence is there of student achievement? The responses to these kinds of questions will often suggest that modifications are needed. It may be wise to slow down and revise some of the plans; other plans may be on target; others still may be accelerated. Such a built-in process of monitoring and review will greatly aid the 'embedding' of the innovation. Even so, pace is unpredictable: there may be great surges forward, then a static period or even regression. These are not to be viewed as signs of failure but as natural occurrences. The important thing is to recognise such pauses, use them to re-assess what has been happening and respond accordingly.

What then are the features and conditions that will most enable the 'embedding' of Flexible Learning to occur? The following observations are based on schools that have already adopted Flexible Learning as a major aspect of their institutional development plan. They could therefore be said to be some way along the road of embedding Flexible Learning.

1. *Ethos.* The grandest design is of little use unless the action is underpinned by a philosophy that has been thrashed out by the main participants. A common ethos is essential both as a backcloth indicating common intent and as a unifying factor. There will be many disagreements but they should not be over fundamental issues such as, for example, the value to be placed on each individual student's work or the need for mutual respect between staff and students.

Part of the maintenance of the ethos depends on a clear articulation and thorough dissemination of the purposes of Flexible Learning to all students, staff, parents, governors and the wider community, including local business and industry.

The head/principal and the management team play a crucial role in maintaining this ethos. A shared understanding of and commitment to the aims of the innovation must be held by this group of opinion leaders. Where this has not happened there is an observable erosion of good intentions.

2. *Planning.* The commitment of management also needs to be seen in practical terms as wholly supportive of change. The importance of this stance cannot be over-emphasised in respect of the planning and maintenance of innovation.

A management style is required that reflects the principles of Flexible Learning: supportive, collaborative, with emphasis on negotiation in decision-making towards a shared, corporate policy.

The high profile given to the innovation should be backed up with appropriate organisational strategies. For example, policy in relation to staffing and allocation of space and time should reflect the esteem in which the development is held by the key decision-makers.

3. *Organisation.* Whatever the scale of change the practical details of how the institution works will be affected. A whole school policy is obviously likely to have far-reaching consequences for the day-to-day organisation. What are the ways in which change or adaptation are most needed in the structure in order to assist the development of Flexible Learning?

Goal-setting and the negotiation of tasks and strategies are expected from the flexible classroom teacher. The same openness in sharing the information on which plans are to be made must also be expected between the *'management'* and the rest of the professional workers. Clear channels of communication and a free flow of information will do much to help shape the whole staff into a team and to dispel the management-worker distrust that still prevails in some schools.

Flexible Learning with its student-centred ethos brings together the academic and pastoral aspects of the institution. It is no coincidence that schools developing whole-institution approaches have decided to rethink what is meant by *'pastoral'*. Responsibility for personal and social development is being put, along with all aspects of learning, back with the tutor, thus softening, if not abolishing, the distinction between the academic and pastoral organisation. Prior to this change teachers holding posts as year heads or house heads were increasingly taking on an impossible case load of problems that should properly have been dealt with by others. The focus now is for such postholders to have a role in co-ordinating matters relating to a particular year cohort and in leading a team of tutors to support and guide their students through all aspects of their learning.

Another organisational problem, especially in larger institutions, is the tendency for groups of staff based on departments, faculties, houses or year-groups to become power bases with vested interests which are resistant to change. Again there is a pattern among Flexible Learning schools to move towards looser structures. There may be new groupings within the curriculum to form clusters or teams to meet particular cross-curricular or related needs. Such teams do not have to have a permanent life. They will serve their purpose and then other groupings will emerge for different purposes. Some of the administrative functions held by heads of department (and year heads for that matter) can legitimately be delegated; and particular jobs can be shared around from year to year so that more staff gain experience of a range of tasks and responsibilities.

One further extension of the argument for more flexible structures is that all teachers within the institution need clearly defined responsibilities. It is to the advantage of the institution to clarify roles to ensure that all staff are aware of their responsibilities, that work-loads are shared and that all curriculum areas are equally accounted for in the efficient running of the institution. Like all bureaucratic mechanisms, the role definition has no intrinsic virtue. But if used flexibly and with imagination it can be a further means of making the organisation more effective.

4. *Staff Development.* Appropriate programmes of in-service training are needed to prepare and to support planned change. Again, by giving priority to such training,

the management team will be sending important messages to all staff about the significance of the developments. Such training should be seen as part of a continuous process in which developments are evaluated and modified. INSET provides an opportunity for staff to experiment with the teaching and learning methodologies to be used with students and to apply Flexible Learning in their own learning processes. Particular priorities suggested from our observations should be the development of skills in tutoring, team building and the design and production of resource materials.

An important but neglected dimension of Staff Development is Management Development. Its scope is essentially that of this report: the management of change, the management of Flexible Learning, the management of staff development and good knowledge of a range of policy options. Nor should management development be confined to the senior management team. It is relevant in some degree to all professional staff.

Barriers to change

Particular problems that have been observed in the development of Flexible Learning are almost certainly common to other innovations.

1. *Attitudes.* Belief in the status quo is clearly inimical to the idea of change. With this may go a resistance to any change in teaching methods and an attack on the 'jargon' which is seen to characterise changes. This negativism can be found as pockets of resistance even in institutions that appear to have whole-heartedly adopted Flexible Learning. The management problem is that negative attitudes can be destructive especially if expressed by people of influence or seniority within the institution.

2. *Resources.* Flexible Learning appears to be 'expensive' in terms of staffing, space, time, equipment and materials. That is, if the best possible plans are to be implemented. But this is a short-term view. In investment terms there is the prospect of a much more efficient use of material and human resources. Centralised materials are available to more students and can be more efficiently maintained and checked. Teachers working in teams can reduce unnecessary duplication, enable ideas to be shared and students to gain access to a wider range of teacher expertise.

However, good resources alone do not create Flexible Learning. Several institutions have been observed where the Library/Resource Base, the workshops and laboratories, the computer technology and consumable materials have been the envy of others but little in the way of Flexible Learning is occurring.

3. *External Relations.* Criticisms about jargon are not without justification nor are they exclusive to Flexible Learning. By their nature new developments coin new terms because innovation is an attempt to redefine the situation. There is a need to educate external constituencies such as parents, governors, local business, industry and the community into some understanding of the purpose and value of Flexible Learning. This can best be achieved through partnership rather than opposition.

This section has, deliberately, not repeated what has been said elsewhere about teaching and learning styles, tutoring, recording and assessing achievement, resources, environment or the finer details of organisation. It has been assumed that these are the basic ingredients of any developments in Flexible Learning. Our focus has been on those factors that have been observed to make a difference between a superficial adoption of Flexible Learning and the 'embedding' of it as a major institutional commitment to more effective education.

Part Three – Using ICT in Learning and Teaching

Information and communications technology has become a permanent part of our lives. It is not something that teachers and students can afford to – or should wish to – ignore. ICT skills are rapidly becoming as essential to future employment as literacy and numeracy, so students and trainees need to be given opportunities at all stages and all levels to acquire and develop these skills. In the future, access to information and learning will increasingly depend upon proficiency with current technology.

Teachers also need to acquire and develop ICT skills as active members of society, but in addition they have a professional responsibility to learn how to evaluate and use ICT effectively in teaching and learning. This will involve reviewing traditional educational practice and re-thinking what is taught and how it is taught – exactly the same characteristics as are required of those who are developing flexible schemes and programmes for their students and trainees. ICT has the potential to increase the flexibility and the quality of learning. The challenge for teachers is to find ways of exploiting this potential to the full.

It is reported that few lecturers and students in colleges, institutes and universities are currently taking full advantage of the ICT facilities which are available to them. Innovative and imaginative uses of ICT can be found in many colleges and training companies, but as Sir Gordon Higginson comments in his Foreword to *Learning and technology in further education colleges*:

> *... they are scattered across the FE sector... If the innovations currently to be found within parts of the FE sector were to be extended to most learning programmes across the majority of colleges, the sector would be transformed radically...*

> (FEDA, 1995: 4–5)

This Part will therefore concentrate upon ways in which teachers can make use of ICT to enhance and support student learning and help students become more effective learners. The readings here show that there is no shortage of ideas, even though we may often find an 'implementation gap' between policies and practice.

The first section presents an overview of prevailing uses of ICT in further education, higher education and training in industry. Much of the material here is drawn from recent government reports and research, and these provide a useful starting point for reviewing current practices and evaluating the progress being made within particular institutions.

In the next extract Paul Helm echoes one of the main themes of the first section, that ICT 'is still peripheral to most students' experience of learning'. Acknowledging that many teachers and students still need to be convinced about the effectiveness of ICT in assisting learning, he argues that innovations need to be carefully and systematically evaluated. He also tries to provide some answers to the question that many teachers ask – is teaching and learning with the new technology more effective than traditional methods?

The contribution by Bridget Somekh and Niki Davis raises a number of questions about the potential of ICT to empower and 'liberate learners' and to change the nature of both teaching and learning. ICT, it is argued, challenges current ideas about teaching and provides us with the opportunity to devise new kinds of learning tasks for students.

The final section concentrates on the use of ICT as a tool for both teaching and learning. Howard Lincoln offers many suggestions for incorporating ICT into the curriculum and provides short case studies of the use of ICT by both students and teachers. He also makes the point that ICT must be integrated into the curriculum if the benefits for student learning are to be fully realised. Though he writes specifically about GNVQ programmes, the issues he raises will apply to all curricula at all levels.

Although the term Information Technology has been used extensively by many of the authors throughout the articles in this Part (and in Part Four as well), other terms are also used which mean roughly the same thing. To emphasise that the technology is not just about using computers to process data and produce information, but is also about modes of communication, some writers use the term Communications and Information Technology (C&IT) whilst others favour Information and Communications Technology (ICT). For reasons explained in the Introduction to this Reader, we have chosen the latter term, though no significant difference is implied by the use of any of the others.

Reference

FEDA (1995) *Learning and technology in further education colleges* Further Education Development Agency

10.   An Overview of ICT in PCET

Lynda Hall

Official interest in the use of ICT for teaching and learning is not new. Since the mid-1980s there has been a steady stream of reports and initiatives from government agencies aiming to encourage the use of ICT in all sectors of education.

This section draws upon a number of recent reports in order to provide an overview of the developments which have led to the current state of affairs in PCET (further and adult education, higher education and professional and industrial training). The reports reveal that progress is being made in the use of ICT for teaching and learning, but that it is relatively slow, patchy and not as extensive as many would like. The reports also reveal that the drive to use ICT more widely in teaching and learning is not entirely motivated by pedagogical concerns.

Further and adult education

In 1993 the Further Education Funding Council (FEFC) set up a Learning Technology Committee, chaired by Sir Gordon Higginson, to examine the current use and effectiveness of technology in colleges and to recommend ways of improving the use of educational technology to enhance the provision of further education. The work of the committee culminated in the Higginson report (FEFC, 1996) published in January 1996.

To inform its work the Learning Technology Committee had asked the Further Education Development Agency (FEDA) to carry out some research into the current situation in the colleges. The main findings of this research had been published the previous September as *Learning and technology in further education colleges* (FEDA, 1995).

The FEDA research

The investigators concluded that 'colleges are looking to new technologies and their applications to learning to help them to improve productivity, to manage planned growth, to help reconstruct the curriculum in modular and unitary forms, and to keep track of an increasingly heterogeneous student population... They seek in particular technologies which will help with managing the shift in emphasis from traditional classroom-based modes of teaching to more independent, student-focused learning...'

In order to achieve these aims colleges were investing heavily in two areas: the IT infrastructure and Learning Resource Centres (LRCs). Although establishing or extending institution-wide networks and upgrading computer hardware was a high priority for many colleges, a more significant development for the future of flexible learning schemes was the widespread creation of Learning Resource Centres. The main purpose of these centres, it seems, was to increase 'the flexibility with which courses can be offered' and to provide 'greater opportunity for students to manage their own learning'. The expectation was that students would spend more of their time studying independently with the aid of learning resources and less time in the classroom.

However, the shortage of suitable software and on-line learning packages meant that the learning materials used in these centres were largely paper-based rather than computer-based. The investigators found that 'the main use of the computers in most LRCs was for students to word-process assignments, followed by their use for spreadsheets and databases. Only a minority of LRC networks carried learning packages'.

Although teachers were 'increasingly being expected to integrate classroom-based work with learning centre activities' less effort was being made to help teachers make use of technology in the delivery of courses. The investigators noted that many teachers were finding it difficult to make the transition from teacher-centred to learner-centred modes of delivery, where 'the teacher's role becomes primarily one of facilitating learning. Teachers need help in achieving the fundamental changes required if they are to effect the delivery of courses by genuinely flexible learning. Investment in teacher development and skills enhancement needs to accompany investment in new technologies if the FE sector and its students are to reap the benefits of the opportunities offered by the new and emerging technologies which potentially can do much to enhance learning'.

In their view 'a key issue requiring special attention throughout the sector is the effective integration of technology-delivered learning elements within an overall framework of mainstream curriculum delivery methods. These may range from using technology-based learning resources to deliver individual topics scattered at various points throughout a learning programme through to the delivery of complete modules...'

The FEDA research found 'little evidence of college strategies which comprehensively address the issues of integrating student-centred learning technologies and related courseware into mainstream curricula. In this respect it supports findings of earlier research work...'

The FEFC follow-up report

Two years after the Higginson report, the FEFC published the results of a further survey, called *The use of technology to support learning in colleges* (FEFC, 1998). Included in the summary of this report was the comment that 'Many of the conclusions of this survey reflect the findings of similar surveys carried out in 1994 as part of the Learning Technology Committee research'. Although considerable progress has been made in the intervening four years in what may be termed the institution-wide IT infrastructure, it seemed that little had changed in terms of the use made of IT to support teaching and learning.

The following extract includes a summary of the results of the survey and the more detailed findings about the use of technology in general and in various curriculum areas. It concludes with a brief outline of the way in which teachers are making use of the Internet.

The use of technology to support learning in colleges

Summary

Many colleges have reviewed the use of technologies to support learning and have encouraged a greater awareness of the potential range of their application. The more wide-ranging vision for using technologies is found in colleges where senior staff have a comprehensive understanding of the possible applications of technology. Few colleges have translated this vision into a comprehensive written statement, with clear targets and timescales in their strategic plan against which progress can be measured.

Many colleges have policies which address the educational uses of computers but less frequently cover the whole range of technologies to support learning...

A strong corporate drive is a key element in making effective use of learning technology. This is best achieved when a senior manager supported by committed staff has overall responsibility for planning and implementation. Frequently, funding pressures make it difficult for colleges to invest in the infrastructure required to develop learning technology. Typically the costs of extending networking facilities can take up to three years of the equipment replacement budget. Annual investment can be as much as 5 per cent of the annual college budget. Variable access to sources of funding other than those administered by the Further Education Funding Council (FEFC) has contributed to the wide differences in facilities between colleges, and there remain some colleges in which facilities for students are less than satisfactory.

Several colleges are developing networks that allow students to use all the electronically stored learning materials and information databases anywhere in the college, including remote sites. These 'intranets' are relatively new and only a few colleges have developed them. Students appear to learn quickly how to make effective use of them. These early developments are a part of the general move towards students studying on their own. At present little use is made of technology to assist students to learn independently. Few colleges have yet devised systems to track students' progress through the learning modules on the intranet although several are working with commercial organisations to develop this essential capability. Videoconferencing is being piloted in a number of colleges. Successful videoconferencing activities include individual counselling for careers advice and tutorial support and the transmission of some lessons to various outlets within the college and to remote sites.

Since incorporation [in 1993] many colleges have made substantial investment in computer technology. There is an increasing number of well-equipped and effectively used learning centres in colleges. These offer general curriculum support or support for specific curriculum areas such as engineering, science and modern foreign languages. The facilities include general computer facilities, computer-enhanced learning materials and other equipment for students to use on their own or with staff support.

Continued...

College facilities often include electronic library catalogues. Their potential to provide comprehensive support to students and tutors is sometimes missed. All colleges in the survey have an internet connection for the use of staff or students. The internet has been a significant factor in increasing the use of IT by staff and students.

Communication networks linking further education sector colleges are increasing through successful bids from groups of colleges for development funds. The networks provide opportunities for collaborative working to develop learning systems but few pilot projects have yet been completed. Several colleges have links with universities to support the teaching of franchised higher education programmes.

Few teachers routinely use IT in the classroom to improve the effectiveness of learning. There are examples of good practice in most curriculum areas but limited spread of good practice between curriculum areas and between colleges. Staff development events to spread good practice do not always lead to action in colleges. Availability of time for curriculum development is often an issue.

In several colleges, students' computer skills are assessed on entry to identify their levels of competence and the need for further development. For students with learning difficulties and/or disabilities there is frequently contact with their former school or local education authority to identify the equipment needed to support them. A few colleges seek specialist advice to select the appropriate supporting technologies. The lack of expert advice hampers the imaginative use of 'enabling technology' to support students with disabilities in some colleges.

The majority of students across the sector have opportunities to develop basic IT skills but the application of these skills varies significantly between curriculum areas within colleges. Their experience continues to depend heavily on the expertise and perception of teachers. The main use of computer equipment by students is in presenting assignments. Information searches using CD-ROM databases or the internet is the next largest use. Video recordings are an underused resource in many curriculum areas although there are examples of innovative and effective applications...

Technology and learning

Range of learning activities

22. Students mostly use IT to present their work and this helps them to acquire general IT skills. Most full-time students are expected to be able to wordprocess and this is the most frequently practised application of IT in most curriculum areas. Spreadsheets are used mainly in curriculum areas such as engineering, construction, business, mathematics and science. Students, for example, present mathematical data in a high-quality graphical format for assignments and presentations though they rarely use spreadsheets to model problems. The use of database applications are limited, are not in a subject-specific context, and are frequently too badly contrived to enable students to gain accredited awards.

23. Few teachers routinely use IT in the classroom to improve the effectiveness of learning. Where it is found, it is often the result of the work of individual enthusiasts.

Continued...

There are, however, isolated examples of good practice in most curriculum areas. For example, on a general certificate of education advanced level (GCE A level) politics course the students were following the progress of the general election. The internet was used extensively to obtain information from a range of websites that the political parties had set up and it was accessed daily to get the latest opinion poll statistics. Students were required to keep a log of the websites used. They were also given a list of websites and this formed a starting point for some research.

24. Although there is a general move towards students studying on their own, little use is made of technology to assist students to learn independently. A major limiting factor is the small amount of high-quality learning material that makes cost-effective use of expensive equipment and provides good feedback to students and teachers. The activities teachers and students find most useful relate to support for students in revising for examinations. Students like the opportunity to test themselves and some teachers have developed multiple-choice and short answer tests that record an overall score and provide feedback to students on incorrect responses. The most popular application of this is in GNVQ programmes. There are also some programmes, produced by colleges on CD-ROM, incorporating video, audio and sometimes animation materials, that cover a range of curriculum topics including woodworking technology, jointing mineral insulated cable, and finance for leisure and tourism...

27. Information searches, as a part of students' research, are a growing activity. In one college there are over 200 different CD-ROMs in regular use. Some of these are totally text-based and fail to make full use of the technology available. The internet is growing in popularity as a source of information. It is highlighted by the national media and has 'street cred' with young people. Students find it a more exciting way to carry out research and use it in preference to CD-ROMs if given a choice. Its use in curriculum areas is wide and increasing. Students in areas as diverse as hairdressing, humanities and engineering use it with equal enthusiasm. Hairdressing students, for example, were carrying out research to find information on new hair care products and examples of topical hair styles.

Technology in curriculum areas

28. This section summarises the developments and practices observed in colleges during the year of the survey to May 1997. There were significant differences in the way in which technology, particularly IT, was used by teachers to support learning. Enthusiasm by individual teachers, understanding of the time needed for developments, encouragement and recognition by managers, were usually the circumstances in which good practice was found.

Sciences

29. Science departments make little use of technology other than in meeting the requirements of the course and, in the case of GNVQs, developing IT key skills. There are infrequent examples of good practice across the full range of science subjects. Students are sometimes directed to use CD-ROMs for individual assignments and some colleges have software packages that students use for revision. In a few colleges, there are excellent examples of the use of automatic data logging, computer analysis of

Continued...

results and the production of graphs and charts. Field trips have benefited from the on-site use of data loggers and portable computers which rapidly produce a printout of results. One college has used the internet to access a simulation of the fruit fly experiments and students' interest was stimulated by the use of this demonstration, which complemented the experiments started in the college laboratories...

31. There is limited use of technology as an aid to classroom teaching in computing courses. Few teachers make use of data projection or large-screen facilities to ensure that all students can see software demonstrations. Formal presentations by teachers, when they are required, rarely make use of the presentation graphics facilities generally available. There are good examples of the use of video, CD-ROMs, multimedia packages and the internet to support learning. Many students effectively use the information from these sources for assignments. However, a minority of students, frequently studying GNVQ at intermediate level, used large tracts of text indiscriminately for portfolio evidence without understanding the content. Students usually make good use of the IT facilities available to them when completing assignments. They frequently use the full range of applications packages and the quality of presentation is good.

32. In only a few colleges is the use of technology an integral part of the study of mathematics. Many GCE A level students are encouraged to use advanced calculators with graphics and statistics capabilities but often only in a limited way. Computer software, which includes graph plotting, solution of simultaneous and differential equations, statistical analysis, and matrix transformations, are used in teaching calculus, algebra and statistics but there is scope for more extensive use particularly in modelling mathematical problems. A few colleges have invested in powerful statistics packages that provide support for mathematics and social science students and these are a helpful preparation for progression to higher education. A significant factor, limiting the use of technology in mathematics, is the difficulty of arranging for whole groups of mathematics students to have access to computer facilities on a casual basis.

Construction
33. Many construction departments have established specialist learning centres of high quality close to workshops. These centres have extensive study areas, often incorporating a well-stocked library of books and other learning materials which are easily available to students during their studies. Supplementary learning aids sometimes include videos, camcorders, computers with industry-standard software, CD-ROM databases, manuals of codes of practice, models, trade literature and technical catalogue systems. Students are encouraged to work on their own using specially designed resources. Staff have developed innovative learning packages which enable students to arrange their studies at convenient times. Over recent years, the quality of learning materials developed by course teams and consortia has steadily improved. However, teachers do not make sufficient use of technology in lessons...

Engineering
36. Most engineering activity requires the installation, use, or maintenance of equipment which has some form of micro-processor or computer control. The use of technology as an integral part of the knowledge and skills required by technician and

Continued...

craft engineering students is usually well developed. Its use for word processing assignments and the gathering of information is generally appropriate although more effective use could be made of spreadsheets and databases.

37. Engineering students use a range of software packages including CAD packages for mechanical engineering. Some CAD packages now include a detailed help system held on a CD-ROM that can be run at the same time as the main package and this demonstrates the particular software feature being used and provides an added dimension to the teaching notes readily available. Electrical and electronic engineering students use computer packages which design and plan circuits. The latest micro-electronics teaching equipment extensively uses software-controlled self-teaching packages which include regular testing of the student's progress. In a few colleges, students use software which mimics the building and testing of circuits. The simulation can be used to supplement conventional laboratory work. Commercial software for designing hydraulic and pneumatic circuits is occasionally available. Some students also become familiar with the design and operation of programmable logic controllers. Installation and maintenance are also key elements of engineering courses. Electrical installation students fit and maintain micro-processor controlled equipment, especially security alarm equipment. Motor vehicle engineering students service and maintain micro-processor controlled equipment such as that used for anti-lock brakes and engine management systems.

38. Most engineering students use general computer hardware and software to produce their assignments. Full-time students use such resources either in engineering departments or within the college. Most students complete some work using wordprocessing software but few are enthusiastic users. There is little use of spreadsheet or charting software and limited use of database software except for a few specific activities...

39. The use of IT to deliver teaching is minimal. Some teachers have used word processors and desktop publishing software to produce their notes... A few teachers use presentation graphics to make their teaching more effective. A few colleges have the latest commercial equipment for teaching electronics which employs software-controlled self-teaching packages. Its use is still being developed in most of these colleges.

Business
40. Computers are used widely in the business programme area as a routine part of the development of skills such as wordprocessing, presentation skills using graphics, and desktop publishing used in business-related occupations. Students also use software for spreadsheets and databases in business applications. There is limited use of computers and other technology to support teaching and learning in other aspects of business-related courses. Few business administration areas have introduced the software available for simulated applications of stock control, simple accounts and records in training offices. There are some examples of interactive software, the most common area being accounting. Packages have been developed for teaching accounting technicians. A number of colleges are using software to provide data sets for business exercises. There is also isolated use of packages for teaching various elements of

Continued...

customer relations, for GCE A level business studies and marketing. There is increasing interest in self-testing software for use on GNVQ programmes.

41. The use made of the internet varies. A number of colleges have now introduced supervised access in IT and 'business' centres. Most activities are searches for information. For example, company, marketing, financial and economic information is readily available and provides opportunities to track real company performance. A website has been developed by a consortium that includes the Economics and Business Education Association. It contains:

- a section on information about companies
- financial and economic data a listing of resources
- a network service of key national and regional contacts
- a study skills support service
- tutor support service with schemes of work and assignments.

It is not used extensively by the sector colleges... Learning packages on topics such as marketing are beginning to be introduced. A recent development is the use of videoconferencing to support applications within the business community.

Art and design
42. The use of technology in the art and design programme area varies widely. In many programmes, particularly the advanced level design courses, technology is an integral part of the curriculum and is well used. There is consistent use of technology in design, media and some specialist music courses... On media courses there are often insufficient editing facilities. Image scanners, laser printers and, increasingly, digital cameras are the most commonly available equipment for use with computers. The use of technology to support students working on their own is still at an early stage of development. Access to the internet provides students and staff with material directly connected to their studies but few colleges have this facility available in art and design studies.

43. The majority of colleges offering a full range of art and design courses have a suite of industry-standard computers on a network. However, in terms of the effective use of computers, there are frequently great disparities between courses in the same departments. For example, media studies courses may be equipped with industry-standard technologies that are effectively used, while in performing arts there is little or no access to the technologies associated with the subject.

44. On some music courses, particularly those involving popular music, the use of electronic instruments and equipment has been accompanied by increasing use of related software applications. In contrast, some vocational course requirements have not kept pace with the increased use of technologies. Art and design students usually take the same key skills programme in IT as other students rather than follow a vocationally relevant programme. A few students and staff continue to cling to the stereotype that artists and designers have no need of new technologies. Most of the courses using computer technologies have appropriate industry-standard software application packages for graphic design, media and music. There are very few

Continued...

performing arts courses equipped with modern lighting systems with computer control... IT support for art and design in these colleges is usually provided in a general learning resource centre...

46. There are a few examples of staff using their expertise to develop teaching methods using new technologies. This is particularly the case where staff in graphic design, media and music courses have industrial or professional backgrounds and experience.

Hotel and catering/leisure and tourism
47. Several colleges have introduced specialist learning resource centres for hotel and catering and for leisure and tourism. However, many still lack appropriate IT equipment and specialist software to support the subject area. A number of colleges are making increasing use of CD-ROM. The best examples include the use of interactive packages of software related to travel and hospitality. The use of the internet is only at an early stage of development, although some staff and students are becoming aware of its potential. In one college, GNVQ leisure and tourism students use it to conduct research for assignments and have been able to gather information on visitor attractions, transport services and tourist destinations.

48. There are a few examples of the good use of technology in realistic work environments. These mainly involve the use of computerised restaurant reservations, billing and stock-taking systems. In addition, some college travel offices have computerised booking facilities and viewdata terminals linked to commercial operators. Students can use the equipment to book holidays for members of the public, other students and staff. The availability of such technology offers students a significant advantage in developing the skills required for employment. In some cases, the hardware and software do not meet industry standards.

Humanities
49. The most commonly used equipment to support teaching and learning in humanities areas comprises overhead projectors, video and audio cassettes and slide projectors... The use of IT is a relatively recent development.

50. There has been a rapid increase in the use of CD-ROMs for general and specific subjects. These are widely used by humanities students to research topics and assignments and as an additional source of information, alongside books and journals, for essay writing. In geography, there is a wider use of software packages which present fieldwork data in formats which are useful for analysis. Water tanks can be used to model deposition, and satellites bring up-to-date information on world climate. Although various specialist software packages do exist in other subjects, for example in history, they are not as widely used and their potential is not yet fully developed. Although students use software packages in timetabled sessions they do not always follow this up with further work in their own time.

51. There is increasing pressure in many colleges for all students to acquire general skills in wordprocessing, and in the use of spreadsheets and databases. However, even when students acquire these skills they are not always subsequently applied within a subject context. Many humanities courses are governed by syllabuses which do not

Continued...

113

have many specific requirements for using IT and so little emphasis is given to developing general skills. There is, however, an increasing tendency to require some wordprocessed work from students. In geography in particular there is some scope for the use of spreadsheets. Many higher education access courses in humanities make the acquisition of IT skills an integral part of the work.

Modern languages
52. Modern language teachers are often enthusiastic about the use of technology in learning. The success with which they use it depends on a number of factors, including development time available, suitable equipment and software, administrative and technical support and the level of their own expertise. Audio and video cassette players are an essential component of modern language teaching... There is growing use of satellite television, electronic mail and videoconferencing with partner institutions abroad to keep staff and students abreast of language evolution, including colloquial expressions.

54. Modern language students make little use of computers for their project work. Work is occasionally presented using foreign language fonts... The use of the internet is growing as the number of useful sites with learning materials for language teaching increases.

Basic skills
55. Teachers of basic skills and English for speakers of other languages (ESOL) usually have adequate access to appropriate computing facilities. However, the time taken by teachers to master the technology frequently hinders its use as an aid to meaningful learning. In community locations, learning technology is used even less because teachers often have to carry equipment to their classes. The software and learning resources for students with basic skills needs are frequently unsuitable or in short supply. Many resources are outdated...

56. The quality of teaching materials varies considerably. In the better lessons they are computer generated, attractively presented, appropriately varied and of a suitable level for the students. In less effective lessons, there is extensive use of poor-quality worksheets. Some teachers do not use IT because of their own inexperience and lack of awareness of its potential. Others have no access to suitable equipment or appropriate software. ESOL teachers tend not to use computers except where there is a focused short course linked with developing computing skills. Although students often have good access to computers in open learning or study centres there may be no facilities for computer-assisted language learning in the ESOL area... In study skills and basic skills workshops, computers are being used to produce good paper-based materials but there is often little use made of technology to assist learning and teachers lack information on the software available.

Students with learning difficulties and/or disabilities
57. Students with learning difficulties and/or disabilities may require specially designed 'enabling technology' to gain access to the full range of learning opportunities. In the best practice, where colleges are committed to ensuring that these students have full access to the curriculum, there is careful initial assessment of students' needs.

Continued...

114

This is accompanied by:

- access to appropriate equipment
- the use of IT as an integral part of teaching
- adequate specialist technical support
- access for students to appropriate technology for home study training for students and staff in the use of the technology.

58. Many colleges have a good range of enabling technology, including: induction loops; videos with subtitles; voice-activated tape recorders for the use of note-takers to support students who are deaf or hard of hearing; mini-cassette recorders for dyslexic students to record lectures; and adapted keyboards, switches, 'glidepoints' and trackerballs to help physically disabled students use the keyboard effectively. One college worked with a local engineering company to develop an adapted darkroom complete with computer-assisted enlargers, finely controlled through simple switches. Other colleges have established a resource bank of adapted and specialist equipment such as laptop computers, voice recorders and spell-check machines. In some colleges, differentiated computer-aided learning programmes are available on the computernetwork. For example, a higher national diploma student receives particularly good study and technical support. He is a switch user and has a keyboard emulator, a modem and access to a phone line so that he can send his tutors his work. Staff have put key material onto disk because he cannot use his hands. Specialist equipment including voice synthesizers allow students with visual impairments to follow computing and other courses effectively...

Development of learning systems and materials

81. Teachers find difficulty obtaining high-quality interactive learning materials. Good commercial products are often expensive and generally cannot be modified without infringing purchasing agreements. Materials that allow students to study on their own are the most difficult to obtain and most of them are not suitable for use with the required range of abilities or adaptable for different styles of learning. Many lower cost materials are effectively electronic books with limited facilities for interactive learning. A few colleges have invested in multimedia authoring systems to produce learning materials that meet specific needs across a range of curriculum areas. There are examples of enthusiasts amongst college staff who have produced this type of learning material through college-based or externally sponsored projects. One innovative project involved learning support staff developing a multimedia low-budget, colourful and interactive induction presentation. This meant that, during induction, students on basic skills programmes were able to explore visually, on their own initiative, the specialist programme areas offered by the college...

82. Many colleges have a substantial quantity of learning materials produced by teachers as a normal part of their work. The majority of learning materials are handouts, booklets, periodicals and books. A small, but growing, number of sector colleges are systematically storing them electronically for use on an intranet. In some of these colleges, teachers are being given guidance on how to develop intranet-compatible materials. Commercial products are frequently the first choice where they are available and of the appropriate quality and cost. Preference is usually given to

Continued...

materials and learning systems which allow teachers to modify them to meet specific needs. Some colleges have produced materials to meet particular needs. Several colleges are able to provide expert technical support and some have design teams who are responsible for the quality and consistency of materials used in college. New projects are sometimes identified and managed centrally. These include the development of multimedia learning systems and pilot exercises in the use of videoconferencing...

Internet access and use

- Most colleges have some form of access to the internet. Some use their data links with higher education institutions to gain access to the internet. Other colleges access the internet directly through a range of providers. Some colleges use a dedicated ISDN line or leased line but most use the telephone network and modems.

- Students' freedom of access to the internet varies from college to college. Some colleges provide unlimited access for students although this is often through a few controlled machines... In other colleges, students may have to obtain the permission of staff, or be under the control of staff, to access the internet. 'Patrol' software can be installed to limit access to illicit information...

- Some colleges have developed their own website. Typically, they provides students with comprehensive information on the courses available, the general college facilities and contact names for students to obtain further information. A few advertise 'open learning' courses on a commercial basis.

- The internet provides a vast database of information. Students can obtain general information on a specific topic to support project or assignment work. They can also obtain specific data such as the specification of an electronic component or details of a railway timetable.

- The internet provides some material of high quality. Many major organisations have websites. Examples include governmental organisations, European bodies, educational sources, military organisations, commercial organisations, and pressure and promotional groups. Information is available on a wide range of subjects and on some subjects which may not be readily available from other sources such as the design of surf boards or help and support with a range of medical conditions. Information on topical events ... and national elections, can be provided in real time.

- Information provided on the internet, and to a lesser extent on CD-ROMs, gains an authority and credibility that may not always be warranted. It is sometimes difficult for students and teachers to determine the status of the information available, especially that provided by non-corporate bodies, individual enthusiasts and/or pressure groups.

- Much time can be wasted whilst carrying out searches for information on a particular topic. Searches often generate results with an American bias. It is sometimes difficult to focus only on United Kingdom or European information. Teachers may decide to restrict students to previously identified websites to help reduce time and expense. To use the internet successfully, students should have sufficient expertise to find their way around and a clear plan of what they want or

Continued...

need to find. This may involve spending time to explore and gain experience in searching the internet. Some colleges have set up as 'simulated' internet which has been previously downloaded and students are free to explore it. This has provided valuable training on using the internet effectively.

- The use and role of the internet in the teaching process is still being explored by teachers. Even with a restricted range of sites students can obtain copious amounts of information very quickly on a chosen subject. Assignments which require only the collection of information can be completed with a minimum amount of effort and understanding may not have been enhanced.

- One modern languages adviser has produced a disk which enables modern foreign language teachers to access quickly sites of real use and interest by setting bookmarks. This use of an expert to provide easier routes to useful information may be the way forward but it needs development time and should not be allowed to block access to information.

- One college is piloting a TEC-funded remote NVQ assessment project for local and more distant employers in the catering industry on the internet. Participating employers and students using passwords can access, electronically, multiple-choice tests relating to specific NVQ units. The programme allows students to have a maximum number of attempts to answer questions correctly, to analyse their performance, and to record results for external verification.

- The internet can be used to good effect to encourage groups of students to work together to seek information. Students working in pairs researched a topic of their choice, obtained pictures and text which they then imported into an electronic presentation they were producing.

- One college's students collect information through the college's electronic mail network and the internet. A student on a computer literacy course gained approved access, electronically, to a space centre in the United States of America and copied digital pictures of the earth to use in an assignment.

- The history department in a sixth form college is exploring the internet as a research tool for GCE coursework, seeking to obtain access to research papers and to take students beyond standard textbooks.

- A few colleges are beginning to explore the use of the internet to provide teaching packages and to communicate with community groups. In one rather isolated voluntary external organisation, the internet provides a means for staff and students to communicate with other colleagues making provision for students with learning difficulties.

- A few colleges have begun to build up an intranet. Several colleges are also in the process of 'unitising' their curriculum. Once this is complete, the next stage is to create learning packages for each unit, all of which will be on the college intranet. Some curriculum material is already on the intranet, though it is not terribly exciting.

- The use of the internet to promote a product should now be part of the curriculum. Students should learn to build a website or develop web pages to market a product. This might be to market a service, such as a privately owned hotel, or to market a

Continued...

commercial product. One college is using the internet as the context for teaching an NVQ level 3 IT course. Students learn how to create web pages incorporating movement and sound. They have links with local commercial organisations and produce web pages marketing products.

(FEFC, 1998: 2–7; 23–24)

Higher education

Over the last 10 years higher education has benefited, unlike further education, from a number of sector-wide initiatives funded centrally through the Joint Information Systems Committee (JISC) of the three higher education funding councils and Department of Education for Northern Ireland.

The Combined Higher Education Software Team (CHEST) provides quality hardware, software and data sets for the higher education community, appraising products and negotiating discounts on behalf of the sector. The National Information Services and Systems (NISS) provides sector-wide electronic access to useful collections of information. Other JISC-funded services include the BUBL Information Service, which provides fast and reliable access to selected Internet resources, an international discipline-based email system (Mailbase) and access to a variety of databases and archives.

Two other higher education initiatives provide direct support for the use of ICT in teaching and learning – the Computers in Teaching Initiative (CTI) and the Teaching and Learning Technology Programme (TLTP). Since 1989 CTI has been providing information and support to lecturers interested in using technology to support their teaching through 24 subject-based advisory centres. These centres act as central reference points for any higher education lecturer and are accessible via the Internet. Since 1992, the TLTP has sponsored 76 development projects intended to produce a wide range of computer-based learning packages, many of which will be produced on CD-ROM. The stated aim of TLTP is 'to make teaching and learning more productive and efficient by harnessing modern technology'. Several of the TLTP projects are developing materials which could support teaching in the further education sector.

The Dearing Report

It may seem that higher education is far ahead of further education in the use of ICT in teaching and learning. However, the Dearing Report on Higher Education (HMSO, 1997) revealed that despite such initiatives as CTI and TLTP, there was little widespread use of Communications and Information Technology (C&IT) in higher education. Here is an extract from what Dearing said.

Higher education in the learning society

The impact of C&IT on learning & teaching

8.20 We estimate that up to ten per cent of expenditure in higher education is committed to C&IT. Our concern here is with its potential contribution to learning and

Continued...

---

teaching. Technological development provides the potential for enhancing the quality of learning for students in an era of attenuated staff-to-student ratios...

8.22 Over the last 20 years, the higher education sector has undertaken a wide range of experimentation in developing and implementing new technology for learning and teaching. This has been triggered by a succession of publicly funded development programmes, and in the last decade has been underpinned by the network of discipline-based Computers in Teaching Initiative (CTI) centres, now numbering 24, all sited in universities...

Benefits of C&IT to learning and teaching

8.24 One of the benefits of new technology lies in providing a learning environment that may succeed in improving understanding where other methods have failed. Computer-based programmes, such as tutorials, simulations, exercises, learning tools and educational games can be highly interactive and provide activities that students need to develop their understanding of others' ideas and the articulation of their own.

8.25 Computers can provide access to information and learning materials through the World Wide Web, datastores, electronic journals and other sources. For students with visual, hearing or motor disabilities, communications and information technology can provide enhanced access to such materials. Given the general concerns of students in our survey about access to learning materials, C&IT provides the potential to ease these difficulties.

8.26 By using computer-based learning materials, students can receive immediate feedback to assist with learning complex concepts. Such materials often provide students with an opportunity to generate as many exercises as needed, as a way of supplementing tutor-marked assignments for certain topics. Simulations of experiments can help students to understand complex or dangerous experiments, or replace experiments that would otherwise use live animals, just as simulators for pilots can be as effective as 'flying hours'. A simulation may replace, or simply supplement, the actual experiment itself. Students can repeat simulations as many times as necessary to enhance their understanding of the procedure and outcomes.

The development of computer-based learning materials

8.27 Despite the potential of C&IT and some major national initiatives, there is as yet little widespread use of computer-based learning materials. This relative lack of use derives in part from the reluctance of some academics to use teaching materials created by others, from the considerable time it takes to redesign programmes to integrate computer-based materials, and from the limited availability of good materials.

8.28 Developing good computer-based learning material is expensive: the Teaching and Learning Technology Programme (TLTP) has spent £32 million, with at least equal contributions from participating institutions. Given the expense of producing high quality courseware ... courseware developers should concentrate on developing materials and systems that can be used by large numbers of students...

8.32 Few institutions will have the resources and expertise to develop high quality material alone. The Teaching and Learning Technology Programme (TLTP) has

Continued..

encouraged departments to produce materials on a collaborative basis, which has been valuable in bringing staff from different institutions together and in assisting wider use of computer-based materials. We support the discipline-based approach of past initiatives as a good way of pooling expertise, achieving synergy and securing ownership of the products...

Implications of C&IT for staff and students

8.34 Increased use of new technology will have major implications for the way in which staff and students work...

8.35 According to our survey of students, the use of computer-based learning packages is, at present, the least satisfactory mode of learning of those asked about. This points to the scale of the task facing institutions in integrating computer-based learning packages into their teaching programmes, in training staff in their use, and most particularly in ensuring that students learn effectively from computer-based materials.

8.36 We have noted during our visits to institutions the growing scale of adoption of C&IT. But its use for learning is still at a developmental stage. For a full and successful integration into learning to take place, staff need to be effective practitioners and skilled in the management of students' learning through C&IT...

8.71 Computer-based learning materials are valueless unless they are actually used by staff and students... The Computers in Teaching Initiative (CTI) has done valuable work in providing institutions with subject-specific advice on technology-based educational practice and by testing and promoting materials...

Networking

13.24 We have observed that, through the Funding Bodies, higher education has in place an enviable infrastructure in the shape of the Joint Academic Network – JANET – which is one of the most technologically advanced networks in the world. The network, and a range of network services, is managed on behalf of the four UK higher education funding bodies by the Joint Information Systems Committee (JISC).

13.25 All higher education institutions in the UK are linked into the network by high-speed connections, as are about 90 further education institutions. An estimated 90 per cent of all significant sites of higher education currently have their own access to JANET. Networks (local, national and international) are impacting upon higher education in a number of ways: as a source of information and software; as a marketing tool; to support learning and teaching; to support research; and for a wide variety of administrative and management purposes.

(HMSO, 1997)

Professional and industrial training

In addition to commissioning FEDA to carry out research in further education colleges, the Learning Technology Committee of the FEFC also asked them to investigate 'the role of information and communications technology systems, platforms and related courseware within companies' internal training programmes'.

FEDA's report was presented in May 1995 and the following extract from the Higginson Report contains a summary of the research conclusions (FEFC, 1996).

The report of the Learning Technology Committee

Internal training programmes

48. The key findings were that:

- Traditional classroom-based instructor-led training still forms a significant component of training delivery, usually supported and/or complemented to varying degrees by the use of technology-delivered training.

- Training managers believe that trainees prefer the classroom-based instructor-led training to other methods of delivery.

- Future planning of training provision is directed towards the acquisition of training applications using new technologies and integrating technology-based training with classroom-based activity.

- Training requirements are determined through internal staff appraisal processes.

- Large companies maintain dedicated training centres with banks of computer workstations (usually networked) as well as videoconferencing and private broadcast facilities for multimedia transmission and Internet access. Some centres mainly provide open learning facilities on terminals which may be networked or stand-alone.

- Custom-designed courseware is used along with customised commercial packages. It can be accessed in some companies from personal workstations outside learning centres.

- Intensive training will be increasingly used to fill perceived gaps in personal, managerial or technical skills.

49. Despite the strong emphasis on classroom-based training, individuals are encouraged take responsibility for their personal self-development, with line managers closely involved in ensuring that individual training needs are met for the people they manage. Individual development plans jointly agreed within the appraisal process form the basis of internal training strategies.

50. Videoconferencing facilities are available but not generally used as an integral part of training programmes. Issues of cost seem to be the main factors currently limiting its use for training.

51. Most of the companies visited are involved in the development of custom-designed courseware, both externally commissioned and internally developed. They work with producers of commercial training software to tailor it to cater for their specific requirements, while in-house units develop additional support materials to complement commercially produced training packages.

(FEFC, 1996)

References

FEDA (1995) *Learning and technology in further education colleges* Further Education Development Agency

FEFC (1996) *Report of the Learning Technology Committee – the Higginson Report* Further Education Funding Council

FEFC (1998) *The use of technology to support learning in colleges* Further Education Funding Council

HMSO (1997) *Higher education in the learning society – the Dearing Report* Her Majesty's Stationery Office

11. Teaching and Learning with the New Technologies

Paul Helm

It has long been acknowledged that some of our thinking about the new technology is skewed by the fact that its detractors seem to be far outnumbered (at least in print) by its champions. Technology initiatives tend to attract the lone enthusiast. These enthusiasts have often spent so long enduring the long dark night of the innovator that they begin to lose sight of the blindingly obvious: subject specialists need to know more about their subject than about educational technology. There is a widespread suspicion in certain quarters that educational technology attracts peripheral figures, and that its use is still peripheral to most students' experience of learning. CAL, CDL, TBT, multimedia, the Internet, the World Wide Web and others can, at times, be all-too reminiscent of the King's new clothes.

Benefits

There is no doubt that teaching and learning with the new technologies require more effort than carrying on as normal. Using the new technologies is a huge learning experience for all participants. Moreover, even the most innovative staff are still 'mixed mode' in that they do not *always* teach using the new technologies, but still adopt traditional strategies as and when fit. Arguments about whether new technologies are a replacement or enhancement of traditional provision still continue; proponents of the replacement argument claim that the emergence of new technologies in education owes as much to the limitations of traditional education as to the benefits of the new technologies. These benefits are defined in different ways by different participants: management views are very different from those of tutors; tutors' views differ from students'. The Higginson Report on the use of new technologies in further education was explicit in its view of the benefits to be gained from a managerial viewpoint:

> *The investigation concluded that colleges are looking to new technologies and their applications to learning to help them to improve productivity, to manage planned growth, to help reconstruct the curriculum in modular and unitary forms, and to keep track of an increasingly heterogeneous student population.*
>
> (FEFC, 1996: Annex D, para 16)

Tutors and students tend to see the benefits of new technologies in terms of *overcoming obstacles*. Obstacles arising from traditional provision for students include:

- costs, particularly for travel and accommodation
- disruptions to work flow and personal life
- rigidity of timing, duration and content

- the number of people who can participate
- possible irrelevance of much of the content to many participants.

With costs coming down all the time, new technology would seem to offer the chance of a flexible, individualised curriculum. Obstacles for staff include:

- limited access to equipment, requiring extensive forward planning
- lack of technical support and appropriate training in the use of hardware and software
- lack of confidence and time to develop familiarity.

Many enthusiasts go all out for the replacement option – thus confusing students who may not be immediately aware of why the technology is being used at this point. Examples include course notes posted on the Web in a variety of formats (.DOC, .RTF, .PS, etc.) confusing to students, when all they want is hard copy. A tutor may not realise who they have to talk to about their intentions regarding, say computer conferencing – leading to libraries and computer centres coping with misinformed students or sudden increases in demand for certain services. This may lead to withdrawal – with the consequent effects on staff and student morale. Experienced practitioners try to slot the technology into the learning process as and when fit; for instance a videoconference may be set up involving a guest lecturer whose script is circulated in advance and questions submitted before the videoconference to stimulate interaction; or computer conferences may be run on quite rigid lines, with introducers, summarisers, secretaries, etc. in order to involve everyone in the conference. Many tutors now find e-mail indispensable to their day-to-day work – that doesn't mean to say their students will feel the same.

Staff development

Confusion is created when the better aspects of traditional and technology-based teaching are not integrated – it is all too easy to see that the answer to everything is technological and thus be tempted further and further away from one's subject discipline. Willing experimenters need to be aware of how hybrid their knowledge is becoming as they delve further into technology and how this changes their colleagues' perceptions of them – and there cannot be many tutors involved in innovative courses who at some stage or other have not had to get a screwdriver out or carry a load of equipment from one building to another... Tutors need access to a two-stage staff development programme. The first level deals with awareness and skills:

- raising staff awareness of the possibilities of new technology, preferably by listening to existing practitioners
- training in the use of the technologies – staff must be at least at the same level as their students.

The second level is concerned much more with the selection, creation, and use of materials using the new technologies, and would include:

- project management – many technological innovations in education are over-ambitious

- authoring skills to transform and adapt existing materials for the new technologies.

Even with a comprehensive staff development programme, some staff will still see obstacles; they may be reluctant to use materials developed elsewhere; they may have concerns about copyright and intellectual property; they may be resistant to changing their role. These obstacles are addressed at the end of this chapter.

Evaluation

Evaluation cannot be tacked on at the end of a project, it should form an integral part of the whole teaching and learning strategy. Evaluators must first decide what to measure, define the instruments of measurement, and then measure the efficiency and effectiveness of the project. Innovative projects need innovative evaluation techniques.

At the University of Bradford we attempt to measure the effectiveness of the technology in assisting learning through a variety of measurement instruments including focus groups, interviews, real time observations, and questionnaires. We collect more qualitative data than quantitative data, in line with our objective of illuminative evaluation. This emphasises the more qualitative aspects of evaluation and has more in common with ethnography and social anthropology. Illuminative evaluation strategies are less likely to take any predetermined stance and ought to be flexible enough to change in the light of experience gained during the actual investigation – it uses observation, interviews, discussion, informal conversations etc. to establish what the people most concerned think and feel about the course, curriculum, and institution involved.

Most of the current work in the field deals with educational effectiveness: advances in evaluation techniques are becoming a major by-product of the Teaching and Learning Technology Programme (TLTP – see Draper *et al.* 1994; Gunn, 1994). We have to be very careful not to impose models and criteria from inappropriate examples; it is worth noting that much of the TLTP work is based on foundation level courses in mainstream higher education and does not focus on some of the most important issues for adult learners coming to technology. All learners, but especially adult learners, do not arrive without preconceptions; they bring with them, amongst other things:

- different levels of prior knowledge
- different conceptions of the subject domain
- different study styles
- different study modes
- different personal objectives.

Illuminative evaluation offers a means of discovering competing interests among the various actors involved in the teaching and learning process. Quantitative evaluation, however, is necessary for measuring efficiency and perhaps cost-effectiveness, and is bound to play a role in summative assessment. Perhaps the key question for us would be, 'is teaching and learning with the new technologies as good as, or better than, the traditional methods – and why?' To this end, we follow a framework of needs analysis, formative evaluation, and summative evaluation.

Needs analysis (preparatory evaluation) means talking and listening to learners and immediate past learners, tutors, and, if appropriate, employers, to explore factors influencing motivation such as expectations.

Formative evaluation measures progress towards achieving programme goals during implementation. When a project utilises new technologies, this stage can all-to-easily turn into monitoring the technology. The risk with all such projects is to allow the project to be driven by the technology rather than by the teaching and learning issues. Students often work in unexpected ways with prototypes – they indulge in unprogrammed interaction and we need to concentrate on the educational aspects of the evaluation as well as the technology. I remember watching students working through a prototype CD-ROM-based economics package that kept crashing (as is to be expected of a prototype). It was our original intention that each student should have their own machine; because of the technical problems they ended up sharing the machines that actually worked. We were intending to evaluate the package's usability, the effectiveness of the interface. As the students worked in groups, and we fretted over the technical problems, we nearly missed the fact that the students obviously preferred working in groups with the materials. Indeed, each group had arranged themselves in identical formations around the machines; the mouse and keyboard were shared around the group with metronomic regularity; and the level and quality of interaction with each other and the materials was heartening. These observations altered the goal of the whole project – we decided to try to replicate the quality of the group interaction by increasing the functionality of the package (in this case, by using videoconferencing and application-sharing for remote group work). This is how it should be – students first, technology second.

Summative evaluation is usually aimed at assessing the effectiveness of a programme on completion, aiming to answer questions such as *'Were the aims achieved?', 'Was it worth doing (this way)?',* and *'Is it worth continuing?'* Often this part needs expert opinion; anyone who has been involved in innovative projects will know that you can get too close and lose the wider view.

Findings: advantages and disadvantages

Advantages

- Most students feel that the technology can be a helpful addition to traditional systems. Praise is given to guest lectures given by videoconferencing, the Internet as a research tool, e-mail as a way of contacting tutors – all equivalents for real life events and actions.

- A substantial proportion of students like to work in small groups with the technology and help other students to use the systems; they feel they learn more by showing others.

- Students being in control of their own learning and greater flexibility are mentioned most frequently as plus points.

- Technological features such as video clips in multimedia or Web access (to sites such as the Vatican Library or foreign language news agencies) are mentioned as being *realistic* as opposed to academic.
- Learning to use the new technologies has a knock-on effect on general IT skills.
- A constant theme is that the technology can help students use their time more efficiently; there is less likelihood that they finish working before they intended to.

Disadvantages

- Reading from a screen is deemed to be less effective than reading from paper.
- Even though many packages try to simulate traditional systems, features such as Notepads are unpopular. There is a general feeling that paper-based materials allow you to have more information in front of you.
- There are many worries about navigation – the novelty of hypertext wears off quite quickly if you are pressed for time or have an assignment to complete.
- A secondary problem with navigation concerns the variety of interfaces used – students often worried if they were using the package the way it was designed to be used.
- The more you know about Windows, the better you seem to do with Windows-based learning materials.
- Video clips and videoconferencing were often described as gimmicks – the quality was deemed poor.
- Many students felt there was just too much jargon involved; computer experience questionnaires, essential for gauging the level of expertise, were seen as threatening and confusing.

Overall, the answer to whether teaching and learning with the new technologies are as good as traditional methods is ... it depends on what it is being used for. *Different* is a word that occurs time and time again in our evaluations. Interviews have shown that students mean different things by 'different': sometimes for adult students it means that the new technologies make them work in different ways (with the implication that they are uncomfortable with the different way); other times they mean that the experience does not meet their expectations, and they obviously feel like guinea pigs. Sometimes, however, they are enthused by the difference – the technology fits in with an image they have of what should be happening in education in the late 1990s. Though some of the disadvantages are clearly technical and will ultimately find technological solutions (video quality, better interfaces, and search engines for instance), some of the problems are to do with the way the various participants interact with the technology – the final section outlines possible developments.

Added value?

Using the new technologies in education can tempt some to conflate what is essentially a delivery system into an educational philosophy (thus mirroring the confusion between open and distance learning). An example is multimedia, which tends to come as two extremes: at one end of the extreme are the large databases with 'user-friendly' front ends and search engines (what might be described as the Encarta or edutainment model); at the other extreme are electronic books, where the main interaction is often to click on a symbol to move to the next page. Both extremes include some measure of hypertext (to give the learner the illusion of freedom?). Yet the use of multimedia for anything beyond foundation learning is problematic. The new communications technologies offer a way out of this 'spacebar mesmerism'. The World Wide Web, the Internet, and videoconferencing promise to take away the solitude involved in learning with technology by offering interaction with peers and tutors. One of the greatest virtues of computers is patience – no matter how many times you get it wrong, you can always try again. This patience is rather inhuman, however, and the promise of contact with your (real as opposed to virtual) tutor should enrich the learning experience. At the moment technology-based teaching aims to either replace or enhance the learning experience, and this often leads to evaluations that try to discover whether the innovative method is better or worse than the traditional method. This seems to miss the point – students feel technology-based teaching is different first, and better or worse second. It is this difference that suggests that a new form of literacy is in the process of formation – it includes basic literacy, but also an understanding of the grammar of film and TV, of the process of browsing through hyperlinks, and the ability to communicate effectively with the new communication technologies. This latter is not to be underestimated; it may be true that e-mail has revived the art of letter writing, but isn't e-mail a rather attenuated form of communication where speed is the dominant feature and emotional nuances very difficult to read?

Some aspects of traditional delivery can transfer across, others cannot: the formal lecture can be delivered via videoconferencing or digital video on a CD-ROM; a tutorial, where the debate is continued over coffee with the tutor and other students who happen to be around, cannot. I believe that the new technologies will give birth to new ways of teaching, but remain reluctant to jettison all of the traditional approach.

Interaction is one of the most widely abused and ambiguous words in the educational lexicon. Definitions exist for open and distance learning, attempts can be made at outlining the parameters that mark out flexible learning from resource-based learning from student-centred learning – but all the time, active learning and interactivity are assumed to be widely understood. Interactivity can be used to mean communication between two or more people; in the context of multimedia, it is often used to refer to the students' ability to follow hypertext links or stop and start video clips. As Mason (1994: 25) points out, 'much of what passes for interactivity should really be called feedback' – and the temptation with multimedia is to have a rather attenuated feedback (typically yes/no, continue to next screen, multiple choice questions which are marked by the computer). The educationalists, then, are convinced of the value of interaction; students, it seems, are less concerned – even though they *insist* on interaction. This paradox of insisting on opportunities for interaction yet not using the opportunities may well be a product of prior learning experiences or, more likely, a failing on the part of tutors to fully grasp the potential of the technologies, often combined with a lack of resources to match their intentions.

New technologies: new learning?

Teachers

The single most powerful determinant of the successful rise of new technologies in education will be the creativity of individual teachers and the strength of their desire to improve their courses. The context of learning and support services must be designed to promote and support this creativity. In the last few years it has become commonplace to refer to teachers as 'facilitators'; over the next few years, they will move towards becoming learning managers, learning resources, and eventually, as learners begin to manage their own learning, information brokers. The potential of the new technologies will never be fully realised unless they are fully integrated into provision, and the critical success factors are as follows:

- management commitment to the importance to the new technologies
- high expectations on the part of management regarding teachers, learners, and the technologies
- ease of access for teachers and learners, at college and at home.

Embedding technology into teaching and learning does involve a leap of faith, not least in trying to optimise the learning environment. Presently, technology-based teaching is a cottage industry: if it is to fulfil its potential, it will become industrialised. The days of teachers as courseware authors are all but finished – in future their input will be content and pedagogics. Multimedia is not inherently educational, at the moment it merely presents information without meaningful interaction; the new technologies will not work if we merely attempt to replicate existing practice through them. Educational technology is at the same stage now as film was at the beginning of the century – the first films were made by pointing a camera at a theatre stage. The first fruits of new technologies are usually more and more of what was possible with the old technology, and multimedia and communications are no different. We will see real interactive learning when teachers become confident with the technology, and are sure of their role in relation to it. Advances in communications technology are going to lead to new ways of learning – teachers have to be part of the process of discovery, otherwise the old dictum will hold true: if you're not hands on, all you get is hand outs.

The focus has to shift from acquisition of the technology to changing the culture(s) of the institution. Teachers have to have a greater focus on how learners learn: the emerging context of learning means that teachers will pay greater attention to prior knowledge of learning; detailed preparation of the learning task(s); the different approach learners adopt; the learners' perception of the assessment; and, the logistical factors. Teachers and learners should know the answer to the question, why use the new technologies here? If the answer is not obvious, the technology is bolted on. All too often, a simplistic equation is made that new technology is the answer to increasing workloads and numbers of learners, as well as the decreasing unit of resource. The real solution to the latter is for teachers to look to adapt rather than create, to drop the 'not invented here' syndrome, and to collaborate with colleagues in their own college and at other educational establishments. Teachers should be pursuing professional development in the area of network skills, pedagogics, and of course, content knowledge.

Good teachers will remain good teachers whatever methodologies they use. Enthusiasts are dangerous if they chase the technology and become technology-driven. Most educational establishments are poor at disseminating good practice, those that improve will gain competitive advantage. Network skills, skills in adapting courseware and 'worldware' are crucial. Those who do not embrace the new technologies will have it thrust upon them.

Learners

In the next few years students will begin to manage their own learning with total freedom to choose modules from any institution in the UK and abroad. Network skills will be crucial to independent and flexible learning – network literacy will become as important as other forms of literacy. Tracking systems will be important to stop open-door policies from becoming revolving door policies; to stop self-paced learning becoming no-paced learning. Whilst there will still be a top-down emphasis on quality, most learners will rely on informal guides and assessments from previous learners (this is already happening with the news groups on the Internet). Learners are already using the new technologies as sources of information, and institutions that do not offer on-line courses, school/industry links, and support across networks will become invisible beyond their immediate environs. Only a small proportion of learners actually want the totally virtual college; most can see the benefits of social development and interaction and peer stimulus. Interpersonal skills will become even more important to avoid isolation and deal with the shorter lifespan of groups. Access will remain a problem with some groups, and there will always be a need for Learning Resource Centres (LRCs). The real challenge is to transform the LRCs firstly into places where learners do more than word process, and then into Intensely Supportive Learning Environments (ISLEs) and, if that is achieved, to make those ISLEs accessible by distributed groups of learners.

Examinations and possibly grades will disappear. New technology will be used initially for tutorial support (asynchronous moving in time to interactive), and remote assessment of competences. Modules will come in a variety of lengths and delivery methods. As now, learners will value support systems as highly as, if not higher than, learning materials. Institutions with high quality support systems will attract learners. Whereas now, learners may buy a textbook that comes with a free disk or CD, in the near future the book will be the freebie. Network skills will move beyond keyword searching to encompass the use of agents and new forms of software called mindtools that will sift information.

Technology

The pace of change in communications technology is much faster than developments in stand-alone PC technology. In order to avoid chasing the technology, institutions will have to anticipate changes from an educational standpoint and base their strategy on perceived present and near-future needs, balanced with delivery constraints. Whilst we are all looking forward to the possibilities that broadband will bring ... the reality is that most companies will expect to have intermediate bandwidth, either through cable connections or ISDN, for the next couple of years... Services aimed at different client groups will have to take account of the variations in bandwidth – we are probably looking at a mean of 10Mb/s by 2002. By 2002, it is to be hoped that the market becomes more market-driven as opposed to the current supplier-driven scenario.

Providers will move away from time-based tariffs. Levels of ownership will rise, (but the PC will not be as ubiquitous as the calculator). There will be more legacy machines. Hardware will begin to include connectivity tools as standard, e.g. modem, videoconferencing unit. Problems with IPR will lead to fewer suppliers of courseware rather than more, and these will be commercial enterprises (perhaps in partnership with colleges). Courses will be a mix of courseware and 'worldware', the latter describing what we now know as personal productivity software being used in an educational context – put simply, the spreadsheet is the best problem-solving tool invented; most courseware is a database in some form or another. Student editions of commercial software are already popular: there will be an explosion in their growth as they mutate into mindtools.

Ten years ago, I had never touched a computer – I found electronic cashpoint machines confusing. Six years ago, I began teaching adults how to use computers – out of 60 people who completed my course in 1990 less than 10 owned or had access to a machine. This year I would estimate that 7 out of 10 students on the course own or have access to a machine (sometimes of a better specification than the machines in the classroom). 18 months ago, nobody had heard of the World Wide Web – today, it is hard to find someone who hasn't. The pace of change is frightening and exciting – frightening in the sense that I have to throw away so much of my materials every year; exciting because I am beginning to realise that I must begin to use the new technologies so my materials are not instantly fossilised.

References

Draper SW *et al.* (1994) *Observing and measuring the performance of educational technology* University of Glasgow TILT TLTP project

FEFC (1996) *Report of the Learning Technology Committee – the Higginson Report* Further Education Funding Council

Gunn C (1994) *Designing and evaluating effectiveness in CBL: defining the problem and designing a solution* Unpublished paper from TLTP CLASS project at Heriot Watt

Mason R (1994) *Using communications media in open and flexible learning* Kogan Page

12. Using IT Effectively in Teaching and Learning

Bridget Somekh & Niki Davis

Teachers' approaches to the use of computers

The computer as tutor

Many teachers who have only recently begun to use a computer assume that its role will be to replace the teacher as a kind of machine-tutor. An example of this was a history teacher ... who told us that he had bought a piece of software and been very disappointed with it because, when he watched his pupils using it, they didn't learn anything of value. It had not occurred to this teacher that he should play any active role in the pupils' learning with this software – instead, he saw it as a complete package which he could load and then stand back and watch while it 'taught' his pupils. In reality, software is not able to fulfil this role unless it is highly sophisticated (and very expensive to develop) – an example would be an expert system flight simulator from which a trainee pilot can acquire experience of flying an aeroplane and in some senses 'learn to fly'. Teachers normally need to play an important part in their pupils' computer-mediated learning: in drawing out points for discussion, planning follow-up work, and (once they are familiar with the software) providing lead-in activities to maximise its impact.

The computer as neutral tool

Other teachers who have begun to be familiar with using a computer often make a different assumption – that its role is similar to that of a pencil: they see the computer as a tool which is virtually neutral and can be used to carry out the same learning tasks their pupils would have undertaken previously with pen or pencil. This is sometimes mistakenly the outcome of advice to make sure that computer activities are 'education led' and not 'technology led'. Arguably, if there is no change in the nature of the tasks pupils undertake when they are using a computer, they might just as well not have used it in the first place. Teachers who adopt this approach often place a high value on the computer's capacity as a presentational tool, because this enhances what was already being achieved rather than changing the nature of the tasks. For example, they may encourage pupils to use a word processor to type out what they have already written by hand and print 'best' copies for display or publication, but deny them the opportunity to write direct on screen and use the power of the word processor to change the nature of the writing process.

The computer as cognitive tool

Those teachers best able to use computers to enhance their pupils' learning are those who have come to understand that computers are powerful cognitive tools which enable them to set new kinds of learning tasks that their pupils could not attempt before. Computer use in these classrooms will be varied – and often computers will be used for tasks similar to those which could have been undertaken without them – but the possibilities they have to offer become integrated with the planning, enactment and assessment of learning activities. To use computers in this way requires that teachers change their pedagogy. An example ... shows how difficult it is for teachers to begin to think in this new way:

A history teacher in a secondary school was experimenting with using a computer database of information about the Spanish Armada. In an interview after the lesson, ... he was unhappy with the program because it 'gave too much information' and this had resulted in the children 'asking trivial questions' so that they didn't learn anything of value about the Armada. He said that he would have preferred to make his own database so that he could have selected a more limited amount of information and in this way guided the pupils to ask important and interesting questions. What this demonstrates is his instinct to use the computer to continue to teach with the pedagogy he has tried and tested over the years. His practice has been shaped in the past by the availability of only a small amount of data, and by the difficulty both he and the pupils have in accessing it – for example finding relevant books in the library. He has been helped by publishers who have produced packages of selected source materials ... and he has gradually built up his own packs which he has been able to use and re-use again and again. Suddenly the computer database on the Armada has disrupted this pattern and provides easy access to a large amount of much less carefully selected information. It is moving towards overcoming the long-standing problem in accessing information (although it is still far from providing all that is available). But, in offering more open access to information, it demands that he sets his pupils a different kind of learning task. Instead of setting them to explore the information provided – in a more or less random way – he must now help them to distinguish what might be an important and interesting question worth pursuing from one which is by comparison trivial and likely to waste their time. They are no longer faced with the artificial situation of information selected to enable them to answer questions apparently of their own choosing, but in reality largely predetermined by their teacher. Instead, they are faced with the more normal situation – particularly in the modern world – of information overload, comprising a very large assortment of disparate information 'to make sense of'.

This is a good example of how the computer often provides both the opportunity of teaching a more difficult and ultimately much more useful skill, and the challenge of having to rethink the purpose of the lesson, the nature of the task which should be set, and the method of assessing how pupils carry it out (should they perhaps be asked to evaluate the questions they have chosen to ask?).

What appeared to happen ... was that teachers began with a concept of 'the computer as a tutor' but moved fairly rapidly to one of 'the computer as a neutral tool', ... but did not use them in any way which altered the nature of their pupils' learning... This learning looked very much like any other learning in their classrooms. It was only ... when their confidence and competence with computers was established, that they could begin to look at the implications of computer use for changing the nature of learning. Even then, sadly, the limited access to the computers available to them made it difficult to bring about radical changes in pedagogy...

The quality of learning with IT

Can quality in learning be enhanced through the use of IT?

Many of the aspirations for quality teaching and learning with information technology are synonymous with those for the curriculum as a whole. However, we will argue that they are promoted and facilitated by new information and communication technologies and therefore can more easily become a reality in everyday class-room practice. What then are our aspirations for quality teaching and learning with information technology?... One 'covert' aim for information technology which might have been regarded as an aspiration by some is the more effective achievement of existing educational goals. Another aspiration is that information technology should act to 'liberate' learners. What precisely is meant by this rather broad and sweeping statement? The central issue is empowerment, that is the pupil's degree of autonomy over the pace and content of his or her learning. The questions which might be raised are: how precisely is this viewed as facilitating quality teaching and learning? In what ways would giving greater control to learners equate with a corresponding increase in quality learning? Indeed, what do we mean by learning and how do we find evidence for it? These are some of the issues which will be explored in depth later...

'Quality' is currently a contested term. If education is viewed as a system for preparing young people to make a valuable contribution to our society in adult life, quality may be seen in terms of the cost-effective use of teacher time and resources and the functional effectiveness of school-leavers in the job market. However, if the aims of education are seen in terms of fostering individual achievement and maximising human potential, quality may be seen in terms of the intrinsic value of educational experiences and the individual achievements and personal fulfilment of school-leavers. These contrasting views are an indication of the extent to which educational debate has currently become politicised – representing extremes between the functionalism of the free market and the individualism of liberal humanism. In looking at quality in teaching and learning we do not wish to align ourselves with either of these extremes. To an extent, what is good for the society is good for the individual and vice versa. However, any discussion of quality in teaching and learning has to recognise its problematic nature. Within a system of mass schooling there has to be a tension between what is ideal for each individual and what is possible for all. It is perhaps in alleviating this tension that information technology tools may be able to make a difference. Let us begin by looking at the implications for teachers if IT gives greater control to pupils over their own learning.

The traditional role for teachers has been as presenters of ready-made information and as organisers of learning experiences. One way in which information technology can be used in the classroom is to take over these presentational and organisational roles. This has implications for both teachers and learners: the computer, by providing an additional or alternative source of knowledge and information, may reduce the dependency of students upon the teacher. The aspiration is that this will liberate the teacher's time and enhance the student's repertoire of learning skills, enabling greater student autonomy. This would allow students to maximise their active role in learning and help to prevent teaching from being construed by teachers as a technical procedure of transmitting knowledge to passive learners. It would also allow a change in the teacher's role: student autonomy in learning means that teachers no longer need to adopt a didactic approach, but gain the freedom to function increasingly as 'enablers of quality learning experiences'. They need to take on a more active and creative role. Through student autonomy, teachers gain the time and mental space to 'see and influence more of the learning process'. This in turn allows greater opportunities for teachers and students to engage in the kind of quality communication which generates mindful, deliberate deployment of higher-order thinking processes such as synthesising, interpreting and hypothesising. As a result of this change in the nature of interaction, the roles of teachers and learners can become less distinct. Indeed, the roles may even be reversed at times, as students find themselves having to explain their thinking to teachers, in order to enable teachers to understand. Operating in such a classroom environment necessitates active cognitive involvement on the part of learners and teachers: it is precisely this aspiration relating to the use of information technology in developing metacognitive or thinking skills to which we must now turn...

One of the most important challenges to an educational system is to empower the young with the intellectual tools of the culture. Children are perfectly capable of incidental learning based on their natural mental functions. The acquisition of more advanced forms of tool use, however, must be deliberate and must proceed in the full understanding of the power of the tool, of its generative capacity and of the demands made on the user during the period of learning. What does this look like in respect of information technology?

Information technology as a tool

Information technology is such an adaptable intellectual tool that it may be better visualised as many tools. Like any other sort of tool, these may be embedded within each other and used in conjunction with other tools and materials in a number of subject disciplines. For example, number is a tool that may be used within mathematics which in turn is used when analysing scientific data, providing access to scientific thinking to those who have difficulty with mathematics... Tools can, of course, support learning at different levels. Kozma (1991) identifies particular features of information technology systems which are of importance in relation to learning: (a) the speed of their processing; (b) the way in which they proceduralise information...; (c) their transformation capabilities (for example, from text to voice, or from equation to graph); and (d) the way in which they 'can help novices build and refine mental models so that they are more like those of experts'. In this discussion of IT tools we shall take four areas of IT capability which are widely used within the UK:

- communicating ideas and information
- handling information

- modelling
- measurement and control.

While considering each in turn, we may be able to illustrate how IT tools can be effective in supporting learners engaged in increasingly decontextualised learning.

Communicating ideas and information

There are many information technology tools which can assist communication and frequently they permit the learner to develop ideas and engage in a creative process. The most widely used of these tools must be a word processor. Those who have difficulty using a pen and paper may experience an intense delight and pride in producing writing in print. At a more sophisticated level, a word processor permits the writer to rework the text without having to 'remember' it as a whole, cut and paste many pieces of paper or rewrite manually. For some, a change in the way text is presented increases its value and provides some 'mental distance' from its production, both of which encourage critical rewriting. Therefore the word processor as a tool speeds the process, reduces the demand on memory and enhances creativity. It also has an effect on the way in which we may work on writing. Collaborative groups of authors can share a screen more easily than a book and the ease of changing or recovering writing increases risk taking. Teachers can organise collaborative writing with a word processor to encourage children to engage in critical review of each other's work (Graves, 1983). Where the teacher takes the role of co-editor, he or she can encourage metacognition and deepen learners' knowledge about language...

Some of the new IT tools promise an apparent explosion of opportunity for communications, in particular in control over the selection and presentation of multimedia material drawn from video, compact disk and satellite sources.

Handling information

Much learning takes place within the context of a large volume of information. For example, historical inquiry necessitates reviewing evidence in order to interpret historical events. However, the volume of information can obstruct learning, and in practice teachers normally present children with only a small selection of information, thereby considerably reducing the authenticity of the task. Information technology provides a range of information-handling tools which can help to alleviate this problem...

Programs which process data into graphs and pie charts reduce the time and skill required to draw them and thereby increase the time available for data analysis. Speed in displaying data is particularly important when dealing with concepts which learners may find difficult. For example, children learning physics can explore velocity graphs by walking in front of a motion detector and seeing the computer plot their own velocity. Information-handling software can search, sort and represent information in graphs and charts, dealing with a range of media including pictures and sound. The data sources can either be local on CD-ROM or video disk, or on a remote computer accessible by means of either a telephone line or a digital line.

Recent developments in the volume and quality of information available have already revolutionised pursuits such as journalism, and have implications for the ways in which teachers can use resource-based learning, now and in the future. For example, a learner who needs to find the meaning of a new word may gain more by comparing ten examples of its use obtained from a CD-ROM containing all the issues of a newspaper for two years, than by finding its 'dry' definition in a dictionary.

Modelling

... Computer modelling also provides support in learning to handle abstract concepts, for example in science. At an elementary level, the spreadsheet tool simply presents rows and columns in the form of a table. However, formulae can be set up which automatically calculate and recalculate results as data are added or changed, hence taking away the need for mathematical calculation and leaving the learner free to concentrate on the scientific concepts under discussion. The facts that the screen can be shared and the model stored for further use on another occasion permit more discussion than a blackboard or overhead transparency. At a more abstract level the rows and columns of boxes may be structured to represent variable factors, and formulae can represent the rules of defining relationships. In this way learners are empowered 'to play' with complex models... The IT tool reduces attention to memory and calculation while increasing speed and accuracy, and so permits learners to be creative in adding factors or changing relationships. Replication allows patterns to be observed and from such patterns learners can generalise and then theorise and so become more formal in their statements of abstract theory drawn from the patterns.

Spreadsheets are a good example of tools which enable learners to operate a high level of abstraction in setting up the model and understanding the way in which a table with changing numbers represents a system in the natural world. These tools have generated other more specific modelling tools, often called simulations... Simulations have the drawback that they are only capable of representing a rule-governed system... In this way they inevitably misrepresent some aspects of what they simulate; and the model itself needs to be subjected to critique by the learner so that its shortcomings stimulate understanding rather than it becoming a tool for misunderstanding.

Such IT modelling tools enable methods of teaching in which learners can pose 'What if...?' questions, such as 'What if gravity was zero?'

Measurement and control

Computers and related devices are also used as measuring tools. The calculating speed of information technology can be used to represent either very swift events, such as dropping an object to calculate the coefficient of gravity, or very slow events, such as the process of photosynthesis. An example already mentioned is the use of motion detectors to plot velocity graphs. Information technology can also permit learners to take many more accurate measurements and so engage in creative exploration of a phenomenon, taking into account more factors than would otherwise have been possible. The drawback, once again, is in the way IT tools may mediate and structure the learning experience, but this is a drawback which up to a point is common to all tools.

... At more abstract levels, control permits learners to appreciate complex interrelationships when they construct systems with electronic switches under the control of a computer program. Many IT tools may be controlled at one time. Themselves made up of electronic systems, IT tools provide the opportunity, for the first time, for learners to explore other electronic systems.

The most abstract and powerful IT tools are frequently created from a number of more elementary IT tools. An integrated package of word processor, database, spreadsheet, graphics and communications software is an example. They are now available on portable 'notebook' computers which easily fit into a school bag or briefcase. We are only just beginning to appreciate the ways in which learning may be enhanced with such tools. Other new tools currently becoming available include expert systems modelled on neural networks with parallel processing of more than one interacting computer system. These may have been set up by 'learning' from an expert, so that children and other users can be encouraged to learn by imitation and playful investigation of an expert's reasoning. Alternatively, some are based on such sophisticated models that they begin to appear to operate with a degree of unpredictability and creativity. The teacher's role may move further towards that of an expert co-learner to support the learner's development of metacognition. There will also be a crucial new role for the teacher. As with all increasingly sophisticated tools there is a risk that the process of learning will become increasingly decontextualised, and the teacher must provide the context linking the learning to the real world.

The information technology tool in the classroom

Classrooms are not ideal learning environments; they are working compromises in mass education systems. In classrooms it is difficult for teachers and children to remain centrally focused on learning tasks. Teachers are always short of resources: space, books, equipment, and above all time to meet the demands of a large number of children... In this context four salient features of school life for pupils are: delay – in waiting for the teacher's attention; denial – in being ignored or refused by the teacher; interruption – in being asked to stop work at an inopportune time in relation to the task; and social distraction – in other children's demands for attention. Frustration levels can be high, noise levels can rise, and the authority of the teacher can be called into question. As a result teachers have a central need to gain (and remain in) control of the class, to organise the children in task-oriented activity and to pace their own work (for example, in keeping the children working at the same pace rather than at the pace which best suits their own needs and abilities). This tends to make teachers managers of learners rather than managers of learning.

Adapting to classroom culture, many teachers concentrate their efforts in planning contexts in which they believe learning is likely to take place, and which at the same time fulfil the conditions necessary for well-organised group activity. Learning can be inferred from the accounts learners give of their thinking, or from an analysis of their products. Additionally, the likelihood of learning taking place can be inferred from an analysis of classroom tasks. Doyle (1979) distinguishes different types of task, depending upon the cognitive demands they make on pupils. The tasks which demand higher-level cognitive operations place pupils in situations of high ambiguity (in which they have to take decisions and solve problems) and high risk (in which they may fail to accomplish the task successfully). These tasks are not only harder for pupils to undertake, but also make classroom organisation much more difficult for teachers because pupils can no longer be assured of doing well in assessment. In Doyle's analysis of the ecology of the classroom, teachers and students normally establish routines and patterns of behaviour which make their respective jobs easier. Through complex and sometimes covert patterns of negotiation they engage in a process of 'exchanging performance for grades', in which teachers set tasks which are less demanding cognitively or socially and students work more efficiently and reliably on those tasks. In contrast, as Stenhouse (1975) points out, when teachers set more cognitively demanding tasks, some students will have quality learning experiences while others may fail altogether to learn what was intended.

This is the classroom context within which learning tools are used... To enable quality learning, IT tools need to support children in undertaking cognitively demanding tasks.

... IT skills are likely to be more easily learned in the context of some other pursuit, focused on more open-ended tasks in which individuals can engage at their own speed; in this context learning to use information technology tools has an obvious purpose which provides the motivation to learn...

To have a positive impact on the quality of learning, the aims for information technology in education must go beyond the acquisition of skills – say to access a database – and engage at a higher cognitive level by asking, 'What questions can I now ask, with the help of this database, that I couldn't ask before – and what supplementary questions may there be?'

In considering the quality of learning with IT tools the most important question seems to be to what extent they change the nature of children's cognitive engagement with classroom learning tasks. In particular, can computer-mediated tasks provide more authentic learning activities? Much recent work has suggested that a crucial determinant of cognitive learning is the authenticity of the task.

Tasks are or are not authentic depending upon whether or not they are supported by, or integral to, the learning context... Activities which engage children in quality learning – in terms of intellectual engagement with valued objectives – need to be authentic with respect to inquiry in a particular discipline or field of study...

To improve the quality of learning there is a need to achieve the best possible match between these two kinds of authenticity: authenticity to the classroom and authenticity to a particular discipline or field of study. For example, Bereiter & Scardamalia (1985) describe a procedure for managing learners' experience while engaging in writing, through a schedule for self-questioning. The whole area is greatly complicated by the fact that central to the context of learning is the learner's own prior experience. This means that a task will be more or less authentic depending upon whether it can be easily integrated with the learner's existing mental models. Authenticity is relative, not absolute. To an extent it depends upon the learner's perceptions of the task and career aspirations, so that it is possible for a task to achieve a kind of authenticity by its academic nature if a pupil aspires to university, or by its vocational utility if a pupil perceives it to be a good preparation for a job.

Despite their limitations, classrooms can be designed to be more (or less) supportive of quality learning. There is a growing body of evidence – supporting our aspirations – that information technology tools can change the social dynamics of classrooms. Their use disturbs the established classroom routines either by enforcing pair or group work, or by necessitating the movement of the whole class to a specialist computer room for part of their time. This disturbance of routine is a necessary, but insufficient, condition for change. In many cases new routines are quickly established which neutralise the disturbance and re-establish the negotiated compromises of Doyle's 'exchange of performance for grades'. However, IT tools can be used as a means of circumventing some of the classroom constraints on setting cognitive learning tasks. Computer tasks, of the kind described earlier, can be more authentic than traditional tasks. For example, through the wide range of information sources that it makes available, information technology can provide many more opportunities for the kind of spontaneity in learning which is characteristic of learning away from classrooms. In addition, the structure of support can be more flexible to the learner's needs in carrying the task through. The degree of interactivity in the software – whether it be through extensions and modifications of the task in response to the learner, or through the demand on the learners to decide upon appropriate questions for interrogating an information bank, or through the tangible products of creativity (in writing, design work or music) – can sustain a higher than normal degree of on-task engagement and 'mindfulness'. This fills a gap otherwise left by the teacher's inability, through pressure of time, to provide sufficient appropriate interventions to sustain the task. Group work around a computer may be more genuinely collaborative than other group work, thereby enabling more focused group talk. This in turn may enable learners to go further in developing their powers of hypothesising and problem-solving without needing to resort to the teacher for help...

It would appear that the conditions for classroom learning can be improved by information technology tools. But, equally, teachers can use information technology to create a new set of mundane tasks which negate the opportunities for quality learning. Word processors can be used solely to produce display copy of previously hand-written work. Chunks of writing can be copied from large information banks to concoct the answers to teachers' questions without any gain in understanding. Simulations can be used to replace experimental work on chemicals or plants, so that instead of close reflection upon one experiment using natural entities, pupils investigate a large number of abstracted examples on the computer screen. In a mass education system the use of IT tools to enable quality learning experiences depends upon the teacher. The need is for teachers to interact creatively with this resource and 'shape its use' (Sheingold, 1987) through the setting of 'framing tasks' (Somekh & Davies, 1991). In this way, computer-mediated tasks are embedded within a wider framework of learning tasks, which are themselves part of the process of task-negotiation between teacher and children.

This chapter has been concerned with looking at the impact of information technology on learning within the existing schooling system. It raises questions about the extent to which information technology tools offer opportunities to 'liberate' learners in classrooms – by giving them a degree of individual control at each stage of the learning process, and by giving teachers freedom from mundane organisational tasks in which to pay more attention to learners' individual needs. There is, however, the possibility that IT tools may lead to a radical restructuring of the education system itself. The impact of these tools is permeating through the infrastructures of our society, making fundamental changes to financial and communication systems, ushering in the concept of the 'global village' and radically changing conditions in the workplace (by no means always for the better). The information and learning tasks presented to young people through new media are already affecting the notion of authentic learning by changing the learning context. IT tools are currently revolutionising school administration – it is possible that in the not too distant future they may also revolutionise school structures. The 'electronic classroom' does not depend upon teachers and learners working in a single location for regular set periods of time: it holds the potential for breaking down the walls of the classroom as we know it and enabling a new form of mass education tailored to individual needs and controlled by individual learners...

References

Bereiter C & Scardamalia M (1985) 'Cognitive coping strategies and the problems of "inert knowledge"' in SF Chipman *et al. Thinking and learning skills vol 2: research and open questions* Lawrence Erlbaum Associates

Doyle W (1979) 'Classroom tasks and students' abilities' in PL Peterson & HJ Walberg *Research on teaching: concepts, findings and implications* National Society for the Study of Education

Graves DH (1983) *Writing: teachers and children at work* Heinemann Education

Kozma RB (1991) 'Learning with media' *Review of Educational Research* 61 (2), pp179–211

Sheingold K (1987) 'The microcomputer as a symbolic medium' in RD Pea & K Sheingold (eds) *Mirrors of minds* Ablex Publishing Corp

Somekh B & Davies R (1991) 'Towards a pedagogy for information technology' *Curriculum Journal* 2 (2), pp153–70

Stenhouse L (1975) *An introduction to curriculum research and development.* Heinemann Educational Books

13.   GNVQ: Integrating IT

Howard Lincoln

Introduction

IT is an integral part of GNVQ courses – that is, IT is a core skill in which students must become competent. For many GNVQ students, however, IT is not an integrated skill. They practise and acquire IT skills as part of their course requirements but do not make use of IT as a natural tool to support their learning. This means that they fail to enjoy many of the benefits of learning using IT.

Many tutors on GNVQ courses – perhaps novices in the use of IT themselves – have yet to take full advantage of IT in their own work...

IT: a toolkit for students

In itself, IT has no intrinsic value – its value comes from enabling users to carry out tasks more quickly, more efficiently or to a higher standard. When applied to a task, IT can provide enormous benefits and this holds true for the task of learning.

The application of IT in its vocational context is a core requirement of GNVQ courses. This makes sense, since there are few working environments where students will not need to use IT in some form. It is clearly important for students to gain a range of IT skills appropriate to their vocational area. This section, however, takes a broader look at the place of IT in GNVQ programmes and examines its potential to enhance the overall learning experience for students.

Word processors, spreadsheets and databases – central to core skills competency – can also be applied to the business of learning, the day-to-day tasks which students need to carry out. These software applications, along with more specialist applications such as desktop publishing and graphics, provide a toolkit which can be used whichever specific course is being followed, or whatever area of employment may be entered thereafter. IT skills – as with the skills of numeracy and literacy – can be applied wherever they are needed.

IT can support students in the production of a wide range of assignment work. Some students may only use a word processor, for example, to fulfil an IT-oriented task or to produce a neat copy of a report which has been handwritten in successive drafts. This fails to take advantage of one of the best features of a word processor – its facility to allow additions, amendments and revisions without starting from scratch. Word processors also offer support to the writing process itself, in the shape of a spell-checker or thesaurus, and most offer an outline facility to help writers to organise their thoughts. Similarly, spreadsheets and databases can offer students support in their learning; there are many everyday mathematical calculations which can be helped by the use of a spreadsheet, and the construction of a personal database might offer considerable help to students in their own research.

IT can also enable users to access information. CD-ROM materials are becoming common in schools and colleges, enabling students to search by keywords through encyclopaedias and newspapers and carry out research into specific subjects such as medicine and technology.

The challenge of the Internet is also being met by an increasing number of colleges and offers both information and a means of communication worldwide. In multimedia packages, where text, sound, still and moving pictures can be incorporated in a single presentation, a new medium of communication is developing, and one which offers interactivity for the viewer. In an environment where reliance on independent, self-directed study is becoming more common, these resources are of growing importance to students.

IT and the business of learning: changing the way we work

IT is changing the way we work, whether in shops and offices, factories, schools and colleges or at home. The changes which IT brings about are often underestimated and in fact we can only expect to reap the full benefits of IT if we allow new working practices to evolve. Use of IT does not have to be sophisticated to take advantage of the resulting changes in process. For example, using the simple editing facilities of a word processor makes the task of revising a document far easier than it would be with handwritten text. The result is to encourage the development of written work and a greater willingness to try out new ideas. The use of IT also supports collaborative work: not only can work be added to by various authors, if electronic communications are also used, joint authors can even be in different locations. In the same way, if a spreadsheet is created to carry out complex operations, it not only calculates data quickly and easily, it also encourages further exploration of the variables involved.

For new ways of working to evolve, however, users will need time to become familiar with using IT. It is also important to allow students time to experiment with IT and discover its benefits to their own work.

Case study – Back to nature with multimedia
GNVQ science students at Hull College of FE use a graphics package to illustrate the structure of DNA. DNA is a complex module which is built up of repeating units within a structure. Using a graphics package reinforced the repetitive nature of nucleic acids (copy and paste functions can be used to construct a long chain) and illustrated the similarity in structure between the two strands of DNA (via the use of the package's rotate function).

Case study – The medium is the message
Studying GNVQ media at Fulston Manor School, Marcus Wright decided to design a multimedia product which allowed the end user to investigate genre through an interactive computer program. After researching the topic he used a multimedia authoring package to design and implement the presentation. The final product consists of 30 screens which the user can explore to find out about genre in media and includes text, graphics, photographs and sound. Marcus was also examining the possibility of including video clips in the presentation.

Multimedia provides a suitable vehicle for developing a theme like genre, and allowed Marcus to combine a wide range of media. It has also allowed him to deal with non-linear subject matter in an appropriate way by making use of the software's hyperlink facilities. The work is to be made available across the school network to support students of English and media.

The project yielded a great deal of evidence for five media units plus a wide range of communication, use of number and, of course, IT core skills.

Making the use of IT meaningful

When students see that the application of IT is directly relevant to their learning needs they are motivated and their learning experience is enriched. For this to take place, IT applications need to be integrated into their mainstream work. Vocationally oriented work is only part of students' learning experience, and a great deal of student activity is concerned with the business of learning: researching information, preparing assignments and maintaining records of achievement.

When applied to these tasks, IT is being used to solve problems of immediate relevance to the student and therefore being set in a meaningful context. A student who is immersed in an IT-rich learning environment will have the opportunity to develop a deep understanding of the value of IT and a set of transferable skills which can be used in other areas of life.

Choosing the right tools for students

For many students, the three office applications (word processor, spreadsheet and database) are the staple diet of IT and this is reflected in the GNVQ core skill specifications. However, they are by no means the only tools available to students nor the most appropriate for students in vocational areas such as media, engineering and art and design

Graphical software such as desktop publishing and art packages is in common use and it is not unusual to find students expressing their knowledge of a particular topic in the form of an information sheet or newsletter. This type of activity not only gives students the opportunity to learn new IT skills, it also enables them to develop communication skills through the use of IT.

A recent addition to the student toolkit is multimedia authoring software. These packages facilitate the production of non-linear documents where, by selecting from the buttons and pages available, the reader has a degree of control over the order in which information is presented. This opens up a new set of communication processes for students both as creators and users of multimedia packages. The ability to communicate using multimedia is going to be increasingly relevant, particularly when it is linked to the Internet. More and more information is becoming available in formats other than the printed page, and in the near future students will increasingly wish to communicate their own work in this way.

Case Study – From genre to generating worksheets

The report which often forms part of the evidence indicators is one medium through which core skills can be evidenced. Allowing students the freedom to choose their own medium for the report can lead to some exciting work. At Fulston Manor School, Robert Shonk approached an investigative report on genre for Unit 1.1 of his media course through the medium of a full-colour DTP booklet. The end-product was a distinctive 12-page booklet which analysed a range of genres and provided a range of assessment opportunities beyond the requirements of Unit 1:1. In addition to evidence for two further media units, a number of core skill objectives have been met. The use of a DTP package clearly involves a broad range of IT and communication skills. Less obviously, page layout and design requires the application of numerical skills...

IT-based learning resources: a library without walls?

More and more information is now stored electronically and may be accessed at a distance remote from its point of storage. So, while CD-ROM material may be stored and administered within the walls of a college library, there is no reason why it cannot be accessed from any location in the college, given the presence of an appropriate networked computer terminal.

Similarly, the Internet provides access to information stored on thousands of servers worldwide, on a scale that could not be accommodated within the walls of any college library. Increased use of the Internet thus brings with it problems and challenges for learning resource staff who have been used to exercising a degree of control over the materials available to learners...

New skills for staff and students

Using computer-based information sources such as multimedia CD-ROMs or the Internet demands new skills. Basic IT skills are needed to enable information to be accessed and transferred between applications – taking an image from a CD-ROM such as *Encarta,* for example, and incorporating it in a DTP document. Although a straightforward task, this can demand a high degree of IT competency.

It is not only technical skills that are required. It is all too easy for students to become overwhelmed by the volume of information available via IT and thus fail to make appropriate use of it in their learning.

Subtle and sophisticated information-handling skills are needed if students are to locate information successfully from CD-ROM discs, on-line databases and the Internet. Students need to learn strategies for searching electronic information sources and how to evaluate the information they find – skills which will be increasingly important as more and more information is published in this medium.

Case Study – Navigating through the Net: 1
At East Birmingham College multimedia has been used in the delivery of GNVQ leisure and tourism programmes since March 1995. The first group to pilot the technology was at intermediate level and came from a local school which had difficulty in providing the resources to support aspects of the course.

There were no textbooks for the unit and collection of the required information had been tried with limited success at the school. My colleague and I were in agreement that much of the required information on UK and European tourist resorts could be found on the Encarta CD-ROM and Virtual Tourist on the Internet. We felt that the high-tech approach might engender more energy and interest during the basic information-gathering stage.

The destinations chosen by the students proved to be difficult to match to the information in the multimedia resources, however. There was little information on Madeira, and Benidorm was lost in the general information on the Costa Brava. Traffic details and underground pipe workings for most European cities is available on the Internet from the CIA, but a 2-star bedroom in Margate proved more elusive.

The lesson learned here was presentation. Had I had the time I would have explored the sources then directed students to those destinations for which information was available. Multimedia is a weird and wonderful master but a limited and vague servant at this stage of development. There is clearly a need for much more specifically dedicated software in terms of content and level of language.

What IT does for learners is place them in greater control of their own learning; it gives them greater autonomy over what they learn and at what pace. The tutor's role also changes, from being the fount of information to being a facilitator of learning – directing the students' learning rather than merely imparting knowledge. Far from being a threatening experience, most tutors have found this change to be a liberation and one which gives them greater opportunities to help individual students. This is particularly important in GNVQ courses, where individual programmes of study are less directed than in GCSE courses and learning is more independent.

New partnerships

For tutors there are additional issues about the integration and management of these new resources in the curriculum. Colleges which have experience of using CD-ROM and the Internet with students stress that staff need to spend a great deal of time on identifying useful resources. This also means that learning support staff will play an increasingly important role in students' learning and that an effective relationship needs to be forged between these staff and curriculum teams...

New resources ... but are they any good?

Both teaching and learning resource staff will need a new framework for assessing the value of IT-based learning support materials on CD-ROM and the Internet. In addition to assessing the content of such material it is necessary to consider factors such as ease of use, suitability of the user interface and compatibility with other software applications.

While many CD-ROMs make imaginative use of this new medium, other resources are little more than electronic versions of existing textbooks. Multimedia resources should be evaluated critically to establish that the format is appropriate and enhances the information. There is little point in committing valuable IT capacity to an information resource when a book or other medium would serve the same purpose.

Case study – Tips on integrating Internet

It is still unusual to find systematic integration of CD-ROM and Internet resources in the Curriculum. The following tips, from staff at East Birmingham College, may be useful for others.

There is a need to construct search guidance sheets to direct students to quality sites.

Multimedia is multi-sensory and can be good for those who have difficulty with text.

It is becoming more difficult to book whole groups into the multimedia centre as demand from the rest of the college continues to rise. Get as many machines as possible – you will probably need more in six months.

There has been a positive effect on two GNVQ grading themes: action planning and information seeking and handling. Students now think about what could be found on the Internet or CD-ROM. They are producing evaluations of how useful the resources have been to their research.

Look at course specifications and match web sites or CD-ROM resources to them. In some cases there will be an obvious match while no suitable material will exist for others.

The number of Internet sites is growing all the time. Staff need time to keep up with what is available. Invest staff development time on hands-on experience and the development of search strategies.

Think about how your students can use e-mail. Do some research on the contacts and set up agreements with institutions to supply information to students.

IT: a toolkit for tutors

GNVQ, with its emphasis on the integration of core skills, has tended to focus attention on students' use of IT. However, IT is a powerful tool which can play a significant role in the professional development of tutors too.

The case studies in this section show that through a wide range of resources, IT supports the development of knowledge and skills. It can also support the production of teaching materials – both print based and electronic – and help in administration...

Using IT to support delivery

The use of IT to produce paper-based teaching resources is now well established. Standard word-processing and desktop publishing packages support the production of professional looking classroom materials which can incorporate text, charts, graphics and (with the aid of a scanner) photographs. This application of IT has led to improvements in the presentation of printed material which is appreciated – and even expected – by students.

Anyone who has recently attended a conference or commercial training course will be aware that the use of technology to support the delivery of information is becoming commonplace. It is not unusual to see a speaker at a conference making use of a commercial presentation package such as Powerpoint or Persuasion. Using such a package through a Liquid Crystal Display (LCD) panel allows the presentation to be displayed to a large audience on a large projection screen in the same way that OHP slides might be.

Trainers also make use of this type of technology to project demonstrations of software packages on a screen. This allows a software technique or concept to be demonstrated to a large group of trainees simultaneously. There are indications, backed up by some of the case examples, that this technology is beginning to be applied to teaching in further education.

Some of the other technologies covered in this section may seem expensive, remote and peripheral to the current reality of teaching in college. It is, however, worth remembering that, not so long ago, the use of DTP software and a laser printer to produce high-quality printed teaching materials seemed an expensive and distant possibility for many teaching staff. Today this technology is in common use and almost taken for granted.

Case study – Projecting an image

Although I did not have access to an LCD panel to project a presentation directly onto a screen, I started to use Powerpoint to create OHP slides. I found that I could incorporate charts and graphics easily and using standard Powerpoint templates saved me a great deal of time on layout as all I had to do was type in the text.

Because it was so easy to make changes to a slide, I found that I was merging the processes of planning a lesson and producing materials to support it. I think it allowed me to be more adventurous.

Since then I have had the chance to base lectures and staff development sessions around full Powerpoint presentations. I feel that using the technology has changed my presentation style for the better – I concentrate more on communicating with my audience because less attention is needed for handling visual aids.

Solving practical problems

The case studies in this section describe a number of ways in which tutors have applied technology to the business of teaching. The tutors concerned have applied IT imaginatively in the classroom but it is worth noting that they are not in the business of using IT for its own sake. In each case technology is being used to solve a problem and enhance the learning experience for students.

A technological solution does not have to be extremely expensive, as some of the case studies show. The use of a presentation package to produce OHP slides, for example, may provide a new teaching tool at no cost. Some solutions will, however, be on a quite different scale and will require major institutional commitment and support if they are to be successful.

Case study – Zooming in
The problem with a microscope is that only one person at a time can look down the eyepiece. This can make it difficult for the teacher to point out important features and to check if a student is looking at the right parts of the slide. Attaching a digital camera to the eyepiece of a microscope had allowed staff at Llandrillo College to display the image in the eyepiece on a standard PC monitor. This technology is used with GNVQ Science students and enables groups to view slides simultaneously. This application of technology has enhanced the delivery of the course in a number of ways:

- The lecturer is able to discuss the content of a slide with one or more students and establish that they can negotiate the slide without missing key features.
- A group of students can view a distinctive slide together and discuss its main features.
- Students can observe and monitor dynamic action such as crystal growth or heart beat in Daphnia.
- Tutors can use the system to help in the assessment of student skills in the observation and representation of slides.
- The system demonstrates the type of technology in use in commercial laboratories.

Because the data is digital a resource bank of slides can be built up and displayed through a graphics or multimedia package. Some students have already used Powerpoint for presenting their work and the potential exists for them to capture and integrate images from the digital microscope.

For students, the technology provides a popular and dynamic alternative to OHTs and handouts. Staff recognise that using the digital microscope has some limitations (low screen resolution for example) but are keen to exploit its potential.

IT and changing processes

It is important to recognise that the application of IT to a task can change the way that the task is performed. In fact, the potential benefits which IT offers are greatest where changes to processes are allowed to occur. Giving up existing work practices and allowing new ones to emerge is often difficult. Staff may need considerable support and development to help them deal with the process of change.

Case study – Learning from the big screen
Large open-access IT workshops optimise the utilisation of IT resources, improve student access and promote individualised learning. From the tutor's point of view, however, intervention to solve a common problem or introduce a new topic can be difficult if it involves a large number of students.

At Halesowen College there is a seminar room attached to each IT centre. The purpose of the seminar area is to allow lecturers to demonstrate aspects of a software package or particular techniques to their students. The seminar areas are equipped with demonstration machines and a large screen. A video machine is also provided to allow lecturers to make short video presentations. The seminar area is bookable on a weekly basis. A timetable for the current week and following week is posted each Monday and lecturers book the area by initialling the required 15-minute time slot.

The success of the area has allayed the fears of many lecturers that the move to a flexible learning environment and learning packages would detract from the students' experience.

Can IT replace the tutor?

Computer-based learning (CBL) involves the application of IT directly to the teaching process. This is just one of a number of IT applications which aim to automate some of the tasks carried out by the tutor.

Some tutors feel threatened by these developments, yet the answer to the question, 'Can IT replace the teacher?' is an emphatic no. This reassurance comes from – amongst others – those actively involved in such developments. The work of a tutor involves a broad range of activities and it is clear that IT can only be directly applied to just some of those activities. What is true is that the application of IT to the teaching process will require a changing role for the tutor.

The role of IT in the teaching process

When the process is managed well, the application of computers to appropriate tasks can provide benefits for both tutor and learner. IT is particularly useful in a number of areas including:

- delivery of factual information
- testing of knowledge and skills
- controlling business and technical simulations
- recording of information on student progress through a system.

Implications for tutors

In recent years, developments in computer-based learning have been closely associated with the need for flexible approaches to learning. In a flexible learning environment students are expected to accept greater responsibility for their own learning, and for the tutor this places a greater emphasis on the management of the learning process. While computer-based systems are able to deliver factual material, they are of very limited value in activities where an element of reflection is demanded. Equally, the tutorial process demands a human approach, although the use of IT-based systems can provide some of the management information to inform the process.

As the demand for new approaches to teaching and learning increases there will be more opportunity for staff to become involved in the development, evaluation and modification of computer-based materials.

The application of IT to the teaching process will present a new skills base challenge for further education. The role of the tutor will evolve and new skills, including IT skills, will be needed. This will be a major issue for those lecturers and other staff involved and for college staff development programmes.

Case study – CBL – one college's view
The initial reaction from the group was that CBL materials are best used to support traditional tutor-led delivery. Used in such a way, they would represent an addition to course delivery costs, whatever the benefits might be. Computer-based learning highlights the dependency that students have on didactic teaching, and the lack of confidence the average student has in their ability to take charge of their own learning. However, as the meeting progressed the argument that the tutor might be partially released from the task of factual delivery in order to manage the learning process and undertake more tutorial functions was accepted as being a better use of tutor time...

Case Study – Using PLATO to support engineering maths
The GNVQ engineering course team decided that the development of core skills was so important that separate sessions should be allocated in the timetable for all mandatory core skills units. Each core element is allocated one hour per week with PLATO software being used to assist in the delivery of mathematics...

Staff involved in the project have reported that the vast majority of students have been happy to use PLATO and have found it easy to use. All staff have been particularly impressed with the management system which allows individual or group work plans to be constructed, initial and final assessment to be carried out on the computer and a wide range of reports to be viewed on screen or printed.

Case Study – Practising for exams
GNVQ Intermediate engineering students are able to take a mock exam on computer during their course. The staff use a commercial package which allows them to construct multiple-choice tests based on past exam papers. In addition to the questions, staff also include supporting text to help students when they make an incorrect choice.

If they wish, students can choose to take the test within a set time, controlled by the computer. On completion of the test, the student is provided with a score. They are generally very positive about the program, which proves very popular in the week before an external test! ...

The role of IT in communication and numeracy development: integrating core skills

GNVQ courses emphasise the need to integrate core skills with the mainstream curriculum. There are, however, potential benefits to be gained from consolidating the three core skills themselves. In the modern world a great deal of communication takes place through the medium of IT. Indeed, many IT applications from the word processor through e-mail to the Internet, are applied wholly to the business of communication. Likewise with the application of number, the use of calculators, spreadsheets and specialist software to support day-to-day numerical tasks is quite commonplace.

Case study – Meeting core skills with multimedia work
Multimedia offers a unique opportunity for the assessment of students' abilities to plan a project, work in teams and respect each other's opinions. Obviously this is ideal on a GNVQ programme as planning is so important and working with others is a personal skill that GNVQ encourages students to develop. Creating a multimedia presentation allows most of the GNVQ Communication and IT core skills to be covered...

Integrating IT and communications

As the case studies demonstrate, communications tutors have discovered IT and are using it enthusiastically and with imagination. This might be expected in courses such as Media and Business Studies where IT and communication are closely linked in the vocational context. It is evident, however, that IT is being used to great effect across the board and that where it is used well, students respond enthusiastically. The use of DTP and multimedia packages in addition to the word processor is creating stimulating opportunities for students to exercise and demonstrate their communication skills.

Case study – Blending IT and communication core skills for presentations
One of the most important attributes for students wishing to work in the hospitality sector is the ability to communicate effectively. The same lecturer was allocated to deliver both IT and Communication core skills to GNVQ hotel and catering advanced students, so the opportunity arose to integrate the two areas.

> *It was agreed that we should use Powerpoint as a presentation aid. Students designed their own presentations, making full use of the facilities that the package offers. The students, although terrified of the prospect of speaking to an audience, soon adjusted to using Powerpoint as a tool. In fact they seemed to be much more confident when using it. I feel it added a most professional touch to the presentation.*

Integrating IT and numeracy

Although the links between IT and number are less developed than those between IT and communication, there is plenty of evidence of activity in this area. The use of spreadsheets and calculators is common in the development of Application of Number skills, particularly where the students are involved in problem-solving activities rather than mechanical calculations.

One obstacle to increased use of IT resources in Application of Number work – and reported by many tutors – is that of access. Compared with tutors in Communication, they were far less likely to have computers available in the maths base room. Whilst it may be that pattern of use and access to IT for number support is different from that for communication skills, consideration needs to be given for improving access to computers in this area.

An interesting approach to the development of number skills is the application of computer-based learning packages to the development of underlying knowledge and skills. While systems like PLATO offer both numeracy and English language modules, it is the numeracy aspect which appears to have been adopted more readily by staff in colleges.

Case study – Using graphic calculators

The use of graphic calculators in the teaching of mathematics has, in the main, tended to concentrate on higher level mathematics. I decided to see if their use would be appropriate with other groups. An intermediate GNVQ engineering class was chosen to pilot this scheme; this was a particularly poorly motivated group and one aim was to develop a more positive attitude to mathematics in the students.

The first time I used the graphic calculators was to tackle the requirement, in Application of Number, for the use of formulae and as an introduction to formal algebra. I wanted to emphasise the concept that the operations within a formula stay the same, only the variable changes to give different values. I chose to use the conversion between degrees Fahrenheit and degrees Celsius – hoping this was a conversion they were familiar with.

On using the calculators for the first time, many students expressed surprise that the screen displayed all their calculations and I could see easily the mistakes that those with the wrong answer had made. This is not possible on an ordinary calculator and is the equivalent of the instruction, 'Show all your working'. One unexpected outcome of the use of graphic calculators has been the increased awareness by students of the usefulness of being able to see their working when looking for a mistake.

Part Four – E-learning and the Virtual Classroom

The readings in Part Three have presented many ideas about the way in which teachers can make use of ICT to enhance student learning. These mainly involve using commonly available software such as spreadsheets and databases, as well as the Internet, as tools to assist learning.

The ideas presented in this Part take ICT in teaching and learning a stage further, suggesting that 'electronic' learning and the virtual classroom have the potential to change education and training radically in the near future. Just as e-commerce seems set to change the way that we conduct trade and business, so e-learning could do the same for education, making access to learning opportunities easy for millions of learners.

E-learning is a relatively new and still ill-defined term. However, it seems to be generally agreed that what distinguishes e-learning from Computer Assisted Learning (CAL) or Computer-Based Training (CBT) is:

- the use of Web-based technology to create learning materials and to deliver courses
- the use of Web browsers such as Netscape or Internet Explorer to provide access to learning materials
- the provision of on-line support for learners.

An e-learning environment contains three main components:

1. courseware – self-study learning materials, simulations, tests, assignments
2. supporting materials – reference materials such as articles, case studies, books, World Wide Web links
3. on-line support – via email, CMC, chat rooms, bulletin boards.

Although it has yet to make a major impact on the delivery of education and training, interest in e-learning is growing. The government announced in February 2000 a plan to create a consortium of 'e-universities' and to provide funding for the development of e-learning in higher education. The government is also promoting on-line learning through the University for Industry. Working with businesses and education and training providers, it will use on-line learning to enable learners to study at home or in the workplace. The initial set of 24 courses will provide training in ICT, business and management skills but courses in a wide range of skills are being planned. It is likely that the University for Industry will use interactive TV as well as the Internet to deliver its training programmes.

The TUC has called upon employers to make on-line learning available in the workplace so that those without access to the Internet at home do not get left behind (see TES, April 14th 2000). The TUC's National Education Centre is using on-line learning to deliver several courses on topics such as employment law.

Annex E of the Higginson Report constitutes the first section of this Part, where the technological developments which have made e-learning (and the virtual classroom) possible are described and discussed. The following section offers a more detailed consideration of the components of the e-learning environment, namely the provision of on-line courses, supporting materials and on-line tutoring. Section 16 presents two case studies which illustrate how universities are currently providing on-line learning and computer mediated conferencing (CMC).

Virtual classrooms can be created in several ways but they all have in common the ability to offer students the benefits (and drawbacks) of the traditional classroom without the need to be in the same location as the teacher or other students. The last section considers videoconferencing as a means of creating virtual classrooms and provides two case studies, drawn from further and from higher education.

14. Emergent Technologies and their Impact on FE

from Annex E of the Higginson Report

1. The impact of technologies makes the lives of students outside colleges radically different from the lives of learners a generation or two ago. Electronic games, personal computers, mobile phones, faxes, compact discs, satellite and terrestrial television channels and a plethora of radio channels influence the lives of college students – but not while at college. These changes have as yet had surprisingly little impact on the classroom. The technological innovations of the past half century which have had the most pervasive influence on college teaching have been the very simple optical technologies of the overhead projector and the photocopier. The classroom model of teaching and learning has not changed significantly in at least a century.

2. Four closely related technological developments have the potential to change teaching and learning in further education in ways that previous innovations have failed to achieve. They are:

- the convergence of previously separate video, telecommunications and computer technologies
- growth in the use of digital technology
- applications, operating methods and multimedia
- information highways and other emerging technologies.

Between them they offer the means of changing the traditional classroom model of teaching and learning.

Convergence and digital technology

3. The separate technologies which provide the telephone, the computer and the television are now converging in ways which increase the educational applications of each. This advance is supported by the additional benefits of lower costs, greater power and portability.

4. Convergence becomes possible when the different technologies share systems for encoding data. Digitalisation entails the conversion of information to manipulable and transferable *bits*. The application of this technique to writing (word processing), graphics, audio signals (voice and music), photography, film and video has led to an information revolution.

5. Digital encoding, which helps to improve the reliability of information, has developed alongside techniques of data compression/decompression which enable more information to be transferred between two points within a given time. For example the combination of digital technology and data compression enables even the simplest telephone lines to carry an enormous range of information...

6. The combination of improved compression/decompression and broader bandwidths allows text, sound and graphics to be commingled to provide *multimedia*. The technical challenges of compressing digital photographic images are still being overcome. However, digital cameras and digital television can now provide further source materials which enrich the multimedia information used to provide entertainment, business tools and education.

Applications, operating methods and multimedia...

8. Hypermedia is the organisation of information in ways which allow users to follow pointers to more detailed elaborations, related ideas and presentations of the same information in a different medium, such as text into graphical or pictorial (still and full-motion video) formats. It brings these together at the classroom (or home) workstation in ways which require active interaction by the user.

9. It has the potential to allow courseware designers to draw upon a wide range of materials. Inputs from cameras, video-cassette recorders (VCRs) and CD-ROMs can be combined with text and graphics 'scanned in' with a computer-linked scanner and materials inputted through computer networks and telephone lines. They can be structured in ways which offer users multiple choices and alternative learning routes, using *authoring* software systems.

10. In consequence, multimedia presentations can organise and simplify data in ways which package information and ideas to match individuals' learning abilities. Processes too small, too distant or too dangerous to be explored at first hand by students can be demonstrated.

11. This need not be a one-way process. The technologies first used by most students for interactive computer games are now being applied to multimedia learning programmes. Multimedia courseware not only enables students to select the information they need in audio, pictorial, graphical and text modes. They can also manipulate the information in ways which require their active responses. Integrated learning systems are now being developed which provide direct individualised teaching. Students undertake regular, structured and assessed computer-based learning activities for short periods each day. They and their teachers receive feedback, diagnosis and direction to further learning...

14. The compact disc was first developed as a means of storing and playing back digitally-recorded audio signals. It is now a prime source of data storage. The advent of personal computers with built-in CD players provides ready access to this data. As the information storage capacity of CD-ROMs increases, they are able to hold interactive multimedia courseware. The availability of these materials is now constrained by market forces rather than technology.

Information highways...

17. Telecommunications suppliers have adopted international standards which now make it feasible to carry full multimedia communications on the Internet. Integrated Services Digital Network (ISDN) establishes a set of *de facto* standards by which

digital voice, data and video signals can be transmitted through the standard 'twisted pair' telephone lines in digital 'packets'. It provides higher quality sound and high definition fax, and is already being used to transmit entertainment videos by phone to domestic televisions. It can make available to learners a vast information resource in audio, text, graphical and video forms, to be summoned up to a desk-top work-station through national and international telephone links at the cost of a local call.

18. The transmission of multimedia information by telephone lines supports videoconferencing. Group videoconferencing systems enable direct two-way communications between groups, as for example between two or more distant classrooms, workshops or conference suites. Desk-top videoconferencing brings these multimedia facilities to the desk-top PC. A camera on or inside the PC enables face-to-face conversations and data transfer across local area networks or ISDN telephone lines.

19. Optical fibre cable *(broadband)* networks are being installed in the urbanised areas of most industrialised nations, initially for multiple television channels but with capacity for telecommunications and related (such as electronic mail) services. The underground cables have the capacity to carry an almost infinite amount of information, and enable central distribution points to take materials from terrestrial and satellite television channels, telephone and computer links and distribute them throughout the network.

Emerging technologies

20. The next stage in telecommunications developments will be Asynchronous Transfer Mode (ATM). This communications technology will provide a common transport mechanism for digital communications traffic, regardless of whether it is between computers on a local area network or across a public telephone network. Within the next few years the standard should be fully installed, opening up opportunities to improve the speed and efficiency of communications. In the longer term, this technology will also tackle problems of moving data from one local area network to another through the public telephone network. Traffic is currently carried across wide-area telecommunications networks in analogue rather than digital form, requiring a modem at both ends of the network to translate data between analogue and digital forms. ATM technology will make it possible to move data between computers without the need for modems...

23. Technological improvements which extend the data-carrying capacity of the CD-ROM may extend its life as an information medium. However in the longer term *on-line services* are likely to replace the CD-ROM as the prime source of data. They will be able to combine:

- encyclopaedic breadth of information
- subject specialist coverage at many levels
- regular and instantaneous updating
- differential pricing structures which can benefit educational users.

24. On-line information services require information about information. The rapid growth of Internet graphical browsers and navigation devices demonstrate the

importance of being able to find out not only what information is available but also how to access it. An increasing proportion of the increased power of the latest generation of computers is devoted to bits providing information about the other bits. This is likely to develop further so that computer software can be instructed to select from the vast body of available information flowing through the networks just those bits which are likely to interest the user.

25. Developments in media, computer and communications technologies are now coming together as *virtual reality* (VR). This is now emerging as an affordable new entertainment technology, but its potential for learning is considerable. It addresses visual, aural and tactile senses in order to immerse the user in a real or imaginary simulated environment which the learner is able to manipulate. The computer-generated world experienced by the learner requires helmets containing tiny screens to produce the three-dimensional imagery, data-glove technology to allow learners to believe they feel the objects in the simulated environment, and a full bodysuit to permit total sensory immersion in the virtual environment. In future, stereoscopic technologies may lead to holographic solutions which free users from the limitations of headsets and bodysuits.

The impact on further education

26. Earlier attempts to develop forms of computer-aided learning often led to dreary programmed learning based on crude behaviourist philosophies. The technologies outlined above have the potential to promote genuinely interactive learning, which can transform the relationship between teacher and student as well as the location of that learning. The basic components – computer networks, telephone systems, televisions and multimedia computers – are already familiar to most students and teachers, and are available in most colleges...

28. Technologies in the emerging 'information society' can be divided into three categories, each of which incorporates hardware and software:

- those that provide an infrastructure for communications, such as the basic cables, satellites and transmission facilities

- those that support the fundamental services, such as telephone, data transmission and network management

- those that directly enable users to engage in applications such as telelearning and remote database access.

29. While technological advances in the further education sector may be dependent on the first two categories, the sector by itself is unlikely to influence them or make any special requirements of them.

Infrastructure

30. If colleges wish to provide effective support for students working remotely from the college, or wish to build efficient links with external organisations then high quality communications are essential. Current technologies supporting the

communications infrastructure include optical fibre fixed links, conventional and satellite TV broadcasting and radio links. All of these can be, and are being, utilised for educational purposes...

Services

31. Once communications channels are established, colleges may wish to use a variety of service functions such as transferring audio signals, still and full-motion video images, text and data files. All of these services are currently available and widely used in corporate networks within large companies. There is no technological reason why such services should not be available within the FE sector, although cost remains a critical factor. Providing data transfer services between colleges, or within multiple sites of a college is now becoming an affordable option. However, it is likely that provision to individual students working remotely will remain expensive for the time being, even though local cable channels are now making some types of data transfer feasible.

Education applications

32. It is in the area of applications that education has special requirements. These centre on the characteristics of the curriculum which technology is being used to support. It is important to recognise that technology must be the servant of learning, rather than its master. This implies that a clear set of objectives linked to learning must be obtained before seeking an appropriate technology to realise those objectives. To acquire technology without a clear idea of its intended purpose is almost certain to be both costly and inefficient.

33. Nevertheless, it is likely that technologies to support learning will share some common characteristics regardless of the objectives to be achieved. These broadly are that networked computers installed throughout the sector will have the ability to:

- transmit information to two or more locations
- store and manage data
- process large quantities of information at high speeds to support interaction with users.

34. Further technical improvements will focus on the links between the computers and video and telephone components, using a common digital base. They will also become smaller, faster, more powerful and cheaper. The most significant change is likely to be the ready availability of a vast resource of digital information – at a price...

35. Emerging technologies should promote much more flexible learning and independent study, but they depend crucially upon the development of:

- learning design skills on the part of teachers and course developers
- information processing skills on the part of learners
- relevant, high quality interactive materials

- resources which make the technologies of business and entertainment available for education and training.

36. Virtual reality environments are being vigorously developed for a range of industries and entertainment applications. At present the cost of these, and their associated technologies, is high in relation to the sophistication they offer. In the long term, however, the delivery of some aspects of the further education curriculum will benefit from virtual reality applications. These would include, for example, those aspects which rely on students experiencing potentially hazardous environments or the use of prohibitively expensive resources.

37. As computers develop the capacity to recognise handwritten and spoken instructions, learners will be able to manipulate flexibly the immense resources available though the computer. This offers the possibility of genuinely interactive learning, whereby students have access to:

- an enormous volume of information
- computer learning aids which select the information required by teachers and students
- simple browsing and selecting techniques to provide immediate access to information.

Such developments will bring particular benefits to students with learning difficulties and/or disabilities.

38. As students follow increasingly individualised programmes of study, this can be personalised to match individual needs. Similarly, teachers are likely to be able to select information for personalised teaching programmes and tutorial support tailored to meet the needs of individual students.

39. Apart from applications which enable the achievement of particular learning objectives, there will be an increasingly sophisticated range of management functions associated with learning which will need suitable support. These include student enrolments, tracking, progress monitoring and assessment. The cost of integrating these functions and adapting them to cater for increased diversity in the range of educational opportunities and modes of attendance will be significant.

40. These will, of course, bring with them new challenges. As students use technologies to help them take control of their learning programmes, teachers will need to learn ways of drawing upon distant resources, including other teachers, to deliver those programmes. They will also need to acquire the specific skills required to deliver teaching across telephone and cable networks to distant groups. College managers will need to be able to call upon a new generation of computerised management information tools, which integrate resource management, marketing, student tracking and support and the management of learning. It is unlikely that the potential for exploiting the available technologies in these ways can be achieved without new forms of collaboration between colleges across and beyond the further education sector.

15.   On-Line Learning

Lynda Hall

The means exist to deliver many further and higher education courses on-line. In other words, it is at least technically possible to provide all the learning materials, learning activities and tutorial interaction and support that a student would need to complete a course of study over a college or university internal computer network, or 'intranet'. Although as yet they may not have brought together all the components of the e-learning environment, many colleges and universities are already providing students with access to some of the elements through their intranets.

Using intranets to provide materials and support

An intranet can be seen as an internal world-wide web, accessible only to members of an organisation. Resources and information are made available in the form of hypertext documents, which include links or cross references to other documents, graphics or video/audio clips. Figure 1 illustrates how a college intranet can be used to make available a large variety of resources and information to support learning.

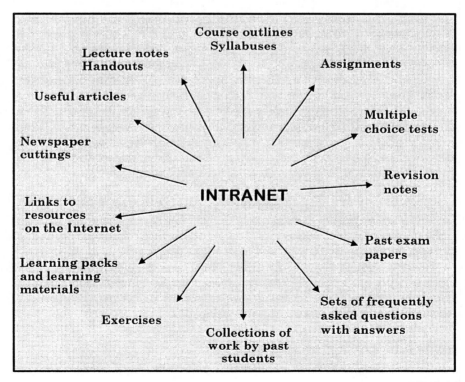

(FEFC, 1998: 36)

Figure 1 Contents of a college intranet

Delivering on-line learning

The main component of an e-learning environment is the courseware – a structured package of learning materials for the student to work through, which may include written information, exercises, tests and assignments, simulations, video and audio clips.

Apart from making education and training more accessible to learners, what are the benefits of on-line learning to students? One of the major benefits has already been mentioned – the opportunity for students to work at their own pace and at a time and place of their own choosing. And good quality interactive courseware can also enhance motivation, reinforce learning and provide students with immediate feedback on their progress. More important however, on-line courses which use hypertext or hypermedia (hypertext plus sound, video, pictures) have the potential to meet learners' needs in a way not possible with traditional modes of course delivery. Any group of students following a course of study will contain individuals with diverse learning needs. One of the challenges for teachers is to cater for students who differ in experience, knowledge, ability, personality and approaches to learning.

Typically, when implementing a course, a lecturer begins by deciding which topics need to be covered in order to fulfil the requirements of the course syllabus or specification of outcomes. The next step is to decide the order in which these topics will be presented to the students and then to decide what material and learning activities to include in lectures, lessons or seminars. Thus, the lecturer determines the sequence in which topics and concepts are presented to learners. He/she decides on a suitable starting point and chooses the route through the course. This may present problems for learners for a number of reasons. What may seem to be a logical order for an 'expert' may not be the most suitable order for a learner. Different students have different preferred learning styles and different levels of pre-existing knowledge. Learners with varying backgrounds have the task of connecting the new material with what they already know and of recognising that links exist between seemingly different aspects of the subject. Some learners may prefer a different approach to the subject matter from that taken by the lecturer.

The major benefit of courseware based on hypermedia is that it has the potential to enable learners to navigate their own way through a course – to choose a route through the material which takes account of their prior knowledge and preferred learning style. Students can decide where to start and where to go next, moving with relative ease from topic to topic in an order which makes sense to them. They do not need to follow a pre-set sequence determined by someone else. Such individualised teaching and learning is not a practical proposition in the average classroom but can be achieved with an on-line course using hypermedia.

Hypermedia and learning strategies

There is now a considerable body of evidence that individuals differ in the way they organise and process information and in the way that they approach learning tasks – the learning strategies they use. The work of one of a number of researchers in this field will suffice to illustrate the way in which hypermedia can cater for students with different approaches to learning.

From a study of how students tackled learning tasks, Gordon Pask and his associates identified two different learning strategies – 'serialist' and 'holist'. Students using a serialist strategy adopt a step by step approach to learning, concentrating on one goal or topic at a time. They build up understanding through discrete steps, looking in detail at the facts and making narrow links between topics. They demonstrate a tight focus of attention, concentrating on detail and procedures. Those adopting a holist strategy have a more global approach to learning, considering many goals and topics at a time in order to achieve understanding. They adopt a broad perspective and seek interconnections between topics. They have a wide focus of attention and try to build up an overall picture before fitting in the details. It was found that when students were given teaching materials specifically structured to match their learning strategies they learnt more effectively than if given mismatched materials (Pask, 1976).

Well-designed hypermedia courseware, providing a variety of links and cross references between topics, has the potential to support different approaches to learning, enabling both serialists and holists to impose their own structure on the material to be learnt. Serialists can follow a linear path whilst holists can adopt a non-linear approach.

However, hypermedia courses are not without potential problems. Research has identified a number of these.

- *Learner disorientation* – Basically this means that learners can get lost. They may not know where they are in the 'system' or where to go next with resulting confusion, time wasting and frustration. They may spend more time trying to decide what to study next than on actually studying the material.

- *Lack of comprehension* – As mentioned above, a variety of links and cross references between topics can be provided. These should help learners to make connections, to see relationships and to integrate information drawn from different parts of the course. However, there is some doubt whether novices can make sense of all the interconnections and therefore construct a coherent overview of the material they are studying.

- *Use of inefficient learning strategies* – Hypermedia encourages browsing, following the links provided, irrespective of whether this is the most effective learning strategy to adopt. Browsing can be purposeful but it can also be time wasting and an inefficient way of finding information.

Making on-line learning successful

What has been said above suggests that students need to be prepared and equipped with the appropriate skills if they are to make the most of on-line learning opportunities. Even so, on-line learning may not suit everyone. Some students are better at organising their own studies than others; some prefer working alone whilst others need the stimulation of interaction with others. Successful on-line learning, like successful distance learning, requires a certain degree of self-discipline, motivation and commitment on the part of the learner.

Crucial to the success of any on-line course is the quality of the courseware and the reliability of the technology used to deliver it. If the courseware is boring, the information poorly presented, the interface confusing or the network slow to deliver the materials, many learners will be discouraged and demotivated. Unless the courseware is of a good quality, well designed and with plenty of opportunities for learners to be active, it is unlikely to hold their attention.

In addition, on-line learning may not be appropriate for all types of learning. For example, it is unlikely to be as successful as face-to-face learning in helping students to develop interpersonal and oral communication skills although opportunities for collaborative learning and discussions can be provided on-line. However, it could be used effectively to help students understand and retain information or to develop and practice skills such as ICT skills.

The experiences of an on-line learner

What is it like to learn on-line? Few people, as yet, have had the experience. In the following extract one teacher who has experienced on-line learning provides a personal account of its advantages and disadvantages. Though on-line learning clearly has much in common with distance learning, the writer claims that it is 'qualitatively different from either distance, or face-to-face, learning'.

A Personal View

From March 25 to August 5 1998 I participated in the online course 'Learning to Teach On-Line', organised by Sheffield City College and Barnsley College. The programme was targeted at teachers and others who may support online learning courses. Its aim was to raise awareness of the skills required and the issues which may arise when supporting or designing such programmes. It was designed as an online distance learning programme to provide participants with first-hand experience of this type of learning. Online collaborative work was built into the scheme.

Building a schedule
... If one's learning group is congenial, then that provides an additional incentive to make an effort. But it is an effort. I spent two years driving down the M1 from Leeds to Sheffield twice a week for an MA course. Sometimes the amount of will-power I had to expend left me brain-dead for the ensuing session. And then I had to drive home...

Distance learning varies. There's the attraction of completing the course in one's own time, but my experience is that the amount of will-power needed to fit in the work to a family schedule is often greater than that needed to get to a meeting. Face-to-face learning is an activity that displaces something else: if I am in Sheffield, I can't be anywhere else. But with distance learning, especially CMC distance learning, we don't displace: we add yet another activity; we multitask, shave our day and night into even thinner salami slices and run the risk of doing everything a little less efficiently.

Continued...

But online learning did mean that, when I had a free weekend, I could move a lot of work out of the way. I could squeeze in an hour's work before I left for work and, perhaps the biggest bonus of all, I had an infinite information source available for a reasonable rate even at peak telephone charge times. In contrast, it cost me three hours and a few pounds' worth of petrol to attend a meeting at Huddersfield University.

The ghost in the machine?

As many teachers will confirm, the 'computer as scapegoat' syndrome is difficult to refute. With CMC this lurks as an ever-present threat, both to the learner and the teacher. My own machine failed a few times during the three months of the course. I lost my email archive and had to reinstall most things. At work the computer network failed once a week, and so on. All of this was absolutely true – and difficult for the tutor to verify.

The judgement must be, however, that the advantages of CMC far outweigh the disadvantages – and we're only at the start of things in this country. In the next three years, we're told, things will become easier: data access through satellite, ISDN or cable modems at home, the use of good graphics, video clips and sound: all will transform the nature of online education.

Collaborative learning

Working with other members of an online learning group was interesting. The first person to reply to a posting or a question from the tutor very often said what I wanted to say. By the time I had thought of something original, things had moved on (by about three weeks, if my past performance was anything to go by). Other contributors approached issues from a different angle: the conceptual shock that this applied jolted me out of routine tramlines of thought. Conversation threads could be followed up with individuals at a later point.

On the other hand, because online conversations are usually asynchronous, you can strip out all the paralinguistic fillers and focus on content. Nobody worries about typos, yet if you indulge in oral malapropism, your listeners automatically discount whatever intelligence you might think you possess. And as I age, my short-term memory becomes less reliable. Part-way through a conversation I sometimes find that I have, as my students would say, 'lost the plot'. With computer-mediated conversation, no matter how heavy a night I may have had previously, the record of a conversation can be reloaded...

What's needed with online teaching and learning?

Online instruction requires the skills of a good primary school teacher. The pedagogical and social requirements promote the features necessary to maintain a learning environment in a classroom where individuals move at different speeds. This is, perhaps, the shift for adults learning to teach online: that content becomes of less importance than process for the teacher – or instructor, or trainer.

Learning to teach online is essentially experiential, and those learning how to do so need to experience the potential sufferings of our students. We all have to get out there

Continued...

and do it for ourselves, because what we're looking for is performance competence, rather than a body of knowledge. We bring our own pedagogical background and expectations to the arena, and try to map those onto the course.

Facilitating collaborative learning is a slippery concept: how can we measure individual success? If we're looking at performance competence, then that's easy to monitor. If we're looking at knowledge, then there must be a point at which a tutor may have to determine strands which are deemed to be missing.

When a tutor assumes the role of moderator in the learning process a level of control over the conversational threads is required, so that contributors who are unaware of their effect on other members should be prompted to behave accordingly. This could be easier than in a conventional class.

The final – and possibly most important – issue is that of time management. Tutors engaging in online work should be able to assign blocks of time to the work in the same way as they would to those conventionally timetabled. There's the rub. The very nature of online work is its ad-hoc nature. The appeal of online work to administrators is its low cost. If the two are combined, the tutor could find herself under pressure to complete the work in fragments, through the day (and night).

The salami factor
This potential for the fragmentation of work is important. I've experienced at first hand the problems inherent in assuming that I can work in short slices of time at work. Short of shutting myself away and locking the door, it's very difficult. I finally had to re-schedule things so that I could work at home – which meant that much of it was done at the weekends. This must inhibit peer interaction, in that responses lack any sense of immediacy.

I soon realised that it was necessary for me to print out the sections of the course, and copies of the directories with messages and tasks in. Despite the fact that my computer is constantly in use, it was very easy to lose track of where I was up to with work. The weight of a file in my briefcase was a tangible reminder that there was work to be done...

Learning gains
The course provided me with the opportunity to carry out a number of very useful tasks. It pushed me to evaluate search engines I might not otherwise have used. There's a temptation to stick with two or three search engines and assume that they're the 'best' for the subjects one habitually researches. I was quite surprised at the range of information that either did, or didn't, come up when I ran searches as part of the course activities. It was at that point that I downloaded a very useful utility called WebFerret, which pulled in sources I might never have found.

Another task involved posting messages in a variety of formats. Ingrained work habits and assumptions were swiftly undermined. After using web-based email on a number of machines I reverted to simple email, rather than that with attachments, providing the document was straightforward. Many institutional networks won't allow

Continued...

attachments to be downloaded. It's a point I'd not considered when I advised my students to use web email.

Ways of learning
Some of the activities provided on the course proved less effective for me than others. Group work raised its ugly head a number of times, then was quickly lowered. It may simply be that learning to teach online is not conducive to group work – or, that the personality types who are drawn to a course of this type are not group workers. The same problem was observed with open conferences. The advantage of an open conference is that the tutor can assume an active role – steering discussion into areas that might prove fruitful; clarifying misconceptions; posing new questions and arbitrating when disagreements arise. The main disadvantage is that the tutor will assume that no postings to the conference = no contributions = no learning. Students will then feel a compulsion to contribute.

The issue is essentially one of learning styles. Some personality types resist group learning, preferring to work autonomously. Despite this, one of the assumptions of much of the literature is that collaborative learning is a very powerful tool facilitated by the medium. This could well be another case of the clash between teacher assumptions and student needs.

Personal experience with clunky web-based conferencing systems suggests that email lists offer a faster way to communicate. I certainly used the group mailing list rather than the conferencing system. Whenever I looked things up in the conference area there was very little that was new, so the compulsion to sign in became less and less every time.

Online courses offer intriguing possibilities: on the one hand, completion of an online course offers a practical demonstration of competence. If a person completes a course, then they're demonstrating that they have the skills to do so. The tricky part is combining that with course content. Understanding and learning can be assessed in an applied situation – through specific questions – but confirming the authenticity of the learner's response is awkward.

Validating learning with online systems
In any course involving certification the authenticity of student work is crucial. On the one hand, can we be sure that the student who registered for an online course is the one who undertook the work? And if we can guarantee that, can we be sure that the answer hasn't been downloaded from another website? On the other hand, who needs the summative assessment? Is it to be used for careers and salary purposes? Is it to be used as a gold standard of competence (as, we are told, are A-levels – until, that is, the results are announced: then standards have fallen).

One of the issues that hasn't been made explicit in the rhetoric of lifelong learning is why people should sign up for it. If it's because they have to, then you'll always have the problem of verification. If it's because they want to, then there's no real problem.

Continued...

Schools online?

Online learning offers schools access to a wider community than that contained within their four walls or their neighbourhood. With an appropriate infrastructure and a committed staff a school could enhance every aspect of the learning experience to which its students are entitled. Post-16 work in minority subjects can develop specialisms which transcend the limitations of timetables and staffing. Videoconferencing offers one way forward. The development of school intranets offers the most cost-effective way for schools to start the process of online learning. Revision courses, minority subjects and additional modules can all be placed on a school intranet. Links can take students to web-based information sources.

(Cuthell, 2000: 8–12)

Support for on-line learners

The third essential component of an e-learning environment after quality of courseware and reliability of technology is the provision of on-line support for learners. For students attending college or university, on-line learning can be supported and supplemented by conventional tutorials or seminars. But this is not available to students studying at home or at work. The lack of human interaction and easily available tutorial support has been one of the drawbacks of distance learning schemes, whether the learning materials are paper-based or computer-based.

On-line learners like all learners need encouragement, feedback and help with resolving any difficulties they may encounter whilst studying. Such support can be provided in a number of ways. Perhaps the easiest way is through e-mail. E-mail is a fast and efficient method of keeping in touch. Students can ask questions of their tutors, seek advice and submit work for marking or feedback just as they can in face-to-face encounters. E-mail also enables students to keep in touch with their fellow students and it can be used as a medium for collaborating on learning tasks and conducting discussions. However, for the latter purpose it has the drawback that there is no means to organise contributions to discussions or to separate one discussion from another. Computer Mediated Conferencing (CMC) provides such a facility.

Computer conferencing systems are text-based interactive systems. As with e-mail, computer conferencing is an 'asynchronous' mode of communication with communication taking place at the convenience of the participant. Computer conferencing software enables students and tutors to send messages to a shared discussion area, where they can be organised, read by everyone involved in the discussion and responded to by anyone. A course can have several conference areas. Tutors may set up a number of discussions or 'conferences', some being accessible to all students and others accessible only to specific groups.

The software makes it possible to organise the contributions of participants by subject (so that you can easily follow a discussion on a particular topic), by author (to make it easy to see what particular people are saying) and by date (the normal way messages would be recorded). Some CMC software makes it possible for discussions to be 'moderated'; in such a case messages go initially to a moderator – the tutor – who decides whether or not the messages should be posted.

Discussions on-line are rather different from face-to-face discussions, having both advantages and disadvantages. They are text-based, so that students who can write well are usually better able to communicate than those who don't. On the other hand, students who have poor oral skills (because English is not their first language, for example) may be more willing to participate on-line than in the classroom.

On-line discussions tend to promote more thoughtful and focused contributions than face-to-face discussions. Participants have the time to compose a contribution or to consider their response before making it, something which can be difficult during a lively classroom debate.

One disadvantage of having discussions on-line is that all the usual visual and auditory 'cues' that people rely upon in social situations are absent. Participants cannot tell how their contributions have been received from the facial expressions, body language or tone of voice of others. This could inhibit some people.

Whilst discussions on-line are different from those conducted in the classroom they present tutors with some familiar problems – finding ways of promoting discussion, keeping discussions on track, encouraging students to contribute, establishing ground rules. Although they may need to be adapted, the skills of a good facilitator are required if on-line discussions are to be productive.

References

Cuthell J (2000) 'The online learner' *ComputerEducation* 94 Feb 2000, pp8–12

FEFC (1998) *The use of technology to support learning in colleges* Further Education Funding Council

Pask G (1976) 'Styles and strategies of learning' *British Journal of Psychology* 46, pp128–48

16. Computer Mediated Conferencing

Two Case Studies

Apart from promoting or facilitating discussion, computer conferencing is an ideal tool for collaborative or co-operative learning, as the following case studies illustrate.

Case Study 1: Computer-mediated conferencing for part-time evening degree students at the University of Stirling

The integration of new information and communications technology in teaching and learning is a field which requires energetic resourcing. This is not just a question of large amounts of funds for hardware and software – although this may help! It is more a matter of staff awareness of the possibilities and limitations of the technology...

CMC refers to software which allows students to input messages to a shared discussion area where they can be viewed, organised and responded to. As a result there is a permanent record of the group discussion.

The University recognises that improving the information technology (IT) situation will require encouraging staff to think more innovatively when designing, delivering and evaluating courses, as well as becoming more familiar with what IT has to offer as a teaching and learning technique. This entails the complementary skills and interests of understanding the practicalities, possibilities and limitations on the technical side together with the particular educational aspirations and objectives which can be enhanced through the application of IT. In our particular case we saw an exciting chance to explore ways of integrating CMC into the experience of part-time adults studying on an evening undergraduate degree programme in Environmental Education. This group is seen within the University as particularly disadvantaged since they are physically isolated from the student body except for a three-hour session once per week...

A course in Environmental Education calls for seeking out all manner of techniques which encourage student engagement in dialogue with the subject material, tutors, and fellow students. Thus we were forever asking ourselves questions such as: What is it about CMC which could enhance the student's learning experience? What different aspects of learning are taking place? What is the 'added value'? Does the technology get in the way of the learning?

This case study deals with the use of networked computers and some readily available free software to permit CMC for students on a part-time evening degree course whose access to one another is more limited than full-time students. It was felt that CMC could provide a forum in which students could develop ideas in response both to the course content and to each other, thus setting up a fruitful educational dialogue. This use of CMC thus has something in common with uses in distance learning – i.e. facilitating access to others' ideas, while at the same time being set in a context where

Continued...

---

students did have limited access to one another. Incidentally students were also gaining confidence in using the technology itself and basic keyboard skills.

The majority of students taking this course are adult returners. The wide variety of backgrounds was expected to enrich the dialogue in the conferences. Consequently there was a very wide range of computer literacy, which naturally raised issues of IT training. Several sessions were dedicated to training and this was provided in contact sessions, with references available on-screen and as hand-outs.

Educational objectives

The CMC software was used as the medium for three different educational techniques:

1. *Collaborative writing...* Students were presented with a theme to debate. Each student was asked to contribute a piece and the 'tutorial' developed through subsequent entries which pursued different key issues with additional supporting evidence brought to the debate from the student's own experience, readings, the Internet and the tutor's comments. The objective of sharing all this information using CMC was to enable students to reflect and comment upon each others' positions and thus to generate a dialogue. Each student was assessed on the quantity and quality of their contributions. One of the main criteria for the success of threads was the amount of dialogue generated.

2. *Journals...* Students were asked to record their developing perceptions of the units. They made critical reflections of the course material and consolidated their understanding through relating concepts and principles to their own personal or corporate experiences. Since they had access to others' journals there were a number of instances where reference to one another's experience helped clarify a position.

3. *Community of inquiry...* This is a rather specialised form of group discussion activity ('conference')... Essentially it is a framework within which a group can follow a line of inquiry which is group-led and involves all members. The inquiry is generated by a stimulus material which is used to evoke questions concerning a controversial issue... From this starting point the group negotiate the key points at issue, and as a community move the conference forward. Thus the conference does not have a stated end point other than the exploration of whether there are some points of mutual agreement and affiliation.

The first and third of these are explicitly group activities which benefit from being pursued over a number of weeks. The second is also one which is often used over the duration of a course, and it was felt that giving all students access to each other's journals would help to enrich the experience. The students reacted positively to the introduction of these techniques although when the technology let us down, or there were serious difficulties of access to computers, there were the inevitable cries of frustration and always a danger that the technology might get in the way of the educational objectives. Where students struggled with access to computers this was most acute.

Continued...

> Training of students was essential and several dedicated sessions within the early weeks of the course were required to get them going. The Research Assistant was also available as a trouble-shooter and to co-ordinate the developing contributions.
>
> We did not use any manuals or training texts: rather, materials were purpose-made with instructions and simple tasks to introduce the application.
>
> (Sankey & Dibble, 1997: 68–70)

The Open University, as we would expect, has been at the forefront of innovations in the exploitation of ICT in distance learning at degree level. Tutors have gained a great deal of experience in using computer conferencing systems.

Case Study 2: Computer conferencing at the Open University

The OU has been using computer conferencing for nearly 10 years. During this time it has conducted numerous trials, but now computer conferencing has a large-scale take up. In 1995 about 5000 students used conferencing, of which about 25% used First Class – a Windows-based conferencing system. The 1996 OU academic year saw the number spiralling to 15,000 as a large foundation course in Technology began to use conferencing.

Range of uses at OU

The following is a brief summary of the way computer conferencing has been used in the OU.

Tutorial support model

This replaces the usual means by which students and teachers communicate, and requires little adaptation of the standard distance course. It can overcome students' sense of isolation as they communicate with each other as well as with tutors.

However, the pedagogical benefits are marginal: partly because the system is optional and only a small percentage of students participate regularly, but also because a significant tutor input – both in terms of quantity and quality – is required to generate any educationally valuable discussion.

High resource model

Here computer conferencing is the primary delivery mechanism for short courses, which are fully resourced with equipment, networks, technical support and high teacher/student ratio. Enthusiasm for such a course is high, the output is educationally valuable, and it sets a benchmark for other on-line courses. But its expense means that it can't be scaled up to large population courses. It is interesting to note that even with this model not all students are active participants. If 60% of students are active, then this is a high take up.

Professional development short course

The Institute of Educational Technology offers on-line professional development courses to teachers and trainers on a global scale. Advantages are that specialised

Continued...

courses can be developed as the catchment area is potentially global, and it is appropriate to professionals – offering a rich environment for multimedia interactive learning that professionals can fit into their working day.

On-line wrap around

This is a combination of a set book with computer conferencing providing student-tutor interactions – at a ratio of about 40 to 60. The on-line interaction is integrated with the course, and requires student participation. It is cost effective, as tutor time on-line is low. In comparison with other OU courses development costs are low and presentation costs are relatively high. This model is adaptable to many disciplines and to global delivery.

Analysis of evaluation studies

OU experiences have built up over time as the various models have been used and refined. The analysis is grouped into seven categories.

1. Structuring on-line systems

As with other open learning media, students need structure to guide them in pacing work, focusing their study and concentrating their effort. Participants continually called for greater structure – through small group work and set tasks – e.g. being allocated the role of proposer in a debate. By providing a framework at the outset there is slightly less need for tutor input during presentation than in unstructured discussion, and this shows possibilities of scaling up to larger numbers on a course.

2. Linking use with on-line assignments

Since students use assignments to focus their work on a course, on-line assignments increase the use of the medium. Most of these involve collaborative work among a small group of students. It has a real educational value, developing a range of analytical skills. Most students accept the compulsory use of the system.

3. Limiting the asynchronicity of the medium

The asynchronicity of computer conferencing is not as flexible and straightforward as it at first seems. People respond to different points of a debate at different times: with one user contributing to an early part of the debate while another is moving the discussion on. This can confuse and inhibit users from contributing. Conferences work best when students participate regularly and equally in small conferences so that in-groups are not formed, and the debate is carried forward at a leisurely week-by-week pace.

4. Enhancing social environment

Computer conferencing can help students avoid feeling isolated, but to become a confident user, students are faced with a big social learning curve. The OU has enhanced the extent to which one is aware of other participants, through First Class, e.g. the use of digital photos accompanying student and tutor résumés and student-only conferences, and through a staff member acting as an interactive media facilitator to help students develop confidence and overcome technical and social difficulties.

5. Training the tutors

Recognising the need to train thousands of tutors, a training programme has been prepared which includes text materials, guided practice, tutoring models and practice tasks, and a structured on-line short course.

Continued...

6. Using the medium for feedback

Formal and informal student feedback are both easier to generate through conferencing than through traditional means. It is usually more extensive, considered and coherent than survey questionnaires.

7. Implementing and supporting a conference system

It is easier than in the past to run conferences. But against high user expectations and management expectations of lower costs than in the past there are a number of issues. Running costs are not low. Support and administration is required which can be time consuming and can demand significant technical skills and discipline. Ensuring the logistics – such as printing of manuals, sending modems to remote students – are right and on time is important for student success. Help desks are not straightforward to run. It is hard to provide a reliable simple mode of operation over a wide range of dial-up networks. Networks are not fast enough at the current state of development to run a world wide course, accessing just one server. However, First Class and other systems allow a distributed network of servers linked together. But users can use modems to access conferences – though speeds of less than 14,400 bps are not advised.

Generalisability

Generalising from the OU experience to other institutions works best when new entrants – including teachers – take the time to learn from the experience of experts, rather than projecting their ideas and values on to the conference system.

It is important to consider how the issues involved in the use of computer conferencing apply to other conferencing-like systems.

Listservers. These rely on e-mail and do not use any centralised system, so don't suffer from network slowness when used world-wide. However, the OU has not been satisfied with the experience of listservers. Possible reasons are that it is more difficult to build up a sense of community, perhaps because it is not as asynchronous as other systems; e-mail can suffer from delays and undelivered mail and there are a wide variety of e-mail software packages.

Usenet News. This is a distributed bulletin board available world-wide that is found on many Unix systems. The strict rules about setting up conferences make it unusable for students. At the moment conferencing and e-mail have better software than Usenet News systems has. The OU has not yet favoured it as a vehicle for supporting conferencing.

World Wide Web. Available systems are rather primitive and hard to use. Current limitations in the interface of World Wide Web mean that it's hard to implement a system which requires manipulation of hundreds of messages in hundreds of conferences.

Scalability

A criticism of First Class has been that it is a toy system, which cannot handle large numbers of users. However, trials proved this unfounded. There are three First Class servers on an OU course with 5000 expected students – and one of these has been provided 'just in case'.

Continued...

A more significant aspect of scaling up is how can computer conferences support courses with large numbers of students? Evidence from the OU experience suggests the following guidelines:

- structure the educational use of the system;
- use student moderators to run various kinds of conferences, including self-help groups, with academic advisers available for backup support;
- introduce an interactive media facilitator role to reduce overload on tutors and stimulate and monitor interactions among students;
- develop effective structures for academic input into conference discussions by teachers, through for example, expert panel discussions.

Conclusions

The OU is now beginning to embed computer conferencing into the organisation as a mainstream support and communications tool. At the same time it is continuing to investigate technologies which will transform conferencing to a multimedia, multi-time learning resource.

(Mason & Bacsich, 1996)

References

Mason R & Bacsich P (1996) 'Computer conferencing university teaching' *Open Learning Today* Issue 33 Sept/Oct

Sankey K & Dibble D (1997) 'Low-cost computer-mediated conferencing for part-time evening degree students' in J Field (ed) *Electronic pathways: adult learning and the new communication technologies* National Institute of Adult Continuing Education, pp68–70

17.   Using Videoconferencing

Two Case Studies

Videoconferencing can create a 'virtual' classroom, enabling students at different locations to see and hear each other as well as the teacher. Obviously this is a more costly way to provide on-line tutoring than CMC since it entails the purchase of expensive equipment as well as the provision of a live link between participants. Nevertheless, videoconferencing is being used successfully by some colleges and universities as the following case studies show.

Case Study 1: Using videoconferencing as a multi-purpose tool in further education

Videoconferencing has been in existence for several years now. Its application in the world of business tends to be the one which most people are aware of, whereby business people can sit in front of a screen or monitor and hold meetings with colleagues on the other side of the world or at the other end of the country from the comfort of their own offices, thus saving on travel time and cost.

In education, videoconferencing has had a mixed reception, being perceived as both an opportunity and a threat. On the one hand, there is the expectation of some that the medium presents an opportunity to reduce staffing costs by having one tutor deliver courses to several groups of students simultaneously; on the other hand, there are the suspicions and fears of teaching staff that that is precisely what will be expected of them. To view videoconferencing in economic terms alone is to undervalue the potential of this medium and the opportunity it affords for curriculum enhancement as well as a variety of other benefits it brings with it.

At Halton College, videoconferencing is used as a multi-purpose tool: a teaching tool, a learning tool, a motivation tool as well as an economic tool.

Halton College began experimenting with videoconferencing as a teaching and learning tool in 1995 as part of a research project funded by the Fairbairn Fellowship. The research looked at the use of videoconferencing as a tool in distance learning and those curriculum areas it might be most or least suited to. The college was particularly interested in exploring additional or alternative ways of reaching out to students in some of its more remote sites.

The college serves twin towns (Widnes and Runcorn) but only has a permanent site in one of them (Widnes). It did and still does rely on good relationships with local schools, libraries and community centres for the use of their buildings as outreach posts. The arguments in favour of Community Education are well known and include the fact that many students feel more comfortable in local, familiar surroundings. In Halton College's case, the socio-economic background of the area with above average

Continued...

---

unemployment and other social problems, meant that, in many instances, travel to and from the main site was beyond the means of a considerable number of students and potential students.

Money from the project enabled videoconferencing equipment to be installed in a number of community sites and the technology was piloted in Communications, Languages and IT with the tutor being based at the college site and the students at the remote site. The research found that student participation, attendance and progress was as good as, if not better, than in the traditional classroom environment, that students experienced increased self-confidence, enjoyment in taking greater responsibility for their own learning and easily embraced the new technology. Inspired by their own success, some of them moved easily to continuation classes in their subject and/or to IT courses.

Since the early pilot, the college has expanded its use of videoconferencing to include a variety of other ventures, both local and international, and covering a range of curriculum areas. At local level, tutors have experimented with teaching two groups at the same time: one at the host site and one at the remote site, with varying degrees of success. Foreign languages, as a subject requiring a high degree of interaction in order to practise speaking and listening skills, seems well suited to a medium which encourages this.

At international level, several curriculum areas have tried out the medium. Hairdressing students have linked up with colleges in Canada and New Zealand. In the latter link-up, students and staff were treated to a demonstration of Maori beading, i.e. the threading of beads into certain hairstyles. Whilst critics might argue that this could have been achieved by watching a video of the same process, if one were available, it must be remembered that videoconferencing has the advantage of being interactive, enabling questions to be asked and responded to as and when appropriate.

A further project involved Engineering students at Halton linking up with similar students in Denmark and working on building a radio together. The language of communication was obviously English. However, not only did it benefit the English language skills of the Danish students, it also helped improve the communication skills of the English students as it encouraged them to think about the language of instruction. In this project, two important key skills, communications and team work, were being covered simultaneously.

In another project, students of A Level English Literature linked up with Advanced students of English in Denmark to discuss certain literature texts together. In between link-ups students communicated with each other via e-mail.

One obvious curriculum area for international links is Foreign Languages. For years tutors have attempted to bring the foreign country and culture into the classroom through a variety of means including audio and video cassettes and the use of foreign language assistants. Videoconferencing offers another choice which has the added advantage that students are able to communicate 'for real' (not just through role play) and 'in real time' (without the delay that accompanies communication via the written

Continued...

word). For groups able to participate in a foreign exchange, videoconferencing can help smooth some of the preparations by enabling exchange partners to see and talk to each other prior to departure. For those unable to afford a trip abroad, videoconferencing may provide the next best thing.

In foreign language link-ups, the language of communication needs to be decided in advance in order to be fair to both/all parties: all in English, all in the foreign language or a percentage of each. In another project that Halton College was involved in, such a decision was not necessary. Advanced students of French, German and Spanish linked up with Advanced students of the same languages in Holland with the target language serving as the lingua franca in each case.

Where foreign link-ups have not been possible because of timetabling difficulties or, indeed, in addition to them, groups of students of the same level on different local sites and the main college site have occasionally linked up to practise what they have learnt with each other. Apart from helping improve the speaking and listening skills of those involved, the experience helps students at out-reach centres feel 'less remote' and contributes to a sense of belonging and group identity. In a similar way, videoconferencing can be used as an alternative medium for tutorial support for those on Open or Distance Learning programmes. It is especially useful for those studying in business or industry if their workplace has the facility. Halton College also offers students or potential students visiting remote sites such as libraries, the opportunity to make enquiries about courses to the Welcome Centre at the main site by means of video-link instead of ordinary telephone call, if they so wish.

Whilst it has not been possible to describe all of the projects in this article, what they do reveal is the potential of the videoconferencing medium for enriching learning and making it more enjoyable and, in turn, the effect this can have on motivation. It has even been used with reasonable success with groups of students of low motivation, including some with moderate behavioural difficulties.

However, what remains to be discussed is the use of videoconferencing as an economic tool. The initial costs of setting up the facility vary according to the standard of the equipment used. A basic desktop facility comprising computer with monitor, camera, speaker attachments and appropriate software costs a few thousand pounds but is only really suited to small groups as it can barely accommodate a maximum of six on screen. For bigger groups a larger, more sophisticated, roll-about version accompanied by various peripherals such as a document camera (capable of visual transmission of OHP transparencies, other documents and real objects), electronic whiteboard and video-playback facilities is more appropriate.

The installation and running costs of the larger equipment are obviously going to be considerably higher. The average desktop operates with two ISDN lines, the more sophisticated model on 6 or more but the latter offers better sound and picture quality which are factors which also need to be borne in mind.

The expectation that the medium can be used to deliver courses to the masses using a single tutor needs to be treated with caution. It may be appropriate in a lecture type situation, such as a talk by a guest speaker, where interaction is restricted as

Continued...

communication is primarily one way. However, this style of delivery would be deemed inappropriate for many classes and, indeed, represents a retrograde pedagogical step since it would affect the quality of the teaching and learning experience for the students which, in turn, would impact on other issues such as motivation, retention and achievement.

Where Halton College has been able to make use of the medium as an economic tool is in merging groups on different sites where enrolments have not been sufficient to allow classes to exist independently. Through linking up those centres, it has been possible to operate as a single viable group, thus reducing student disappointment of having classes cancelled and sparing those involved additional costs and time in travelling to other centres. In the same way, savings can also be made in tutor travel time and costs. Colleges operating on multi-sites may also find, on occasions, that it makes more economic sense to hold meetings in this way.

Whilst videoconferencing has its advantages, it is not without its disadvantages. As with any technology, there are occasional technical problems. Technical support, therefore, needs to be available though that does not necessarily mean a technician being permanently present for every link-up. The system is relatively straightforward to operate once training has been given, with the teacher taking control of the operation of the equipment at the host site so that students at a remote site may need do little more than press the on/off button or turn up the volume control.

However, it must also be borne in mind that technophobes do exist and that for this reason or because of student preferences, this delivery may not appeal to everyone. Should it be forced on them, some students will only respond by 'voting with their feet'.

Research also revealed that some individual work is not suited to the medium, for example in some basic skills work or for dealing with sensitive or confidential issues.

The mode of delivery also demands a lot of teacher effort and energy and meticulous preparation, far greater than for a traditional class. There are additional points to think of: room layout for camera and sound, resources all to hand since any item left behind cannot be retrieved, the physical delivery of a hand-outs/worksheets to the remote site (sent in advance or faxed?). Furthermore there is the protocol of videoconferencing to ensure that all students feel involved and part of the same group. This requires a well-structured approach and early familiarisation with members and their names since usual cues afforded by body language tend to be lost. Some of these points also represent good practice in traditional groups and one of the findings arising from the research project was that the medium encouraged organised teaching and learning habits.

For international links there are time differences and timetabling obstacles to overcome, in addition to trying to plan sessions across continents. E-mail has proved an invaluable asset here, far easier than trying to make contact with colleagues abroad by telephone.

Videoconferencing also demands a lot of concentration both on the part of tutors and students. For the tutor it involves delivering the lesson while trying to operate the

Continued...

equipment at the same time. It would be impractical to expect a tutor to deliver every lesson on his/her timetable in this way. For the students, constantly looking at a monitor can be tiring and, as with work in front of a computer screen, is not recommended for lengthy periods of time. With larger television-type screens the effect may be less pronounced; nevertheless, videoconferencing is perhaps more suited to sessions not exceeding one hour.

Like other forms of technology and modes of delivery, videoconferencing has its advantages and disadvantages. It requires investment in money, time and energy but institutions and students in particular can and do reap the benefits. At Halton College, we have been surprised at the opportunities the medium affords and look to new ways of developing its potential.

(Parhizgar, 1999)

Case Study 2: Videoconferencing: active reflection on new technologies when lecturing

Introduction

There are many diverse views on what constitutes learning. At its best it is the active process of acquiring new skills, knowledge and attitudes. Many factors affect the ways that students learn not least of which are the personalities of both the teacher and the learner. It has been stated that the teacher's task is to tell the learners what to look for, without telling them what to see[1]. In most traditional learning environments this is a sufficiently difficult task when dealing with students at close quarters.

The subject of this project was to evaluate how this task might be altered when using videoconferencing as a method of delivery and what could be learned about teaching strategies to assist learning. The project's aims were to gain feedback from the staff and students involved which would provide information on best practices for future videoconferencing sessions. The sessions consisted of a series of lectures and modified lectures on various topics. The distinction between a lecture and a modified lecture was in the degree of participation expected by the receiving student group and in the structure of the lecture delivery.

The Project

For many years students from Queen Margaret College (QMC) in Edinburgh spent time at the School of Textiles, Heriot-Watt University in Galashiels receiving specific specialist instruction in textile and clothing subjects. This involved the transportation and accommodation of the students at the remote site and the carrying out of intensive specially prepared classes. QMC could never justify the employment of the variety of specialist staff required to teach various aspects of their Consumer Studies course when these staff were available at other institutions. More recently, QMC decided to provide textile specialisms which were industry relevant, by a remote videoconferencing link with the School of Textiles. Core modules would be delivered by videoconferencing links and by more traditional face-to-face methods. The remote

Continued...

183

communication was supported by funding from the Scottish Higher Education Funding Council (SHEFC). It was initially proposed that the teaching by videoconference could occur simultaneously with regular classes on the same subjects at the School of Textiles thus avoiding duplication and additional preparation. This was not found to be possible due to clashes in term times, timetabling difficulties and the small size of the videoconferencing suite at the delivery site[2]. The student participants had never experienced videoconferenced classes in the past although they had attended many face-to-face lectures and modified lectures.

Technology used and system etiquette

The communication link between the two centres was initially by ISDN6 telephone, using Satelcom videoconferencing equipment, in both locations. Later links were established on the Metropolitan Area Network (MAN) using MPEG technology. There were no apparent quality differences between the systems used and this did not impact on the users' impression of them.

A series of 'practice' links were undertaken by lecturing staff at both sites before the formal classes were undertaken. These links were structured so that an etiquette for the links could be established. This etiquette detailed who should formally initiate the link, who should control what the students could see and how to formally end the link. In the later session, using the MAN network, the contact was externally controlled but the etiquette for vision control was maintained.

Methodology

Seven lecturers at the School of Textiles delivered a total of twenty-one lectures, with one lecturer providing six of these. Therefore the lecturing input ranged from a 'one-off' lecture to a series of six lectures. The delivering lecturers had industrial experience in either the clothing or textile industries, or both. Additionally, half had received at least basic training in teaching methods. The lectures were spread evenly across three textile-based modules: Textile Product Development, Quality Appraisal of Textile Goods, and Advances in Clothing and Textile Research. The selection of modules to receive videoconferenced input was determined by the gaps in the receiving institution's specialist knowledge of the subject areas to be covered and by the practical consideration of timetabling restrictions.

Nineteen students at QMC attended the videoconferenced lectures, with most of them being in smaller groups ranging from five to eight student participants. The students and the lecturers were asked to complete questionnaires to give their feelings and perspective on the use of videoconferencing as a transmission method. Feedback was obtained from students after the final videolinked class in each of the modules delivered. Students were asked to complete a short questionnaire, which comprised Likert-rated questions plus open-ended questions. They then participated in group discussions to focus on the strengths and weaknesses of videoconferenced classes compared to more traditional classes.

The videoconference suite was set up so that the students could see two monitors simultaneously, one which showed the remote lecturer and one which showed the student group. When the lecturer was making use of visual examples, using a

Continued...

visualiser, the students were not able to see the lecturer. The visualiser enabled the students to see written text, diagrams and objects at the delivery site and it was also possible to see other visuals such as fabrics and designs. Although not an ideal experience for the students this set up was used due to equipment restrictions and technical considerations.

Results

Feedback from students

The main points to emerge from the analysis of the fourteen student questionnaires were:

- The most successful lectures were those which involved a high degree of interaction between tutors and students. This was particularly evident when modified lectures were delivered. There appeared to be more inter-student interaction in these instances.

- When a wide variety of audio-visual material other than traditional OHPs were used the class was more effective, with students commenting that this held their interest and prompted them to ask questions about the presented material.

- Students preferred classes where they could ask questions and become fully involved in the class.

- Students found the slight time lag between institutions quite disconcerting.

- Some students felt that being able to see themselves on screen during the class was distracting, whilst others viewed this as a positive item.

- Students sometimes could not read items on screen, as the print size was small.

During the group discussions it was identified that students particularly enjoyed sessions where the lecturer had good personal delivery and a lively personality. They felt that if the delivery had been boring they would have switched off. Students appreciated being questioned by their own name and felt it encouraged them to review notes before the sessions, although some students felt this approach rather intimidating. Nine students disagreed that the classes were impersonal, with two believing they were and three giving no definite feelings either way. They did not believe that the experience was similar to watching a video or television and they were aware at all times of the interactive nature of the classes. It was suggested by the students that the video link made them work harder although some thought this might have been due to the novelty of the approach. The students felt excited at being involved with the technology. Overall the classes were seen to be very interesting, with all fourteen students asked responding with agreement. The students considered the use of visual elements essential and that the advanced receipt of notes and other materials plus a telephone link made the classes more acceptable. Although they enjoyed the variety of lecturers who delivered material, the students felt it was essential to have a specialist on site.

The students expressed concern that the practical elements needed in their teaching could not be delivered by videoconference and that due to the nature of textiles and clothing, there would at some stage be a need to feel and experience fabrics and

Continued...

garments. The students suggested that some facilities be available for them at their site to allow for some practice. Students found it was easy to ask questions during the sessions. The students felt that they were able to consider teaching standards from another institution and enjoyed the novelty of having a variety of different lecturers.

When asked if they would like to be involved with further videoconferenced classes the majority of students said they would like to be. Some students felt intimidated by the presence of cameras and other technical equipment during the sessions but the majority of them did not think this hindered their learning. They had mixed feelings about how effective the sessions were when considering how much they had learned. As they had not been taught the subjects previously it was hard to estimate if the use of the link had increased learning.

Feedback from lecturers

The lecturer comments indicated that students involved in the videoconferenced sessions came across in a negative manner. Students appeared to be passive recipients of information and extremely still and quiet during the classes. Students did not appear to be able to communicate well across the medium. Student questions were hesitant and the students appeared aware of the need for microphones to transmit their voice to the lecturer. The main psychological difference when using videoconferencing was in the level of student participation. The lecturers felt that they were unable to maintain eye contact with students, as their image was so small. Gestures were also negligible and needed to be exaggerated to assist in communication. They felt the need for practice sessions which would give them time to become acquainted with the equipment and to prepare special visuals for each class. It was also recognised that initial exposure to videoconferencing can be stressful and practice sessions might reduce this. Lecturers felt the need for more information about the courses and students involved to provide them with a clearer context into which they could place their lectures.

Critical evaluation

A wide variety of options were open to the project team when deciding how to monitor and evaluate the videoconferencing experiment. There were a range of sources which could be used to assess the success of the teaching programme: evaluation by external examiners, colleagues, self, students and former students[3]. The associated methods for these evaluations were the use of questionnaires, group discussions, interviews and observation. The number of students involved were so small that it proved impossible to split them into meaningful groups and carry out elaborate measures of effectiveness[4].

The evaluation had therefore to rely on subjective assessments from the students receiving the classes and from the lecturers delivering them.

The equipment used when carrying out a videoconference was found to be initially intimidating. The class was seen on a small television screen, their size being vastly reduced and details were limited. The lecturer was alone in the delivery room with the equipment and a distant audience. This situation was uncommon for most lecturers

Continued...